The Stai

Radical feminist and pacifist Alice Chown was born in Kingston, Ontario, in 1866. Until the age of forty she cared for her devoutly religious mother and acted as matriarch of the family household. When her mother died in 1906, Alice was at last free to live as she chose, travelling widely and exploring a number of avenues of social reform. The diaries she kept for the next thirteen years were the basis from which she wrote *The Stairway*. First published in 1921 and for many years out of print, *The Stairway* is one of Canada's early feminist classics.

It tells of an extraordinary life: suffragist, settlement worker, peace activist, journalist, labour activist, college teacher, and itinerant catalyst for social change. During the First World War her pacifist stance brought about a bitter split with the mainstream women's movement in Canada, and in 1917 she moved to the United States. She lived there for the next ten years, during which time *The Stairway* was published in Boston. In 1927 she returned to Canada, where she continued to live until her death in 1949.

Inspired by a belief in a new age of humanism which gained significant popularity in Victorian Canada, Alice Chown was in many ways a woman very much of her time. She was also far ahead of it: to feminist and pacifist ears today, the voice in *The Stairway* rings true.

DIANA CHOWN is the great-great niece of the author. She lives in Edmonton.

The Stairway

Alice A. Chown

with an introduction by Diana Chown

UNIVERSITY OF TORONTO PRESS

Toronto   Buffalo   London

© University of Toronto Press 1988
Toronto   Buffalo   London
Printed in Canada

ISBN 0-8020-5769-1 (cloth)
ISBN 0-8020-6683-6 (paper)

The Stairway was first published in Boston in 1921 by the Cornhill
Company.

Canadian Cataloguing in Publication Data

Chown, Alice A. (Alice Amelia), 1866–1949.
The stairway
Bibliography: p.
ISBN 0-8020-5769-1 (bound). – ISBN 0-8020-6683-6 (pbk.)
1. Chown, Alice A. (Alice Amelia), 1866–1949 –
Diaries. 2. Feminists – Canada – Biography.
3. Radicals – Canada – Biography. 4. Pacifists –
Canada – Biography. I. Chown, Diana, 1939–
II. Title.
HQ1455.C46A3 1988   305.4'092'4   C88-095153-2

PICTURE CREDITS:
Edith and Lorne Pierce Collection, Queen's University Archives: Alice
Chown 1886, Amelia Chown, Alice's card 1941; Margaret Chown
Leslie: Edwin Chown, Alice and niece 1911; Beth Pierce Robinson:
Alice and nieces 1907, with Edith Chown Pierce and Bruce 1934 or
1935, Alice early 1940s; Dr William H. Cobb: Commonwealth College
Faculty

Publication of this book has been assisted by the Canada Council and
the Ontario Arts Council under their block grant programs.

INTRODUCTION

DIANA CHOWN

Aunt Alice was the black sheep of the family. Her idealism and unrelenting hopes for a just society were often misunderstood, causing her to be labelled eccentric. My acquaintance with her was limited to a family gathering when, still an infant, I was produced for her approval. Not until forty years later did I realize, after reading an article about turn-of-the-century Canadian idealists,[1] that there was much more to my great-great aunt than family lore had suggested. Finding in the Toronto Public Library one of the few known copies of *The Stairway*, I soon became fascinated with this extraordinary woman. *The Stairway* reveals much about Alice Chown's life and thought and points to her importance in Canadian feminist history. Printed in Boston in 1921, it is here reprinted for the first time after many years of being almost unobtainable.

Except for the few who have already read it, *The Stairway* will be a welcome new source in the unearthing of the history of women in Canada; it will speak directly to both historians and supporters of the movement for peace and disarmament, a reinvigorated force in the 1980s. Alice Chown's approach to women's emancipation and abolition of war were connected to each other by her social gospel belief in the evolution of a new age that would reveal a higher dimension of human potential. This belief places her in the company of many pre-First World War reformers, including Canadian feminists like Nellie McClung and and Francis Marion Beynon. Her perceptiveness and her activity as a pacifist and proponent of disarmament, as revealed in *The Stairway*, have impressed several recent scholars. Canadian women's peace historian Barbara Roberts mentions her support of the International Congress of Women in 1915 in *'Why Do Women Do Nothing to End the War?' Canadian Feminist-Pacifists and the Great War* (Ottawa 1985) and Thomas Socknat places her within the context of pacifism in Canada in *Witness against War: Pacifism in Canada, 1900–1945* (Toronto 1987), while Veronica Strong-Boag describes her role among Canadian women in the peace movement during the inter-war years in 'Peace-Making Women: Canada 1919–1939,' in Ruth Roach Pierson, ed., *Women and Peace: Theoretical, Historical and Practical Perspectives* (London 1987). Carol Bacchi discusses Alice Chown's interest in many aspects of women's lives, including sexuality, education, and economic conditions, in *Liberation Deferred? The Ideas of the English-Canadian Suffragists, 1877–1918* (Toronto 1983). Bacchi thought Alice Chown of such importance that she tried, without success, to have *The Stairway* reprinted in the mid-1970s.[2]

Doing the research for this introduction has been both an exciting and a frustrating experience. All the elements of historical research were heightened by an evolving sense of identification with the subject. What began as frustration and incomprehension in the face of seeming missed opportunities and uncompleted work has become admiration for the life's work of another woman – a kinswoman. I can now appreciate the diversity of Aunt Alice's career: feminist, suffragist, pacifist, settlement worker, writer, home economics advocate, journalist, labour activist, labour college teacher, and peace activist. At times, she seems like an itinerant catalyst who provided her analysis, along with knowledge, energy, and enthusiasm (and sometimes funding) to far-seeing projects and then moved on to what she viewed as the next manifestation of the evolving new age of democracy. It is perhaps because of a lack of comprehension of her role as catalyst that some historians have either ignored her or trivialized her accomplishments.

My pursuit of Alice Chown's story led me, either in person or through correspondence, to Kingston, Toronto, the United States, England, and Europe. I was fortunate to find private and public sources which greatly assisted the search. The papers of Aunt Alice's niece, Edith Chown Pierce, now in the Edith and Lorne Pierce Collection at Queen's University, were of particular value. Also, family members have unearthed letters and documents and shared memories and recollections. The Elizabeth Smith Shortt Collection at the University of Waterloo provided material that illuminates the long friendship between these two women. Archival collections related to Commonwealth College, Arkansas, have been valuable, as have many smaller, but no less exciting, finds. Unfortunately, Aunt Alice's personal papers seem to be lost, and her short stories, plays, and other fiction writings have not yet been located.

As my search progressed, the initial impression that Aunt Alice was not well regarded by many family members was soon confirmed. In *The Stairway* she wrote that her six brothers 'always thought me erratic' (16).[3] One of her nephews, who knew her in New York when he was studying there in the 1920s, recalled that 'her brothers thought her utterly wrong. Imagine! Treating black men as equals! ... She was someone one didn't speak of.'[4] At least one of her sisters-in-law refused to allow her son to read *The Stair-*

way. As her opinions became more radical, to embrace trade unionism, the abolition of private ownership, and a wartime commitment to pacifism, she became gradually estranged from the established Kingston and Toronto societies to which the Chowns belonged. These beliefs also alienated her from the mainstream Canadian women's movement, represented most significantly by the National Council of Women of Canada. Like two other female wartime pacifists, Francis Marion Beynon of Winnipeg and Laura Hughes of Toronto, Aunt Alice moved south of the border near the end of the First World War. She returned, however, after spending most of the years between 1917 and 1927 in the United States. For the rest of her life she lived in Toronto.

Although *The Stairway* is in the form of a personal journal, much of it was written during the three or four years preceding its publication. Thus many of its so-called daily entries describe events which took place earlier. (An example of memory actually being acknowledged as the source is found in the entry for 15 November 1911 on page 93.) Published women's diaries in English were not uncommon when *The Stairway* appeared, although narrative forms of autobiographies, such as memoirs, were more prevalent.[5] Why Alice chose the diary form can only be suggested. Just prior to the publication of *The Stairway*, Canadian feminists Nellie McClung and Francis Beynon also published on the themes of social regeneration and anti-militarism. They chose the polemic essay and the novel, respectively.[6] Alice obviously felt more freedom to get her views across in the diary form, which lends itself to reminiscence and spontaneity. Moreover, the intermittent time structure permitted by the diary form allowed her to relate events without having to connect them. This discontinuous and fragmented presentation seems to mirror the way she experienced life for many years.

Alice wanted to reach the reader directly, both non-intellectual and intellectual. The veracity implied in a diary facilitates a relation of trust between the reader and writer. It provides for 'an immersion in the text which parallels the immersion in life.'[7] This attempt to reach a broad public, rather than an intellectual elite, dominated her educational work with the Women's League of Nations Association ten years later. The exploratory element in *The Stairway* may be said to be related to traditional published travel journals. Rather than an account of travels through new or exotic countries, this is an account of travels through new understanding, new relationships, and ideologies. Alice herself applies a sense of physical journey to the women's movement. 'In many of the explorations that women have made during the last quarter of a century, I have been one of the party' (15). Besides suggesting a voyage of discovery, she employs the image of a stairway to evoke an evolutionary consciousness. It appears in the title and from time to time in the text to portray new insights experienced by the author. Twenty years later she called her column on postwar reconstruction 'The Next Step' to suggest a progressive attitude towards the task.

The intention of *The Stairway* was not strictly autobiographical. It was written, said the author, in the hope that it 'might give individuals faith in themselves' (4). Her social gospel belief in the innate goodness of individuals is apparent in a letter written just before publication. 'I am anxious to get one thing across,' she wrote, 'that truth in the individual soul may be trusted.'[8] Mention must be made of the self-consciousness of some of the writing. Alice seems to overstress, for example, her pioneering spirit and eccentricity. This self-consciousness and the frequent changes in tense detract from the formation of an integrated, complete personality. Alice's letters from this time are more open and spontaneous. The wit and mischievousness they sometimes contain is less apparent in *The Stairway*.

With few exceptions, existing documentation supports Alice's portrayal of the events as presented in the book. Sometimes dates are wrong by a few months, probably because she was relying on memory. As her purpose was to advise her readers, she included events which she felt most effectively conveyed her message, and omitted others. In 1912, for instance, she records her experience as a suffragist and a supporter of trade unionists, but not as a student at the University of Wisconsin where she studied for a few months in the fall.[9] In some cases in the book names have been changed: for example, pacifist Crystal Macmillan becomes 'Hester Maclean' and Edith Chown becomes 'Agnes.' The changing of names has made identification difficult; disappointingly, the identity of 'Norman,' to whom the book is dedicated, has not been discovered.

When *The Stairway* was published in 1921 its forthright and idealistic tone was seized upon by some reviewers who acknowledged, with almost a sense of awe, the courage and sense of mission of the author. The sharing of experience, that time-honoured means of communication between women, seems to have been particularly appreciated. Thus, although reviewers criticized the book for not extolling more pragmatic aims, they responded to its personal tone. The more conservative the reviewer, the more the review concentrated on the book's radicalism. A Canadian reviewer seemed affronted by Alice's view of marriage as an impediment to women's autonomy.[10]

The span of *The Stairway* encompasses the years 1906 to 1919, when Alice Chown was between the ages of forty and fifty-three. As the story opens, her mother has just died after twenty years as a semi-invalid cared for by Alice, her only daughter. Released at last, Alice wrote: 'Today I am free. My first day of freedom! It is my new birth!' (5). By that time she had already been involved in reform work related to women for several years. Her work had included direct involvement in the United States settlement movement and in the Lake Placid conferences on the future of home economics. During the period covered by the book, Alice's concerns took her to Toronto, the United States, and England, where she worked for women's suffrage and the improvement of women's working conditions and lived among anarchists in New York and 'Utopians' in Letchworth 'Garden City.' Her wartime experiences saw her declare herself a confirmed pacifist and attempt to set up co-operative communities outside Toronto and Boston.

Although Alice's intention was admittedly didactic, *The Stairway* also tells the story of a single, middle-aged Canadian woman who was a radical intellectual during the first quarter of the twentieth century. It not only relates the tale of her work and achievements but also reveals the problems she sometimes encountered – loneliness, rejection, semi-poverty, and illness. To portray herself as lonely and rejected was not, of course, Alice Chown's intention. She hoped that she could reach others, particularly women, with a message of love, empowerment, and truth to oneself by telling her own story from a particular point of view. However, to us, *The Stairway* is also a rich source of information about the life of a remarkable Canadian woman and the context in which she lived.

Alice Amelia Chown (1866–1949) was the only daughter who lived to adulthood of Edwin Chown and Amelia Anning in a family of six sons. She did not come from a family of intellectuals. Although most of his children attended Victoria College or Queen's University, Edwin Chown began to work at the age of eleven, eventually becoming the owner of a successful Kingston hardware store. Her mother had been permitted only minimal education. Married in 1850, Amelia Anning lived too soon to take advantage of the inroads women had made into Canadian universities by the 1880s. Moreover, her father had denied her the chance to attend one of the ladies' colleges which did exist in Ontario. Both Alice's parents were devout Methodists. She summed up her father's belief in the power of righteousness as 'Do justly, love mercy, and walk humbly with thy God' (11).

By the time of her adolescence Alice had developed a strong sense of independence. Years later she recalled her outrage when her brothers were allowed to climb trees and go without gloves while she was not. Along with her resentment at such restrictions, she embodied a spirit of service, typical of a well-brought-up young woman of her time. Strengthened by her Methodist upbringing, this Victorian ethos, whereby middle-class women were socialized to serve humanity in many capacities, formed much of the context for her life.

Her mother lived a life of service. Alice recalled the hours Amelia Chown spent working at household chores and tending to the large family as well as to apprentices from the hardware store and visiting missionaries. Alice was keenly aware of her mother's frustrations. She felt that she had 'always cried out for a larger life and had had visions, long before votes for women or even secondary education were considered, of the time when women should have opportunities equal with men' (7). This vision led to Amelia's insistence that Alice receive an education equal to that of her brothers. The right of women to higher education was to become one of Alice's most passionately held beliefs. She wondered if her mother's long illness had been due to 'doing of the thing prescribed, being shut out from large activities, from large deeds, so that her spirit beat itself against the cage of her environment until it bruised her body?' (6).

Illness was also part of Alice's life. As an adolescent she was an invalid for four years. This experience meant that she missed years of the socialization that contributes to effective human relationships. It could partly explain her later tendency towards isolation. Although the nature of the illness is never stated, until she was at least in her fifties she experienced headaches and periods of extreme weakness and fatigue. These symptoms are typical of those endured by a large number of North American and British middle- and upper-class women of the late nineteenth century. Well-known reformers like Jane Addams and Charlotte Perkins Gilman were stricken in their twenties but managed to break out of a pattern of illness from which many women never recovered. Cases of invalidism are now known to have been widespread. For some women illness was an escape from the stultifying effects of middle-class marriage, in which Victorian society's expectations often resulted in their becoming what Olive Schreiner called 'female parasites' with little connection to the world outside the home. For single women with aspirations to be more than maiden aunts on the fringes of extended families, the inner conflict between society's expectations and their own need for useful work often led to illness. In Alice's case, her desire for meaningful work in the face of family expectations that she devote herself to the care of her mother certainly contributed to her illness.

Alice Chown was better educated than most women of her time. She attended a Kingston high school[11] as well as

Wesleyan Female College in Hamilton.[12] In 1887 she entered Queen's University where, intermittently until 1894, she studied mathematics, philosophy, English, and political science, but never completed her degree.[13] Her years at Queen's, in spite of the ostracization of female students, were almost certainly more influential on her social thought than she maintained. She took junior philosophy in 1888 and 1894 and would have been influenced, if not taught, by John Watson, one of Canada's best known idealist philosophers. Watson believed in the possibility of the attainment of ultimate truth through the evolution of human consciousness firmly connected to a commitment to social good. In his view, self as a spiritual being could not be separated from self as a member of society.[14] The intellectual climate at Queen's during these years is credited with influencing the social gospeller Salem Bland. In political science, Alice was almost certainly taught by one of Watson's best pupils, Adam Shortt, who, by 1888, was the instructor of that course.[15] Shortt insisted that students take philosophy as a prerequisite to his political science course and Alice took both courses in the required order during the 1894–5 academic year. Besides teaching the standard texts for traditional political and economic theory, Shortt was interested in the application of theory to society as a whole and had developed a curriculum which expanded the study of politics and economics to include investigations of social conditions.[16] It is likely that Shortt, who believed in moral reform as an answer to capitalism's shortcomings, was the economics professor Alice recalled trying to convince her of the dangers of socialism (15). Thus, Alice's experience at Queen's, while no doubt exasperating due to the misogynist attitude of many of the male staff and students, provided encouragement to her developing idealism and her search for means to social reform.

By 1888 Alice had begun a friendship with Adam Shortt's wife, Elizabeth, who was seven years her senior. In 1884 Elizabeth Smith had been one of the earliest female medical graduates at Queen's.[17] After marrying Shortt, she returned to her alma mater in 1887 to teach medical jurisprudence and sanitary science. That Elizabeth was a continuing source of encouragement and support is seen in Alice's letters to her over the next sixty years. Frequently a mentor of female students at Queen's, Elizabeth had befriended Alice during the younger woman's first year at the university. By this time Alice was burdened by household duties and the care of her mother. She was also suffering bouts of illness. In a letter to Elizabeth in April 1888 she agonized over the fact that a severe headache had prevented her from writing the final mathematics exam.[18] Whatever the cause of her distress, it was Elizabeth to whom she turned for comfort. Alice, who felt called to champion women's emancipation, was inspired by Elizabeth's courage and determination, which had seen her through her fight for both admission to and graduation from medical school.

In 1892 Alice accompanied the Shortts to Europe where Adam, by then university librarian, was to buy books for the library. Elizabeth's diary of the trip frequently mentions Alice, who, at twenty-six, seems to have been a companion for the sometimes ailing Elizabeth.[19] Even after the Shortts' departure in 1908 for Ottawa, where Adam had accepted the position of civil service commissioner, the friendship between the two women survived. The fact that Alice's interests and analysis of the underlying causes of society's inequalities became decidedly more radical than Elizabeth's did not destroy their bond.

Alice's writing as well as her life place her securely within the pre-First World War reform movement. She believed in the essential goodness and truth of each human being and in the coming 'age of humanism.' Besides being related to secular humanism's concern with moral progress, these beliefs connected her to the late-nineteenth-century and early-twentieth-century social gospel movement which viewed social, political, and economic oppression as the only barrier against the coming to earth of the Kingdom of God. Originally a strong supporter of the doctrines of social responsibility of the Methodist Church, she served the church faithfully through such projects as her 'young men's missionary society' in 1888.[20] In later years she referred to her former church-related missionary zeal as having been replaced by a belief 'in the life force in every individual' which needed to be set free through truth and freedom from societal and other oppressors.

It was with a view to this sense of optimism and hope for moral progress that she worked for women's suffrage, combined with higher education and better working and living conditions for women. Alice's feminism can be compared to that held by a number of American and a few Canadian feminists who believed in the natural rights of women. This view has been distinguished from the more conservative 'social' or 'maternal' feminism. Of these two streams, Linda Kealey has written that the former 'argued for equal rights as a part of the legacy of the eighteenth century revolutions; the latter abandoned social criticism of the family and separate sexual spheres for a concern with social reform issues and justified women's involvement in the public sphere on the basis of their supposed special characteristics.'[21] Of course, in many instances the interests of these two groups overlapped. For instance, turn-of-the-century conditions of the urban poor, exacerbated by rapid immigration and industrialization, were of concern to all reformers. The Canadian women's movement in 1895, when Alice left Queen's, was predominantly Anglo-Saxon, middle class, and conservative with 'maternal' feminist views. Thus, the main organizations, the National Council of Women of Canada and the Women's Christian Temperance Union, directed their efforts to such concerns as urban reform, improved public health, child welfare, and prohibition. Largely absent in their campaigns was strong support for labour unions or for socialism as answers to the exploitive effects of capitalism. As might be expected, these latter two issues were of particular concern to Alice. Besides holding more radical views than most of her Canadian contemporaries in the women's movement, Alice rejected the two most prominent criteria by which Canadian society measured women reformer's credibility. Working within their roles as wives, mothers, and church-goers was the means by which women maintained the public view of women as morally superior. Alice neither married nor remained in the official church.

Like many socialist feminists, Alice was attracted to a kind of utopian socialism. Her view of the individual capacity for good and for responsibility towards others made her suspicious of dogmatic socialist programs. Although she was sympathetic to Soviet Russia and likely read Marx's writings, this belief in individual freedom prevented her from seeing oppression in strictly economic or class terms. She saw a connection between the Christian sharing of her own resources and the societal sharing that would result from a socialist system. 'If my conscience is not alive enough to make me act,' she wrote late in life, 'how can I expect other people's conscience to prompt them to action? ... There must be sharing and an economic system that makes co-operation and democracy possible.'[22] Alice's socialism could be described as 'ethical socialism,'[23] a term employed by Sheila Rowbotham to describe the creed of Edward Carpenter, the British socialist and writer to whose ideas, found largely in *Towards Democracy* (1883) and *Love's Coming of Age* (1896), Alice often refers. The term was intended to distinguish it from the more utilitarian reformism of the British Fabians. It involved a moral view that required action. Like Carpenter, Alice believed in a socialism inseparable from a vision of a new life, seeing the means and ends as one entity. She also shared his contention that private property and the class system bore partial responsibility for the inequality of society and that a connection existed between war and the oppression of workers and minorities; socialism, to her, could lead to a system that did not promote war.

As her mother had done before her, Alice spent many years caring for others. By the age of twenty-two she was devoting much of her time to her ailing mother. These years of service resulted in a desperate desire to be free and to live her life with as few rules as possible. She spoke out against women's restricted role in marriage both in her correspondence and in *The Stairway*.[24] In addition to her mother's circumscribed existence, she saw the oppressive effect of marriage on her friends. She was convinced that, whether married or single, women must become better educated to escape from their limited role in society; their inferior educational and economic status merely encouraged domination.

Alice's thinking reflected Carpenter's *Love's Coming of Age* wherein he somewhat ambiguously opposed women's oppression and advocated female emancipation within marriage. He focused on sexual liberation for women and men. It is likely that the ideas of Charlotte Perkins Gilman also influenced her attitude towards marriage. By 1898 Alice was on the fringes of a milieu in the United States where the ideas of Gilman and other prominent feminist writers were discussed. Although Gilman did not firmly advise against marriage, she set out some of the perils of contemporary matrimony in *Women and Economics* (1898). It is likely that Alice read this well-known work soon after its publication. Unlike Carpenter, Gilman stressed economic inequality rather than sexual repression as the basis for the oppression of women in marriage.

Alice's views on women's sexuality as referred to in *The Stairway* suggest that she was receptive to ideas like those found in Olive Schreiner's *Woman and Labour* (1911), which claimed women's right to meaningful work. Like Schreiner, Alice extolls the beauty of sex and even suggests the right of a single women to bear a child at the same time as she counsels self-restraint. Accompanying this attitude was a belief in the need of the will to overcome a woman's sexual desires in order that she might serve humanity better. Schreiner's biographers suggest that she had not read Freud when she wrote the book.[25] Alice, who knew some of Freud's work, wrote of her inability to accept his theories of the sexual origins of human development. A description of Schreiner's view of female sexuality as being centred on the 'progressive, evolutionary [and] historical' could also be applied to Alice, who considered that once society had 'begun to busy itself with all the delightful possibilities of human nature and talent, the sex question would take care of itself' (104).

Alice supported the view that women had suffered from sexual repression but not as it applied to herself. In *The Stairway* she agonizes over a marriage proposal she had received; she could not accept that 'sex relations are natural and inevitable' (88). Part of this reluctance to countenance herself in a sexual relationship was likely due to her age (forty-four), which she would have considered as beyond the age of sexual activity. Although her attitude seems now like sexual prudery, to women before the First

World War, including feminists, sex was a more complex issue. Regardless of the rise of sexology in the 1890s, women's socialization continued to stress the need to be feminine and to regard sexual desire as something to be repressed.

Alice did regret that she would not have children. However, like many other pre-war spinsters she vowed to live her life as a single woman. Her views on marriage went further than Carpenter's in their condemnation of its effect on women's lives. Personal autonomy, she felt, had no chance when a woman was constantly preoccupied with maintaining peace within a marriage. 'I am debating most seriously,'' she wrote in 1919, 'whether marriage is not the greatest drag on the individual that has ever been created. I believe that, free of marriage, people would develop better ... The constant negation of oneself for the sake of peace is damnable.'[26] Other single women in Canada came to this conclusion. The opinion of Agnes Macphail, shared by hundreds of capable spinsters with whom she had discussed the subject, was that *the person* could not be subjected.'[27] Alice's letters, however, reveal a devoted aunt who kept in close touch with her nieces and nephews and carried on the family traditions as if she were the matriarch. In 1920, for example, she wrote delightedly from her primitive cottage in New York state that she would send the family christening robe to her niece, Edith (by then married to Lorne Pierce), when she heard of the arrival of the Pierces' first child.[28]

Three years after leaving Queen's University Alice began what was to become a long association with advocates of reform in the United States. Following another serious illness she became a resident of one of the more progressive social settlements, Whittier House in New Jersey. Her first contact with the American settlement movement had been in 1893 when she visited Hull House while attending the World's Fair in Chicago. The movement, which effectively began in England with Toynbee Hall in 1884, was established by middle-class reformers trying to help the urban poor of London. Based on the English model, Chicago's Hull House, the best known of the early American settlement houses, was founded by Jane Addams and Ellen Gates Star five years later. The settlement residents worked for improved urban conditions; they also provided education, cultural occasions, and many other activities considered beneficial to the urban poor. The movement, which provided the context in which many well-educated and capable women reformers carried out their work before the First World War, was part of a larger revolt, as Allen F. Davis wrote, 'against the vulgarization of society.' Its ultimate goal was 'the spiritual reawakening' of the whole person. The settlement worker or resident lived and worked with the inhabitants of the house and the neighbourhood. In the United States and Canada many of the settlements were affiliated with religious institutions. Through their settlement house residency, women learned much about the conditions of the urban poor. Some of the workers, like Jane Addams and Cornelia Bradford, head resident of Whittier House, came to understand the underlying causes of urban poverty and were skilled at lobbying governments at the municipal, state, or federal level for changes in legislation and other reforms. Sometimes the settlement movement propelled its leading residents into civic government positions. Florence Kelley, who Alice knew personally, became an Illinois factory inspector after working at Hull House in the 1890s. Some settlement houses, not so cognizant of the difference between settlements and charity organizations, were accused of merely providing 'cultural comfort stations' or endeavouring to enhance the industrial efficiency of the poor.[29] This attitude denied the philosophy of Jane Addams, who envisioned Hull House as founded on the theory that the dependence of classes on each other is reciprocal and looked forward to an economic unity of society.[30]

Situated in Jersey City, Whittier House had been established four years before Alice's arrival in 1898. By 1900 it had established Jersey City's first kindergarten, district nursing service, dental dispensary, and public playground.[31] In a letter written soon after her arrival, Alice revealed her delight in leaving the stifling atmosphere of her life in Ontario. She praised the founder and leader, Cornelia Bradford, with whom she felt a personal bond. Bradford, she wrote, had travelled extensively in Europe, spent a winter in Berlin, studied at Oxford, and been received by the Pope, all of which greatly impressed the young woman from Kingston. 'Her life has been full of association with people who are only honored names to us,' Alice wrote. Bradford's views were obviously stimulating to one whose faithful church-going was being challenged by the settlement leader's belief that 'she can serve God in secular work quite as well as in Church.'

The new Canadian resident was thrilled with the number of 'wide-awake women' she met at Whittier House; she felt as if she had 'been shut up in a dark room and had suddenly emerged into the free air.'[32] Soon after her arrival she had been asked to represent Whittier House at the 'Social Reform Societies of New York,' where she would meet some of the people she admired such as R.W. Gilder, editor of *Century Magazine*, who, like Bradford, was concerned with poor housing conditions. Alice also likely met Jane Addams, if she had not already done so in 1893; in the same letter she referred to Addams' imminent arrival at Whittier House. She described the prominent settlement head as 'a disciple of [Tolstoy's] principle of non-resistance,' a principle she herself held for much of her life.

Alice seems to have spent only a year at Whittier House. The following spring she wrote that she dreaded having to return home because of lack of strength.[33] According to *The Stairway*, however, it was her father's request that she resume the care of her mother (12) that led to her reluctant return to Kingston. Whatever the reasons for returning home, the period at Whittier House had been very satisfying to her; she considered that she might never again have the same opportunity (12).

While she was at Whittier House, Alice's evolving commitment to the new 'scientific' attitude that rejected charity for the practice of social work is obvious in her letters. She described the work there as 'along sociological lines.' She believed that the alleviation of poverty could only be achieved by understanding its underlying causes. Later, she severely criticized the settlement movement, stating that the average settlement worker 'rarely has any real conception of unity with [the poor] patronizing them only less in degree than the Lady Bountiful of the past, for whose gifts she substitutes diversions' (25). Ironically, what came to be one of her own solutions, getting the urban poor out of the city and into co-operative communities, also avoided a confrontation with the causes of urban deprivation. That period of her life, when she tried to develop co-operative living conditions for city people, began in 1915. Before then, she was involved in more socially acceptable reforms, such as the introduction of home economics.

In 1900, as the recently appointed field secretary of the Canadian Household Economic Association, Alice became the first Canadian to participate in the Lake Placid conferences which examined the philosophy behind home economics as a discipline. The connections she made at Whittier House would certainly have acquainted her with women reformers in various fields, including home economics. The discipline was defined at the Lake Placid conferences as 'a study of man [*sic*] as a social being and his physical environment and especially the relationship between the two.' This definition coincided with Alice's view of the subject. She considered it as a means to 'the application of science to release women from the home and the economic dependency of marriage.'[34] These views were far from those held by the best known proponent of home economics in Canada. Adelaide Hoodless had just officially introduced the subject into Ontario schools by successfully promoting the establishment of the Ontario Normal School of Domestic Science. She viewed home economics as a means to bolster the status of the homemaker. This approach maintained the sexual division of labour, a position which facilitated her support by the Ontario Board of Education.

The papers Alice gave at the Lake Placid conferences help to illuminate her own views on education for women and her philosophy of home economics. She attended the second, third, fourth, and sixth of the ten conferences. In 1901, at the third conference, she gave a paper titled 'Courses in Home Economics for Colleges and Universities' in which she set out her views on teaching the subject. Like many of the university-educated participants, she was against the introduction of home economics into the university level curriculum unless it was integrated into the study of society as a whole. This view coincides with the Lake Placid definition of home economics as the study of the relationship between the individual and his or her environment. It rejects the inclusion of Hoodless' perception of home economics (domestic science) in university curricula. It also implies revisions of such curricula to suit the needs of female students. This above all is implicit in her articles of this period: that the evolution of humanity must include increased opportunities for the education of women.

To illuminate her views, Alice delineated three classes of orientation for education and applied them to home economics. The first two were appropriate to a university, she maintained, and the third to a professional or trade school or similar institution. The first, which she calls 'truth for truth's sake' may be described as an examination of abstract principles and aims 'to train the student in logical thinking, to incite the passion for original research.'[35] Practically, it would 'treat the development of the home with as much dignity and consideration as the development of the state or commerce.' Alice stressed the need for higher education for women who could follow this line of study in which one must refuse 'to be swayed by utilitarian values in the pursuit after knowledge.'

The second orientation for education is for those who, unlike the first, do not 'gain their mental development thru [*sic*] abstract thought' but rather through the 'discernment of the relationship between the concrete and the abstract.' Thus, she asserted that colleges should provide women with opportunities for the specific study of the home. Such studies would teach that 'phenomena are valuable as illustrating and making clear scientific principles.' Thirdly, she described the category 'applied science' whereby the phenomena are studied, that is, the home is studied from a utilitarian point of view and science is only important if it provides explanations. 'All our schools of applied science, our professional schools and agricultural colleges, come under this head,' she explained; 'their value is largely utilitarian.' She was of course thinking of Adelaide Hoodless' domestic science classes at this point.

Although she acknowledged the value of domestic science schools, Alice warned against having 'a large body of women specifically educated for the home without a sufficient number of women broadly educated for life with all its manifold complexity of interests.' In a letter written on her return from Lake Placid that year, she was sharply critical of Hoodless who she blamed for the fact that 'the American experts' at the conference considered the 'Domestic Science work in Canada somewhat of a freak.'[36] She cited the reluctance of American participants to invite Hoodless to the conference and while acknowledging the domestic science advocate's value in popularizing the subject, she criticized 'not only her lack of science' but also the 'lack of mental training which makes Mrs. Hoodless incapable of doing real first class academic work.'[37]

That year Alice published an article which further advocates reform of women's education in Canada. It appeared in the *Methodist Magazine and Review*, one of the Methodist publications that periodically printed her work until 1916.[38] Implicit in it was her belief in women's right to higher education and her concern that the proliferation of domestic science schools could lead to the ghettoization of women's education. Although she acknowledged the value of woman's role as homemaker, she clearly affirmed that 'the preparation of the individual to attain her highest possibilities is of more importance to the state than the perpetuation of any of its institutions, even the time-honoured Anglo-Saxon home.' Statements such as these, with their emphasis on women's right to autonomy and economic and social independence, point to the gap between Alice's feminism and the maternal feminism of the mainstream Canadian women's movement.

The paper she gave at the 1902 conference examined the emancipation of women as revealed by their progress within the home.[39] Tracing women's emancipation in regard to marriage, she cited the right gained during the Renaissance to marry on the basis of personality rather than family arrangement, and the opportunity developed during the early nineteenth century to earn one's living and thereby avoid reliance on marriage. This process she regarded as part of the evolutionary emancipation of one class after another.

To Alice, historical changes in marriage patterns coincided with her evolutionary view of life. She maintained that the home must not be excluded from the gains made by society. All women must take part in the 'age of the new humanism' in which the aim of the sociologist and the politician will be 'to provide the fullest opportunity for everyone, rich and poor, gentle and simple, without regard to sex or social condition.' Thus, she makes a plea for raising the status of the female household servant, whose choice of housework as an occupation, because it 'affords better mental and moral discipline than mechanical work,' should not exclude her from gaining the self-respect and better wages and hours for which workers outside the home were fighting. Stating goals unattained to our present day, Alice wrote that 'democracy must teach us ... to put [housework] on such a plane that the social ostracism accompanying it will cease.'

Concern for the conditions of female servants also appears in the paper Alice gave during her fourth and last appearance at Lake Placid in 1904. No longer representing the Household Economic Association, she spoke on housing conditions in Boston, stressing the low wages and poor living conditions of female servants in some apartment houses.[40] Another aspect of her contribution to the conferences was her participation in a committee which submitted the report *Practical Suggestions on Courses of Study in Home Economics in Higher Education.*

In recent studies of the history of home economics in

Canada, Alice is considered to have made a significant contribution during the four Lake Placid conferences she attended. Her paper given at the third conference, on women and home economics education, has been called 'a revolutionary proposal [which] was not fully appreciated or understood at the time.'[41] The fact that she never returned after the sixth conference has left historians baffled. However, by late 1905 Amelia Chown was needing constant care and this may have prevented Alice from leaving Kingston.

Although she apparently never joined the National Council of Women of Canada (NCWC), Alice acted as convener of the Committee on the Care of the Aged and Infirm Poor at the 1904 and 1905 general meetings.[42] Her experiences at Whittier House would have acquainted her with the issues related to poverty of all ages. In neither case did she attend the meetings. In her 1905 report to the NCWC, read by someone else, she urged the group to advocate the adoption of old age pensions, rather than continuing to lobby the provincial government for legislation compelling relatives to support the aged. At the 1904 general meeting she submitted a paper entitled 'Modern Experiments in Housekeeping,'' which discussed one of her central interests, co-operative forms of living.[43] She regretted the absence in Canada of co-operative experiments in housekeeping in which the participants had a voice in the organization. Her solutions to this situation, which included the professionalization of domestic work, suggest that she was aware of such undertakings in the United States as well as Charlotte Perkins Gilman's similar proposals in *Women and Economics*. Rather than the usual response of increased immigration of domestic servants as an answer to women's housework problems, Alice outlined the 'business enterprises which are successfully ministering to the household needs of their community.' She proposed apartment houses that would provide meals and other services, employment bureaux for domestic servants, take-out food kitchens, and other services originating outside the home, based on an adaptation of United States models to Canada.

During these years, as Amelia Chown's death approached, Alice became even more tied to running the household and caring for her mother. She also kept in close contact with several of her nieces and nephews. Her life was sometimes lonely and isolated; during this period she seems to have had less contact with Elizabeth Shortt.

Alice's grief was mixed with relief when her mother died in 1906. 'Now I am to begin life,' she wrote at the beginning of the *The Stairway*, and after a pleasant summer of entertaining in the garden she 'turned the key on the old home' (16–18). Her refusal to observe some of the grieving rituals met with disapproval, which stung yet challenged her. 'Once more I have insulted all the traditions of my native place.' The suffocation she had felt in Kingston was finally relieved when she began to travel; for the succeeding twenty years she never remained in one place for any length of time.

Like many reformers of the period, Alice Chown believed that co-operative, communal living arrangements were foundations for the coming new age. On a smaller scale, she saw co-operation as a means of alleviating the isolation and poverty of both married women and domestic servants. When she was able to choose her own living arrangements, she began to experiment. Soon after her mother's death she went to New York where she visited a group of women who had set up 'co-operative, democratic housekeeping' in a large house with courtyard, pond, and fountain. In a regrettably short reference to this apparently feminist community, she praised the participants for 'creating a home where co-operation would make possible better opportunities for the educated woman to follow her profession and at the same time have her family needs satisfied' (30).

Probably for the first time since her 1892 trip with the Shortts, Alice visited Europe in 1907. The high point of the trip was a visit to Millthorpe, near Sheffield, where Edward Carpenter lived with his long-time companion, George Merrill. Various visitors who sympathized with Carpenter's concept of simplified living stayed in cottages on the property. Carpenter also operated a market garden and sold produce to the local market. His biographer views his belief in co-operation as the social and economic manifestation of his egalitarian sentiments.[44] Alice considered him to be a prophet of the new age, a man who held no theories to which he had not applied the test of practice. She felt that he had thrown aside 'all conventions which men deem necessary, and which in return choke their souls.' Her own life suggests that she sometimes saw herself too as a prophet. Alluding to the title of her book, she wrote that the insight she had gained from Carpenter would be her 'vaulting pole' which would 'carry me up my stairs according to the clearness of vision and tenacity of purpose with which I grasp it' (51). This ascending image is a reminder of the spiritual evolution which accompanied Alice's concept of the dawning age.

In late 1907 Alice was once more called on to care for family members in Kingston. Little is recorded from then until mid-1909 in *The Stairway*. She intended the book to concentrate on her spiritual and intellectual odyssey, and presumably she did not regard this return to Kingston as a period of growth. She later recalled these years with her niece Edith and nephew Gordon, then Queen's University students, as a time of darning socks and teaching lessons as

well as serving eight hundred extra meals to 'the nieces and
nephews and their chums who adopted me as aunt, and all
the lonely people whose paths crossed mine, as well as the
old friends and comrades' (56–7). When she was free to
travel once more, she went to England to experience life in
the recently completed 'Garden City,' Letchworth, north
of London.

She was enchanted with the place. She felt she had found
the co-operative living experiment she had been looking
for. 'My Utopia exists!' she declared. 'Not in dreams, not in
books ... but bodied forth in bricks and wood – principally
wood – plaster and mortar, trees and gardens and real people living in them' (61). Letchworth had been designed by
Ebenezer Howard, who became interested in co-operative
living concepts partly through the writings of Edward
Bellamy and Marie Howland, Americans who advocated
co-operative communities. The utopian vision in Bellamy's
Looking Backward (1888) had influenced many; it is considered to have made socialism respectable among the
American middle class. Feminist Marie Howland was instru-
mental in developing a co-operative community in Topolo-
bampa, Mexico, which influenced Howard's Garden City
designs. At Letchworth, Howard was consciously trying to
meet the needs of women. He referred to co-operative living schemes as pragmatic responses to 'the servant question' and 'the woman question.' By 1909, Letchworth consisted of detached and semi-detached houses, garden apartments, and row houses with private kitchens. That year
Howard began the addition of a "Co-operative Quad-
rangle,' a plan which permitted the sharing of housing and
domestic work by tenants. Considering her long interest in
co-operative housekeeping, it is likely that Alice stayed in
one of these apartments during her 1913 visit. At the
Columbian Exposition in Chicago in 1893 she would have

had the opportunity to see a model of row housing with co-operative housekeeping facilities.[45]

At the time of her 1909 visit there were five thousand people living in Letchworth. Having already experimented with reforming women's fashions, she appreciated the simplicity of dress worn by many women. Letchworth's avowed aims – the substitution of service for profit in business, creation of beauty in one's surroundings and of fellowship in relationships – were overwhelmingly appealing to her. 'Words cannot utter,' she wrote, 'the charm and glory of living when one is controlled by a new idea' (72). The inhabitants she described as socialists, single-taxers, syndicalists, communistic anarchists, Tolstoyans, and people against private ownership (65).

A humorous contemporary description of a typical male Letchworth resident viewed him as 'clad in knickerbockers and, of course, sandals, a vegetarian and member of the Theosophical Society, who kept two tortoises which he polishes periodically with the best Lucca oil. Over his mantlepiece was a large photo of Madame Blavatsky and on his library shelves were *Isis Unveiled* and the works of William Morris, H.G. Wells and Tolstoy.'[46] This mocking description should not obscure the idealism and determination of the residents of Letchworth; although it is satire and describes only the male residents, it does suggest the milieu which Alice found most stimulating during this period of her life.

Alice once more fell ill and was cared for by the women of the Garden City. After her recovery she returned to Kingston, where her enthusiastic descriptions of Letchworth fell on deaf ears. 'Things that seem quite a matter of course there are too Utopian here to seem rational,' she wrote sadly (74) after unsuccessfully trying to launch a co-operative residence in the area.[47] However, she did arrange for Letchworth inhabitant Bruce Wallace to visit Canada soon after her return. Wallace, part of the brotherhood movement in England, published *Brotherhood*, formerly the *Christian Socialist*, which criticized capitalist society and promoted co-operation.

Although she visited Letchworth at least twice in the next few years, Alice does not seem to have returned after the war. During her 1913 visit she became involved in a dispute over the right to live in the Garden City without being legally married. After witnessing the community's rejection of the couple in question, her conviction that Letchworth was 'imbued with a faith in love's being the actual life force of the world' was shaken. She was concerned that the community was becoming dominated by followers. 'When the idea for which the pioneers are willing to sacrifice life itself becomes definitely outlined and adopted by the multitudes ... once more the everlasting element in life must reveal itself in new guise' (151).[48]

During the summer of 1911 Alice moved to Toronto where she had a job with the *Toronto Daily Star* (referred to as the 'Daily Herald' in *The Stairway*). She shared a house with two other women during the succeeding year which she later described as one of the 'most momentous' of her life. Her assignment was to write articles about 'civic betterment' as it applied to Toronto. Relishing the opportunity to put forward her ideas on co-operative living, she wrote about the merits of garden cities and the possibilities for co-operative building schemes. These articles appeared for only a short time and after the first one they were not signed. The fact that she condemned private ownership and emphatically stated that 'the rising spirit of democracy demands that there shall be no class consciousness, that the smaller shall be swallowed up in the larger,' may have been too much for the editors who would not permit her even to mention women's suffrage (93).[49] She also had been asked to write a series on the life of the working woman (99). This seems to refer to a series of articles for the Methodist Church's *Christian Guardian* that year. Although she suggests in *The Stairway* that they were about factory workers, the articles dealt with the church's deaconess movement.

In writing on both these subjects, Alice's guiding principle was her evolutionary vision. The creation of co-operative living schemes and the improvement of working conditions for women were merely two of the necessary reforms. Some of her other concerns are also evident, such as the inadequacies of women's education and the need for professionalization of services for the poor. In strongly worded articles she criticized the poor education and inadequate wages of the deaconesses. Of the course of study offered them, she wrote that 'every subject which a supporter of the movement deems beneficial has been hay-forked into the course – a little smattering of everything.' 'Perhaps the purpose [of the deaconess society] is to furnish nice little satellites for Methodist ministers,' Alice wrote caustically, 'women who will clasp their hands with admiration at the greater knowledge of the pastor ... It seemed to me that the course of study was aptly framed to fill Ruskin's ideal education for women, the ability to appreciate other people's learning, not to be competent oneself.'[50] She condemned the narrow outlook of the deaconesses, related to their limited education, and viewed them as handing out charity to the poor without questioning the causes of their poverty.

Alice stressed the importance of the developing social movement then taking place in the United States, and in Canada to a lesser degree.[51] The understanding of the causes of poverty was part of this movement, as was the evolving discipline of social work. The fact that the deaconesses seemed disinclined to join the movement was of particular concern to her. Moreover, she viewed the church as doing little to prevent poverty among the deaconesses themselves. Concerned as she was over women's lack of economic independence, she was aware of the deaconesses' inadequate remuneration; they were paid ten dollars a month plus room and board and several minor allowances.[52] The officials who had authority over them seemed unconcerned with providing a living wage or improving the standards of the training school. In ignoring the plight of the deaconesses, the church was guilty by implication of the same exploitation of women as other employers who refused to pay women a living wage. The provision of room and board permitted the church to avoid paying a living wage, just like the employers of women living in Barbara House, the deaconesses' boarding house. As the well-known American feminist and activist Florence Kelley had recently pointed out to Alice, such homes were 'bonuses to manufacturers, enabling them to pay less than the girl could live upon if she were dependent strictly upon her own resources.'[53]

Her articles were interpreted as attacking deaconesses themselves, to Alice's dismay. 'I am too much a lover of my sex,' she responded, 'not to understand how our very weakness of self-sacrifice and self-negation has come from long years of regarding other people before ourselves.' A few others shared her views. J.S. Woodsworth, then at the All People's Mission in Winnipeg, wrote that 'Miss Chown has rendered a valuable service to the church by daring to frankly criticize things as they are.' In the United States, he pointed out, 'the charity organization societies and social settlements are decades ahead of the churches in their understanding of social problems.' The year after Alice's

articles appeared, modest reforms in the treatment of deaconesses began: the principal of the training school was
replaced and deaconesses' travelling expenses were increased.[54]

Alice was often concerned about her own financial
resources. Her work as a journalist served to supplement
her small investment income. The capital which yielded
this income was partially derived from contributions made
by some of her brothers and, later, by Edith and Lorne
Pierce. She must also have received an inheritance from
her parents. Allotments of income to her, overseen by her
younger brother Stanley,[55] were gratefully, if reluctantly,
received, but she frequently expressed concern over how
to earn an adequate income through her own work. She
seems never to have acknowledged that the years of caring
for her mother might have deserved financial remuneration. Her continuing periods of poor health meant that
weakness and fatigue usually prevented her from holding a
full-time job.

During this period Alice had also become involved in the
suffrage movement. When she took her twenty-year-old
niece Edith to Europe in 1910 they both took part in a large
suffrage march which, according to *The Stairway*, was
organized by the 'Women's League for Social and Political
Equality' (likely, in fact, the Women's Social and Political
Union). Alice saw the suffrage march in the same light as
she viewed higher education for women and co-operative
communities: 'the procession of the great democracy – the
democracy that includes women as well as men' (79). Edith
('Agnes' in *The Stairway*) wrote in her diary that their small
contingent consisted of 'four English ladies, three Canadians ... and one African.'[56] At the end of the march she was
thrilled at the sight of Albert Hall 'filled with 10,000 people, mostly women.'

By the following year, when she moved to Toronto, Alice had joined the Canadian Suffrage Association (CSA),[57] the most progressive women's suffrage group in the city. Headed by Flora MacDonald Denison, a more radical feminist than most of the Canadian suffrage movement's members, the association's government lobbying and publicity had contributed to the NCWC's 1910 decision to support women's suffrage. Alice's relationship with Denison is not known; although many aspects of their social criticism were similar, their approaches to suffrage obviously differed. In January 1912, as part of a group of women refused the vote in the association's elections, Alice called a large meeting at which the Toronto Equal Franchise League was formed.[58] The new league, with Alice as first vice-president and Constance Hamilton (Mrs L.A.) as president, intended to convince women of the need for the vote by implementing educational programs. The vote was seen as a way for women to gain power to carry out reforms. Unlike the CSA, Alice saw female enfranchisement as a means, not an end.

Alice's role in the Equal Franchise League was consistent with her previous concerns. The emphasis on women's education and an insistence that it was 'first necessary that [a woman] should feel her sense of responsibility in the community' had been implicit in her article of 1901 on women's higher education. She would have understood the word 'empowerment.' Newspaper accounts state that the new organization's membership would include both professional women and homemakers. Alice's priorities are suggested in the group's purpose which was 'the attainment of the municipal and parliamentary franchise for women on the same terms as ... men and the education of men and women both in town and country in social, economic and political matters.'[59] The league's program began with a series of 'parlour' and public meetings and an attempt to co-operate with other women's groups. By March, the organization had given about twenty parlour presentations, some of which had occurred in houses where 'hard workingmen and women ... listened to an informal talk on some vital problems needing re-adjusting.' Alice's influence can be seen in attempts to cut across class lines. Besides efforts to reach the uncommitted elite, the league promoted a 'Working Girls' League' whose membership included office workers.[60]

A month after Alice founded the Equal Franchise League the well-known Eaton's strike took place. Alice's inquiries into women's working conditions had acquainted her with conditions of female factory workers, including instances of sexual harassment. As she wrote in *The Stairway*, 'Often a factory girl's job or, if she did piece work, the kind and amount of work given to her, depended on her courting the favour of the foreman' (99). The main strikers consisted of about 575 members of the International Garment Workers' Union, but over 275 female cloakmakers walked out at the same time in sympathy with the male strikers.[61] Arriving at the strike unexpectedly, Alice felt such solidarity with the female strikers that she allowed herself to be arrested along with them. At the courtroom she was regaled with stories of foremen's harassment and bullying of female (and male) workers. She was in tears by the time she left and accompanied the strikers to a labour meeting where she volunteered to publicize the strike. This endeavour soon made her aware of the reluctance of newspapers to publish news about the strike because of large advertising accounts with Eaton's.

These experiences made Alice a firm believer in trade unionism. She wanted middle-class women's organizations to acknowledge the appalling working conditions that many women endured in Toronto. The fact that the strike was focusing attention on this issue convinced her that the time was right for more privileged women to become involved. Consequently, she tried to interest women's club and suffrage organization members but was 'amazed because they had no sympathy with the strikers, unless I had some tale of hardship to tell' (120). When she arranged for an American strike organizer to speak at a suffrage meeting, she was denounced for introducing the subject of female strikers in a discussion of women's suffrage. Later, she bitterly recounted this experience, citing the women's lack of concern for social justice.[62] 'I did not expect an audience who had never considered that justice to working people was a higher virtue than charity, to respond any more cordially than it did,'' she wrote (121). As she does not mention the Equal Franchise League again, it is likely that she broke from the organization at this time. Her efforts to persuade the employers of the strikers were also rebuffed: the head of the firm was so sure of his good intentions, she wrote, 'that he refused to listen to anything that would cast a slur on them' (120).[63] Her commitment to justice rather than charitable works was understood by few. To suggest in 1912 that Eaton's should share authority with its employees, and to support openly the strike, was to distance herself effectively from the established society from which she sprang.

Alice's belief that strike action and subsequent improvement of working conditions and wages was one of the paths to the new age resulted in her decision to go to New York the following January to support striking women members of the International Ladies' Garment Workers' Union.[64] As she travelled to New York she was convinced that 'a new era was dawning, when women ... were coming out a regular army, to take their ranks with men in organized labor' (124). She was particularly interested in sup-

porting the attempt to gain the protocol, a uniform agreement for whole sections of the industry.

In New York Alice listened to the speeches, learned of
the grievances, and joined the picketers. She was impressed
by many of the young women strikers. 'It has been wonderfully interesting to see the young girls in the strike,' she
wrote to Edith, 'young girls of sixteen and eighteen who
have shewn such wonderful ability to lead their shop-
mates.'[65] She also commented, as she had before, on the
difference between her life in New York and that in Kingston. The people she knew in New York 'would all be so abnormal in [Kingston people's] estimation while here they
arouse no curiosity, they are taken for granted and their
ideas are expected to be the coming ideas.' She was impressed by the reading material of the strikers, noting that
favourite authors were Carlyle, Morris, and Ruskin. There
were more idealists, she maintained, among the ranks of
the labour leaders than in the churches. Once again, as she
had during the Eaton's strike, she criticized the daily newspapers which 'preach almost constantly that the labor
troubles are due to agitators who are seeking their own
profit' (130). Alluding once more to the image of the staircase, she wrote that her new understanding of 'the necessity for economic freedom for the workers' was the next
step on her stairway (132).

Alice's last known direct involvement with the suffrage
movement was in the United States. While living in New
York at the beginning of 1914 she secured a part-time job
with one of the suffrage associations. She arranged meetings and demonstrations and apparently produced dramatic sketches on the theme of women's suffrage. In March
she wrote that one of her plays was 'on the road.'[66] This interest in drama as a vehicle for social comment was related
to her association with the Ferrer Center in New York. The

centre, a meeting place for intellectuals and anarchists, and one of the few places where Jewish immigrants and middle-class Americans met in an atmosphere of respect, was congruent with Alice's conception of a tolerant and democratic society. Besides being a forum for experimental theatre, it provided lectures, concerts, plays, and discussion groups. Lecturers might include artists such as Robert Henri and George Bellows or birth control advocate Margaret Sanger. Sixteen years later, Alice's interest in drama as social expression was to resurface in the form of peace pageants for the Women's League of Nations Association.

Alice sought out the lectures of Emma Goldman. The well-known feminist and anarchist, whose interests included drama, had published *The Social Significance of Drama* the same year. Hearing Goldman, Alice felt she was in the presence of 'the best piece of work that was being carried on in New York,' and was tempted to join the New York anarchists. However, she felt that Goldman's 'work was not the work for me' (170). As she wrote in *The Stairway*, 'I am quite willing to think hatred may be necessary in certain stages of development, but it is not necessary to me.' She acknowledged that the religious viewpoint of her youth still 'so clings to me that I cannot postulate freedom without relating it to my faith in spiritual forces.'

In New York, Alice lived alone in an apartment, having temporarily rejected communal living. However, she still hoped to find a group of people who 'based their hope for a new society' on the fundamental principles of 'love and truth' (169). Glad to be away from Kingston where she was considered 'erratic,' she wrote to Edith, with tongue-in-cheek, that she had had two offers of marriage by mail but would 'not give up my freedom for any man.'[67] Among the tenants in her apartment house she was amazed to find un-educated young factory workers who shared her own ideals. Of one young tenant she wrote: 'her idealism and her vitality are a great joy to me.' Another girl and her brother became her protégés for several years.

Just before she left New York in June 1914 Alice took part in a demonstration protesting the killing in Colorado of wives and children of striking miners, known as the Ludlow Massacre. The demonstration, organized by writer-reformer Upton Sinclair, consisted of a silent parade in front of mine owner John D. Rockefeller's church. Alice recalled the experience of this protest as one of social significance and personal frustration, a reminder to her that once 'a lady' committed herself to radical causes she was liable to be treated with hostility by both uncomprehending workers and middle-class radicals. 'Poor me!' she wrote, 'Here I was, falling between two stools.' (188) The demonstrations against Rockefeller became more hostile after Alice's departure. A few days after the silent parade a bomb meant for the millionaire's house went off and killed several protesters. Fortunately, Alice was then in Toronto.

There, she suffered one of her periodic attacks of unexplained illness. As at Letchworth five years earlier, she was extremely weak and often had to be carried to her small apartment. In early August Britain declared war on Germany. After her recovery Alice moved to Clarkson, about thirty kilometres southwest of Toronto, where she began an experiment in co-operative living. She rented a cottage on a fruit farm where she hoped to establish a community for ex-labour leaders and women who had spent their lives doing social work.

While Alice was moving to Clarkson, a year into the war, the International Congress of Women at The Hague, chaired by Jane Addams, was taking place. The congress, an extraordinary feat of organization and faith, resulted in a plan for mediation between the opposing sides in the war.

Over a thousand women from twelve countries partici-
pated. The fact that British and German women sat peace-
fully together and tried to devise a strategy for ending the
war flew in the face of contemporary Allied conceptions of
German people as the enemy.[68] The congress authorized a
party of delegates to visit heads of state and present the
mediation plan which had been largely drawn up by a
Canadian expatriate, Julia Grace Wales.

One of the members of this delegation was Crystal Macmillan, a Scottish lawyer and secretary of the congress. In
the fall of 1915, six months after the congress, Macmillan
was invited to speak in Toronto at the annual meeting of
the National Council of Women of Canada. The women
most responsible for bringing her to Toronto were Harriet
Dunlop Prenter and Christine Ross Barker, who represented a more radical approach to the war than was to be
found in NCWC policy. The fact that they were permitted to
bring Macmillan to the annual meeting, after the NCWC had
refused to condone The Hague congress,[69] was likely due
to Macmillan's reputation as a women's suffrage spokes-
person. That she was considered a controversial figure is
suggested by the fact that she was given only three minutes
to speak. Her presentation, 'What women can do to prevent war,' was summarily described by the press as present-
ing 'two special aspects from which to view women's
responsibilities. One, to do what they could to promote
good feelings among the nations, and the other to work for
political emancipation.' However, an editorial in the same
newspaper suggests that Macmillan said a lot more and that
her analysis of the war was considered unprintable by
some Toronto papers.[70]

Soon after this presentation, according to Alice, the
'Women's Patriotic League' passed a resolution condemning Macmillan. This organization may have actually been

the Women for Patriotic Service whose national committee, acting as an umbrella group for national women's groups, had officially refused to participate in or condone the congress at The Hague. Thus, no official Canadian delegates attended, although Laura Hughes of Toronto went unofficially.[71] Not only was Macmillan condemned by the female patriots, but she was harshly attacked by at least one Toronto newspaper which described her as being 'under the influence of the German plotters at the alleged peace conference held [in The Hague],' and as one of the 'purveyors of scandals and slanders.' Alice protested Macmillan's treatment in an angry letter to the editor. To begin with, freedom of speech was at stake, she declared. 'Despite the strictures of the Woman's Patriotic League on the address of Miss Crystal Macmillan ... militarism has not so far succeeded in curtailing the right of free speech.'[72] Her belief in the need for personal responsibility, rather than faith in institutions, was restated when she put some of the blame for the war on German people who had 'obeyed and not thought' and had been 'too content to leave their government in the hands of their ruler.' In this, she was likely suggesting that those who condemned Crystal Macmillan were doing the same thing. Alice affirmed her conviction that 'the causes of war are not national, they are human and economic. They cannot be overcome by force.' Her absolute opposition to force was clearly expressed. 'If we are ever to be free from militarism,' she declared, 'we must do away with the spirit that causes war. We must believe that ideas are more powerful than machine guns, and to love our enemies is a surer way of defeating them than to fight them.'

As the newspaper had attacked Crystal Macmillan, so it condemned her supporter. 'Miss Chown' had put herself in the company of women who were conducting 'an in-

sidious campaign with the object of undermining British
influence and British prestige.' She 'is determined to dis-
associate herself from the rest of her kind.' Letters to the
editor suggested she be put in a lunatic asylum or sent to
'ravished Belgium.' Alice defended herself with renewed
vigour. 'Long before I had ever heard of Jane Addams or
Miss Macmillan,' she wrote, 'I was an anti-militarist.'[73] As
J.S. Woodsworth would state in his letter of resignation
from the Methodist Church two years later, Alice wrote
that her belief in the teachings of Jesus prevented her from
accepting war. She challenged her critics. 'Like Bernard
Shaw,' she asserted, 'I tell everyone who is encouraging
war in any way, at least be honest with yourself; if you
believe in force, acknowledge yourself a pagan.'

In the three letters she wrote in support of Crystal Macmillan, and an open letter to pacifists written to the *Christian Guardian* in the spring of 1916, Alice set out her
belief in pacifism. She could not view the war, as did Nellie
McClung in *In Times Like These* (1915), as a product of un-
christian nations inhabited by Christians who were powerless to prevent it. Alice believed women could speak out
against the war and live out their beliefs as she did. 'There
is only one way for women to put an end to the war,' she
wrote, 'that is, to refuse to countenance it.' As for church
support of the war, that institution was denying 'the principle for which Christ was willing to die – the brotherhood
of man.' That the church did not support her position is
revealed in the attack on pacifists by the *Guardian* later
that year.[74]

Alice's pacifism was of course related to her commitment
to working towards the coming of the new age. In this, she
was in the spiritual company of the social gospellers who,
as Thomas Socknat points out, believed that by taking the
pacifist stand 'they were remaining faithful to pre-war

social gospel pronouncements on the necessity of attaining world peace before the Kingdom of God would be realized.'[75]

Alice placed great emphasis on education and the availability of information. She condemned press censorship during the war, insisting on the individual's democratic right to know the facts. She deeply resented the Canadian government's refusal to allow the entry into Canada of publications which stated the enemy's case. In the letter to the *Guardian* she called on people to 'pledge themselves to work for a non-partisan knowledge of both sides.' Her strongly anti-militaristic attitude led her to be investigated by government officials and, she suspected, to have her mail censored (222).

Whether she was living in Canada or not, Alice attempted to educate her own family on the importance of informed opinion. In 1915 her Christmas present to Edith was 'a subscription to the best democratic paper. ... I want you to commence to get the social viewpoint concerning events as that is the only preventive of war.'[76] She read their essays and sent material such as 'literature about the Freedom of India movement' to one of her nephews at Queen's in 1921. Writing to Lorne Pierce after the war, she restated her absolute rejection of censorship: 'I believe in freedom for every individual to develop [the] life force within him, I would give free and full education of facts without regard to their desirability but no propaganda, no creed, no censorship of thought either by Church or State. I believe in self determination for individuals and nations and in co-operation likewise.' At the end of the war, when she attacked her cousin Dwight Chown, general superintendent of the Methodist Church, for his position during the war, her strongest criticism was reserved for his ignorance and reliance on a censored press.[77]

Promoting ideas that were seen by many as naïve or worse, Alice, and the few Canadians who held her position, had great difficulty in getting their pacifist message across to the general public. In 1915, when patriotism was being carefully promoted by government propaganda and even by fiction writers, few could understand the message of the wartime pacifists. With a hint of despair, she wrote that 'there are surely Canadians who believe that the time has come in the world's development when ideas, intelligence and good-will should take the place of force in settling disputes between individuals and nations.'[78]

For two years during the war Alice isolated herself at Clarkson. Her attempts to create a co-operative community were not successful. She continued fruit farming and caring for the people who came to her door needing food, money, or shelter. In 1916 she seemed bemused, yet pleased, that her niece Edith had decided 'not to follow your aunt's example and keep your freedom,' but was to marry Lorne Pierce. She welcomed Pierce, who was studying theology and had not yet begun the editorship of Ryerson Press, as a nephew-in-law and assured him that Edith would never worry him 'as the aunt may, by her radical opinions.' Her letter marked the beginning of a long and close relationship. Soon after the engagement was announced she delightedly gave her old 'theological works' to Pierce. She agreed to go to the wedding in Kingston, stating that 'nothing but a wedding or funeral would take me back.'[79]

In 1917 Alice moved to the country outside Boston, according to *The Stairway*. No correspondence has been found dating from this period. In leaving Canada to live in the United States that year, she had settled on the same solution as Winnipeg journalist Francis Beynon, who also experienced the difficulty of living in Canada and holding anti-militarist beliefs. Also that year, J.S. Woodsworth, having been fired from the Bureau of Social Research in Manitoba for his pacifist position, considered moving to the United States or joining a Doukhobor community which held pacifist views. After leaving the Boston area Alice lived in various parts of New York state, often returning to Ontario in the summer. Sometimes she considered returning to Canada for good but felt that this would be 'like going back into another age, another era, a foreign land where people do not speak my language, and yet one reason they do not is that just as soon as people get a little progressive they desert Canada and leave the old conservatives there. It is quite a question in my mind if I could do work that was not controversial there and quietly educate the people.'[80]

Alice's despair over the war is evident. In early 1918 she wrote that she was 'sick with dismay' about the German offensive. In a letter to Lorne Pierce written from Croton-on-Hudson, New York, she poured out her doubt and grief. She had lost faith in non-resistance, she wrote, after the German brutality against Russia. Only through resolute action, she felt, could the spirit for change be re-established. 'I have come to the conclusion we must create the spirit in men we desire,' she insisted. The new world must be created by doing, not by preaching, sentimentalizing, or theorizing. Thus, she implored Pierce to delay entering the church and attend an American political science college which was to prepare students for reconstruction after the war.[81]

Her disillusionment affected her attempts to complete *The Stairway*, but she apparently finished the first draft by May 1918. The following year, after a major revision, she was still tormenting herself over it. 'What worries me,' she confessed, 'is that while I am writing a book to prove that

there is only one law in life that is fundamental, un-
changeable and always desirable to follow, I am tormented
by doubts about the possibility and desirability under present conditions of always following it.'[82]

Although *The Stairway* ends with an entry for June 1919
which implies a sense of harmony in her life, letters from
Alice suggest that such was not the case. In that period of
the 'red scare,' wartime pacifists and those with sympathy
for the Russian experiment were subjected to widespread
hostility. The Pierces worried that she had 'thrown everything overboard,' perhaps because of her friendship with
American socialists. At least two of them, Roger Baldwin
and Kate Richards O'Hare, had been jailed for their anti-
war activities. Alice's reaction to the Pierces' concern
reveals that, like many reformers, she considered herself to
be part of an enlightened elite. 'Unless you get joy out of
defending me do not do it,' she wrote, referring to herself
as 'on the foremost ship blazing the new trail' and pitying
those in the back ships who 'catch only the far off echoes
of our virile songs of faith.'[83]

By the middle of the next year, 1920, Alice's mood had
shifted. She reflected on the effects of the difficult climate
for people on the left in the United States. 'For a time I was
in a very bellicose mood,' she wrote the Pierces, and 'felt
like saying all sorts of hard, strong things but I am once
more a pacifist ... I think we pacifists who came through
the war had a hard time this spring with the re-actionaries
[*sic*] and were inclined to lavish some hatred on them.'[84]

In the 1920s Alice expanded her acquaintances among
American liberal and socialist circles, wrote stories (none of
which have been found) and essays, and continued to pon-
der the best way to live out her beliefs. Her life during
these years seems less focused as she travelled, visited, and
searched for the ideal community. The intensity of the pre-

war women's movement had been severely circumscribed. Reasons for this included internal philosophical differences over equal rights, the 'red scare' and its accompanying fear of socialism, and the drive to return women to the patriarchal authority of the home. One of Alice's essays of this time suggests that she viewed herself as part of a progressive, but not necessarily feminist, elite. Titled 'The Joy of the Minority,'[85] it told of the joy, as well as the pain, of members of the 'initiative minority' who possessed 'the consciousness of ever growing, expanding life,' and understood that 'facts are not enough, convictions are not enough. One must feel the spiritual impetus.' Similar to *The Stairway*, with which it shares some passages, the essay describes the initiated few as being able to comprehend a world where 'latent possibilities' may be developed through freedom and 'self realization.' The forms may vary. 'The Bolshevik may find it in Russia, the Guild Socialist in Britain, and the Co-operators elsewhere. New forms will be created to answer to the new spirit.'

Besides being interested in the drive for self-determination in Russia, Alice followed the struggles in other countries. She apparently went to southern Ireland in the early 1920s.[86] Unfortunately little is known about that trip. In the United States she continued explorations of co-operative and non-exploitative living arrangements. In 1922 she was living on a poultry farm, 'not because I am interested in poultry,' as she explained to her niece, 'but the great problem for everyone who tries to free himself from living on the profits of labor is the question of earning his own living. I thoroughly believe that we are going to have a great deal of experimenting in self productive groups. As I am free, I am a good one to experiment.'[87] Her next endeavour, of which only the early planning stages are known, also took place in New York state. Probably in

1923 she announced that forty-six acres and a Dutch colonial cottage had been purchased with the intention of organizing 'a Land and Craft Guild among people who believe that if joy in living is to return to us that we must simplify life in both its needs and pleasures.'[88] The plan included common ownership of land and an emphasis on co-operation.

It is not known how long Alice stayed with this scheme. By late 1923 or early 1924 she was completely involved in a more consciously socialistic experiment with co-operative living and the education of the children of workers. This involvement lasted for three years and took her to Louisiana and Arkansas. Two of her central concerns were manifest in Newllano Colony and Commonwealth College which grew out of it: co-operative, self-sufficient living schemes and education for all, including oppressed groups. Alice's connections with the Socialist party would have acquainted her with communities like Newllano. The colony itself had begun in California in 1914 but, due to shortage of water, had moved to Louisiana in 1917. In 1923 Kate O'Hare, a prominent member of the then-waning Socialist party, moved to the colony with her family. O'Hare had attended a Florida labour college and become interested in establishing a self-sufficient teaching institution for workers. She had persuaded educator William E. Zeuch to set up a college at Newllano. Tentatively opened in the fall of 1923 with Zeuch as director and O'Hare as field secretary, the college was 'an overt manifestation of American general discontent in the between-the-wars era with the economic, social, and political inequalities under the capitalist system in the United States.'[89]

After taking up residency at the Louisiana site of the colony, Alice unwittingly became involved in the hostility among the school and colony administrations. Resentment of her as a woman who wanted to be directly involved in administration seems to have interfered with her efforts to mediate agreement between the groups. As she was to encounter within the League of Nations Society a few years later, difficulties appeared between herself and the male hierarchy. In both cases, she did not set out to challenge the monopolization of power, but simply viewed it as a temporary wall blocking her path. The main problem appears to have been a lack of any real conception of co-operation among the community members. Except for O'Hare, women seem to have had no voice. Alice involved herself with a women's group and spoke out at meetings on the silencing of the women by the men.[90] Although disturbed by such shortcomings, and especially at the exclusion of blacks from the colony and school, she believed in the ideology behind the school and committed herself to seeing it firmly established before she left.

Alice worked hard at raising funds. In late 1924 she went to New York (apparently with Kate O'Hare) to approach the American Fund for Public Service, among whose board members was her acquaintance Roger Baldwin. She arrived back at Newllano with a cheque for $35,000 to be distributed to Commonwealth College and a group of seceded Newllano colonists who had re-established themselves at Ink, Arkansas.[91] However, as the two administrations were unable to settle their differences, which was a condition of the grant, Alice was obliged to return the cheque to the donors. Likely encouraged by her enthusiasm for the college, the fund did later make substantial grants to Commonwealth College, contributing over $30,000 between 1925 and 1928.[92]

During the summer of 1925, when the college moved to the country outside Mena, Arkansas, Alice 'worked harder than [she] ever worked before' to establish the new site. By then a woman of almost sixty, she lived in a tent, planted the garden, and involved herself in work which resulted in 'crops harvested for food for winter ... four large buildings and three cottages.' Conditions were primitive; she wrote that 'the college is running smoothly altho [*sic*] we have neither doors or windows to our houses.'[93] Revealing both her sense of humour and her Kingston middle-class background, she confided to Lorne Pierce the following year: 'In many ways, I like the pioneering altho I am very tired of white oil cloths for table cloths and the rough and ready table manners.' Besides teaching English composition, she became the college's comptroller, store proprietor, and sometime benefactor. A colleague recalled that 'whenever need arose, [she] advanced the cash to pay the baker's or milkman's demands.' Years after she left, she was remembered for her 'brilliant intellect' and as 'a strong example of what the spirit could do when in the grasp of a great principle or idea.'[94]

During the twenties the college conducted Sunday evening open forums. At one of these, in 1926, Alice presented 'The things that cannot be shaken.' According to the college newspaper, which described her as the 'gracious, white-haired comptroller,' she discussed 'The Joys of Life, the Reality of the Cosmos, the Soul's Strife for Perfection through Heroic Action, the Yearning for Beauty, the Harmony of Nature and the Power of Love.'[95] That Alice's beliefs had moved away from the church's teachings, to a commitment to inner spirit and mysticism, is emphasized by this presentation.

In late 1926 or early 1927 Alice returned to Toronto where she devoted the rest of her life to the peace movement and the promotion of tolerance and co-operation among individuals. By now in her sixties, she put aside her quest for the ideal community and turned her attention to the community of nations, the League of Nations. Her commitment to both pacifism and social justice put her in an isolated position in Canada, where peace advocates of the 1920s, with some notable exceptions, tended to 'fight militarism without directly challenging the state.'[96] Thus, the fact that she put her energy into the League of Nations Society (LNS) rather than the more radical Toronto branch of the Women's International League for Peace and Freedom (WIL), which more closely reflected her views, is possibly explained by the pressure of family and friends. The WIL was considered far left and radical by the Toronto establishment which included her brother Edwin, a United Church minister. Soon after her return she visited the Shortts in Ottawa; Adam Shortt was by that time involved with the League of Nations. Besides these influences, Alice may have felt she could be more effective within the established LNS which she viewed as 'a great co-operative society.' Many women are already involved in the LNS; in fact the society relied on the League of Nations committees of women's organizations for its survival. The Woman's Christian Temperance Union was active as was the National Council of Women of Canada, which included such committees in forty-two of its fifty-six local councils.[97] In 1927 the WIL in Toronto was not a strong organization; it was not until the 1930s that an official Canadian Section was established to co-ordinate the branches scattered across Canada. Alice's concern with popular education on peace issues, with combating racial intolerance, and her belief in the economic causes of conflict closely paralleled significant concerns of the WIL. It is possible that she first joined the organization in the United States after the war. She did, in fact, work jointly with it in Toronto.[98]

Basic differences of approach soon became apparent between Alice, who was the representative of women's church organizations for the League of Nations Society, and the LNS central and local executives. Colonel Colborne P. Meredith, the secretary-general of the society, has been described as a military man who 'sometimes forgot that he was no longer at Camp Petawawa and tried to run the office with the precision of a General Staff Headquarters.' By December, Meredith was writing anxious letters to W.L. Grant, head of the Toronto chapter, about Alice's procedure in organizing a membership drive without giving due credit to the central executive. The fact that she was undertaking a membership drive with little support from the head office coincides with the experience of women in other groups: Veronica Strong-Boag states that by the mid-1920s 'conduct of [LNS] recruitment campaigns was assigned to women's organizations.'[99]

For three years Alice worked within the structure of the society. Aware that she held a more radical view than the LNS hierarchy, she managed to proceed with caution for some time. As she humorously explained in 1929 to Madeleine Doty, editor of the WIL's *Pax International*, 'Here I am back in Canada doing a perfectly proper job in a very diplomatic manner, getting occasionally a little radical information across to very stodgy people. It is a case of boring from within. My good Methodist name carries me far and I have opportunities which another radical might not have. I am severely proper but the day may come when I am thrown out of the League of Nations Society. In the meantime I sow my seed.'[100]

In June 1929, before she was, in effect, 'thrown out,' Alice visited the Soviet Union, a journey she had wanted to make since 1919, when her known criticism of the Canadian government prevented her from doing so. However, she was at last permitted to see the country she described as witnessing 'the wonderful task of changing the ideals of the people from self-interest to service and co-operation.' Like J.S. Woodsworth, who toured the country three years later, she was amazed at the 'versatility of finding new methods, new stimulants for people to learn' and of the campaigns to abolish illiteracy and alcoholism. 'Culture is the goal,' she wrote, 'the culture that gives the individual faith in his own ability to do creative things.' The experiment was too new to judge it economically, she wrote to her old friend and mentor Elizabeth Shortt, 'but culturally, I admire.'[101]

On leaving the Soviet Union, Alice journeyed to Geneva where she stayed at the Maison Internationale and attended the League of Nations Assembly. Saskatchewan feminist and journalist Violet McNaughton, also a member of the WIL who had attended its international meetings, described the Maison as an 'informal gathering place for women delegates to the league [of Nations] where they meet other outstanding women who happen to be in Geneva at the time.'[102] That summer, Canadian MP Agnes Macphail represented Canada at the assembly and as a delegate to the late-August WIL congress in Prague. Alice may have also attended the WIL congress where, expectedly, the connection between disarmament and economics was intensively discussed.

Alice's relationship with the hierarchy of the LNS deteriorated further after her return from Europe in 1929. The following spring her prediction came true and she was virtually purged from the society and prevented from holding any significant office in it. Grant advised Meredith that she 'has now no status with us whatever.' Meredith's reply, that he was pleased to know that she was 'no longer to be feared,' would certainly have amused her.[103] Alice and the women who had been working with her in the LNS immediately founded the Women's League of Nations Association (WLNA) and continued to work for the society. Now less hindered by the local and central LNS executives, they resumed their work with increased energy. As there is little mention of other women's groups in the LNS after Alice left, one can presume that the active women in the society became members of the WLNA. Their efforts towards increasing LNS membership and their innovative educational programs soon caused Grant to switch from refusal of recognition to enthusiastic praise of the new association, which, between 1930 and 1935, seems to have done most of the LNS work in Toronto. The difference between the methods of the LNS and the WLNA prompted Alice to observe in 1935 that 'men are all for tactics and women for results.'[104] Correspondence suggests that the central executive of the society tended to confine its activities to board meetings, luncheon meetings, fund raising, and model assemblies whereas the WLNA, less concerned with organizational structure, organized membership drives, study groups, lectures, dramatizations, and conferences whose influence went well beyond the confines of Toronto.

The WLNA's first major undertaking was to campaign for support of the 1932 Disarmament Conference. One of its most effective tools was the use of drama. Having become interested in drama as a means of communication in 1914, Alice once again wrote 'dramatized sketches' as she called them. 'The United States of Europe,' written to promote the conference, was one of these. The plays were popular with other women's groups who were promoting the Disarmament Conference. In late 1931 Alice received requests for copies from Violet McNaughton and the International Council of Women. That year, the Local Council of

Women in Toronto performed one of the plays at the Canadian National Exhibition. Further illustrating the WLNA's intensive work for the conference is the fact that it sent speakers to fifty women's organizations per month near the end of the campaign.[105] The contribution of the WLNA to the campaign and the accompanying petition drive, which collected 200,000 signatures, has yet to be evaluated by peace historians.

After its work for the Disarmament Conference, the association turned its attention to the evils of private arms manufacture, a concern of both the LNS and the WIL. Alice's plays, 'Salesmen of Death' and 'Enemies of Peace,' were presented to bring attention to this issue. By June 1933 the association had sent publicity on armament manufacture to all members of Parliament in the Dominion. Again, speakers, lantern slide presentations, and study groups were organized. During the campaign Alice consulted Dorothy Detzer, the secretary of the U.S. section of the WIL, who had been one of the most prominent promoters of the Nye Senate inquiry into arms manufacture. When the Canadian government finally spoke out in the League of Nations against unregulated arms trade, Alice gave credit to the WLNA's effort, calling it the 'most vital and far reaching piece of work for the League of Nations done in Canada' and lamented the 'deficiencies of the [LNS] Central Executive.'[106]

Alice's main source of support within the LNS hierarchy was R.B. Inch, editor of the society's publication, *Interdependence*, in Ottawa. At Inch's request, she suggested people for the LNS executive or topics for *Interdependence*, which she frequently criticized as too highbrow to reach ordinary people. She herself sometimes despaired of educating the women in her group. In her attempts to bring the message of personal and international co-operation to a broader section of people, she differed from the hierarchy of the LNS. As she wrote in 1933, 'Colonel Drew [president of the Toronto branch] wants to enlist influential citizens. We are more interested in the masses of people.'[107]

By the mid-1930s Alice was tiring of the struggles related to shortage of funds, inadequate support from the LNS, and the difficulty of affecting public opinion. 'I wonder why the world is so stupid,' she wrote to Elizabeth Shortt just before Christmas 1935. 'Why does it not learn that the laws of truth and justice, love, good will and harmony are eternal, universal and breaking them carries its own penalty.'[108] Her efforts to 'keep the Toronto [LNS] chapter from dying' went largely unrecognized; she was rejected as a member of the League Council of the LNS. Her frustrations were apparent to those around her. A Chown family member, who as a young university student in 1935 knew Alice, remembers her as a woman whose eccentricities and delight in appearing outrageous weakened her credibility as a peace activist.[109] Other recollections of her during the period point to her continuing intellectual curiosity and interest in socialism. Among those invited to her tea-time discussions of world problems were socialist intellectuals, such as David Lewis, and University of Toronto history professors.[110]

The WLNA's work after the 1932 Disarmament Conference included promoting the resumption of the conference in October 1933, publicizing the effects of the arms trade, and producing study guides for reading circles and other groups. Despite the difficulties with the LNS, Alice maintained a commitment to the League of Nations at least until the end of her active membership in 1936.[111] By March 1935 the association had been integrated with the LNS's Toronto branch; Alice was considered to be chairman [*sic*] of the women's organizations within the society.

Alice's last known trip abroad was in 1935 when she went to Geneva for the League of Nations Assembly. On her return she was interviewed for an article which aptly described her as devoted to 'achieving peace in a world that is under the death-sentence of war,' and applauded her for having 'raised her voice against private profits in the armaments industry, against false patriotism, against national rivalries and imperialist ambition.'[112] Along with many members of the WIL, Alice believed that capitalism had failed. Like them, she viewed with alarm the growing fascist movement and saw socialism 'as a preventive of war.'[113] 'There must be sharing and an economic system that makes co-operation possible' was a variation of a statement she repeated throughout her life. She greeted the formation of the Co-operative Commonwealth Federation in 1933 as a means to put the words into practice.

Alice was able to express once more her belief in the connection between personal and international co-operation when she attended a reception in 1941 in honour of her seventy-fifth birthday given by the Women's Section of the League of Nations Society. To each guest she gave a card bearing her photograph and an inscription which reiterated her belief in the transformative power of love and her commitment to working for peace: 'Let us as members of this League of Nations Society express love in every relationship that we may bring peace and good will, unity and co-operation in all the world. My love and my faith that we shall become a Society of lovers.'[114]

As one of her last undertakings in the years of work towards a just and peaceful society, Alice began in 1941 to edit a feature in the *United Church Observer* entitled 'The Next Step.' This was the first known instance of the church publishing her work since her open letter to pacifists in 1916. Perhaps her age or a promise to avoid radical subjects convinced the church to publish her work once again. For the column's title Alice used the same imagery to evoke her view of the evolutionary nature of human awareness as she had for *The Stairway*. Obviously enjoying the work, she wrote to Elizabeth Shortt that 'it is a very easy task for I have no refusals.'[115] Continuing until 1945, the column consisted of general articles on post-war reconstruction in Canada and discussions of specific issues to be addressed after the war such as women's equality, housing, health, education, and trade unionism. Contributors tended to come from a religious, moral or socialist perspective and included writers such as Frank Underhill, Margaret Fairley, and Rabbi Maurice Eisendrath. The immediate need for Canada to accept more refugees was also discussed; Canadian government resistance to Jewish immigration was particularly painful to many pacifists. Although not written by Alice herself, a few of the articles are reminders of Alice's belief in women's right to autonomy and their special understanding of the issues of war and peace. One of the pieces, 'Women's Role in Building the Peace,' asserts that women's participation at all levels of government, in the professions, and in social services was essential to effective post-war reconstruction. Moreover, the writer calls for women to educate their children that 'wars can be stopped only by an extension of social and economic justice.'[116]

In her own contributions to the column Alice criticized Canadians' racist attitudes towards Jews and blacks. Now an old woman, her sphere of action was more circumscribed. Accordingly, she organized tea parties to encourage co-operation and tolerance. Calling them her 'venture in understanding,' she described how they promoted interaction which had not previously existed between Jewish and non-Jewish women.[117] Two Chown family members who assisted at the teas recall the sense of purpose as well as the unceremonious repast at the gatherings.[118] Alice was saddened at the racism she encountered towards blacks in Toronto. 'It is hard,' she admitted, 'to persuade even individuals who are supposed to be broad minded that people stand on their character and not on the color of their skin.'[119]

Alice's work since the publication of the *The Stairway* had been a continuation of her life as described in the book. Experiments in co-operative living and education, concern for oppressed peoples, and concentrated work for peace had taken up most of her time since the First World War. In her seventies, she continued her efforts, permitting neither age nor despair at finding herself living through another world war to end her lifelong mission. Her work as a feminist, pacifist, and socialist had been directed towards her perception of the coming age of equality, social justice, co-operation, and love. Always acutely aware of women's oppression, she viewed their struggle for autonomy as necessary to the realization of this goal. Her understanding of the underlying causes which prevented them from gaining that autonomy set her apart from the maternal feminists of the mainstream Canadian women's movement. She promoted these ideals both through her work and her daily life, assisted by her inextinguishable spirit, intelligence, and sense of humour. The story of her life, its significance largely unrecognized since her death in 1949, can serve as an inspiration to many women and men of today who are similarly working towards a more peaceful and just world.

NOTES

I am particularly grateful to Frances Early, Susan Jackel, Barbara Roberts, and Thomas Socknat; at different stages in the work, their suggestions resulted in major improvements. I wish it were possible to acknowledge all the help I received. Besides scholars already mentioned, I very much appreciated Veronica Strong-Boag's insightful suggestions, Margaret Prang's guidance in Canadian religious history, and Gregory Kealey's information about RCMP files. Talking over this project with scholars working in Canadian women's history such as Georgina Taylor, Anne Hicks, and Kathy Cavanaugh provided new understandings. Archivists who were particularly helpful were Susan Bellingham at the University of Waterloo, David Fraser at the Public Archives of Canada, George Henderson of Queen's University, and Jim Lewis at the University of Saskatchewan, as well as the staff of Special Collections, University of Arkansas. Chown family members have contributed a great deal, particularly William S.E. Chown, Margaret Chown Leslie, who like Beth Pierce Robinson spent hours going through trunks of letters, Sylvia Woodsworth Campbell, Kenneth Woodsworth, Allison Chown, Jean Woodsworth, and Peggy Patterson. My sister Nora Clarke provided valuable criticism, and my husband Jan Van Stolk, as well as Sylvia Gorchynski, suggested thoughtful psychological interpretations of Aunt Alice. Eunice Scarfe's insights were always important to me. Finally, for the patience, enthusiasm, and skill of history editor Gerald Hallowell, which made my relationship with the University of Toronto Press so pleasurable, I am sincerely grateful.

1 Michèle Lacombe, 'Theosophy and the Canadian Idealist Tradition: A Preliminary Exploration,' *Journal of Canadian Studies* 17, no 2 (summer 1982)
2 Besides these writers, Richard Allen and Ramsay Cook mention Alice Chown in the context of the social gospel movement in *The Social Passion: Religion and Social Reform in Canada, 1914–28* (Toronto: University of Toronto Press 1971) and *The Regenerators: Social Criticism in Late Victorian English Canada* (Toronto: University of Toronto Press 1985), respectively.
3 Numbers within parentheses refer to page numbers of the text of *The Stairway* that follows this introduction.
4 Dr Bruce Chown to Beth Robinson, 28 Feb. 1978, collection of Beth Pierce Robinson
5 See Estelle C. Jelinek, *The Tradition of Women's Autobiography: From Antiquity to the Present* (Boston: Twayne 1986)
6 Nellie McClung, *In Times Like These* (New York: D. Appleton 1915); Francis Marion Beynon, *Aleta Day* (London: C.W. Daniel 1919)
7 Judy Nolte Lensink, 'Expanding the Boundaries of Criticism: The

Diary as Female Autobiography,' *Women's Studies* 14, no 1 (1987) 43

8 Alice Chown to Edith and Lorne Pierce, 25 July 1920, Edith Chown Pierce Papers, in Edith and Lorne Pierce Collection, Queen's University Archives

9 Bernard Schermetzler, archivist, University of Wisconsin-Madison, letter to author, 8 Oct. 1987

10 *The Survey* (New York), 23 April 1921, p 123; *Boston Transcript*, 23 April 1921, p 7; *Freeman* (New York), 17 Aug. 1921, as quoted in *Book Review Digest: Review of 1921 Books* (New York: H.W. Wilson 1922); *Mail* (Toronto), date unclear, 1921

11 This was Kingston Collegiate Institute (now Kingston Collegiate and Vocational Institute) which first admitted girls in 1877. Alice attended it from 1878 to 1880 and in 1885, if not longer. Ronald A. Ede, letter to author, 11 May 1988; A.P. Knight to registrar, University of Wisconsin, 6 Nov. 1912, University of Wisconsin-Madison Archives. The years she was absent, 1880-5, coincide with her adolescent illness, referred to in *The Stairway*.

12 Margaret Houghton, archivist, Hamilton Public Library, to the author, 11 Aug. 1987. See Marion Royce, 'Methodism and the Education of Women in Nineteenth Century Ontario,' *Atlantis* 3, no 2 (spring 1978) 131-43.

13 Register, 1869-93, Queen's University Archives. Queen's University first admitted women in 1878.

14 See A.B. McKillop, *A Disciplined Intelligence: Critical Inquiry and Canadian Thought in the Victorian Era* (Montreal: McGill-Queen's University Press 1979)

15 See S.E.D. Shortt, *The Search for an Ideal: Six Canadian Intellectuals and Their Convictions in an Age of Transition, 1890-1930* (Toronto: University of Toronto Press 1976) 97

16 Bruce William Bowden, 'Adam Shortt,' unpublished Ph.D. thesis, University of Toronto, 1979, p 64

17 See Veronica Strong-Boag, ed., *'A Woman with a Purpose': The Diaries of Elizabeth Smith, 1872-1884* (Toronto: University of Toronto Press 1980)

18 Chown to Dr (Elizabeth) Shortt, 16 April c. 1888, Elizabeth Smith Shortt Papers, Special Collections, University of Waterloo

19 Elizabeth Smith Diary, *ibid.*

20 R.W. Anglin to Edith Pierce, 15 March 1949, Chown Pierce Papers

21 Linda Kealey, ed., *A Not Unreasonable Claim: Women and Reform in Canada, 1880s–1920s* (Toronto: The Women's Press 1979) 7

22 Chown to Edith Pierce, c. 1940, collection of Beth Pierce Robinson

23 Sheila Rowbotham and Jeffrey Weeks, *Socialism and the New Life: The Personal and Sexual Politics of Edward Carpenter and Havelock Ellis* (London: Pluto 1977) 75

24 See Chown to Edith Chown, 8 Aug. c. 1913, 4 July c. 1916, 28 Aug. 1919, Chown Pierce Papers

25 Ruth First and Ann Scott, *Olive Schreiner* (London: André Deutsch 1980) 294

26 Chown to Edith Pierce, 28 Aug. 1919, Chown Pierce Papers

27 Margaret Stewart and Doris French, *Ask No Quarter: A Biography of Agnes Macphail* (Toronto: Longmans, Green & Co. 1959) 31

28 Chown to Edith and Lorne Pierce, 25 July 1920, Chown Pierce Papers

29 Allen F. Davis, *Spearheads for Reform: The Social Settlements and the Progressive Movement, 1890–1914* (New York: Oxford University Press 1967) 7, 17

30 See Allen F. Davis, *American Heroine: The Life and Legend of Jane Addams* (New York: Oxford University Press 1973)

31 *Notable American Women, 1607–1950* (Cambridge, Mass.: Belknap Press of Harvard University 1971) I, 218

32 Chown to Minnie Chown, Oct. 1898, collection of Stanley Chown descendants, Renfrew, Ontario

33 Chown to Stanley Chown, April 1899, *ibid.* Claudia Clarke, who has researched the Whittier House Collection, New Jersey Historical Society Library, Newark, NJ, found no mention of Alice in the Whittier House annual report for 1899–1900. Letter to the author, 30 Nov. 1987

34 Mary Morley, 'Home Economics in Canada,' unpublished Ph.D., thesis, Teacher's College, Columbia University, 1973, p 16, as quoted in Patricia Saidak, 'Home Economics as an Academic Science,' *Resources for Feminist Research* 15, no 3 (Nov. 1986) 50

35 *Lake Placid Conference on Home Economics: Proceedings of the Annual Conference, 1901* (Washington, DC: American Home Economics Association 1901) 105–8. With appreciation to Pro-

fessor Linda Peterat for sending me the American Home
Economics Association articles.

36 Chown to Richard Harcourt, 7 July 1901, RC2 D7, Box 3, Archives of Ontario. Professor Terry Crowley first brought these
letters to my attention: see 'Madonnas before Magdalenes:
Adelaide Hoodless and the Making of the Canadian Gibson Girl,'
Canadian Historical Review LXVII, no 4 (Dec. 1986).

37 Chown to Harcourt, 2 July 1901, *ibid.* Home economics was, in
fact, offered at the university level in Canada that year when the
University of Toronto introduced a degree course. Described as
heavy in pure science and languages, the course was initiated by
Lillian Massey-Treble. Patricia Saidak, 'The Inception of the
Home Economics Movement in English Canada, 1890–1910: In
Defence of the Cultural Importance of the Home,' unpublished
MA thesis, Carleton University, 1987, p 69. This valuable thesis
discusses Alice's role in the home economics movement in more
depth.

38 Chown, 'The Supplement of Higher Education for Women,'
Methodist Magazine and Review (Nov. 1901). No letters or articles by Alice have been found in Methodist or United Church
publications between 1916, when she wrote an open letter to
pacifists in the *Christian Guardian*, and 1941, when she began
to edit 'The Next Step.'

39 Chown, 'Effect of Some Changes on the Family,' *Lake Placid
Conference on Home Economics: Proceedings of the Fourth An-
nual Conference, 1902* (Washington, DC: American Home
Economics Association 1902) 31–5. That year also, Alice arranged
for the prominent American home economics advocate, Ellen
Richards, to visit Canada.

40 Chown, 'Non-Resident Household Labor: A Study in Economic
and Ethical Values,' *Lake Placid Conference on Home Economics:
Proceedings of the Annual Conference, 1904* (Washington DC:
American Home Economics Association 1904) 32–3

41 Eleanore Vaines, 'Pause and Reflect,' *Canadian Home Economics
Journal* 34, no 3 (summer 1984) 139, 138. Patricia Saidak considers Alice to have been one of the participants who broadened
the base of discussions within the home economics movement.
However, 'the dynamics of the Lake Placid debate did not
translate to reality within the academy when reform became in-
stitutionalized' Saidak, 'The Inception of the Home Economics
Movement,' 143

42 National Council of Women of Canada, Yearbooks for 1904 and 1905. Yearbooks for 1893 to 1912 reveal that Alice never joined the Kingston local council.

43 Yearbook for 1904

44 Chushichi Tsuzuki, *Edward Carpenter, 1844–1929: Prophet of Human Fellowship* (Cambridge: Cambridge University Press 1980) 51

45 Dolores Hayden, *The Grand Domestic Revolution: A History of Feminist Designs for American Homes, Neighbourhoods, and Cities* (Cambridge, Mass.: The MIT Press 1981) 231, 186

46 W.H.G. Armytage, *Heavens Below: Utopian Experiments in England, 1560–1960* (London: Routledge and Kegan Paul 1961) 374

47 Julia Firth to Edith Chown, 11 Aug. 1909, Chown Pierce Papers

48 Another community in Great Britain that Alice visited was the one she refers to as Ariel Colony. Based on an interpretation of Ruskin, the colony fostered agriculture, and arts and crafts such as spinning, weaving, pottery, dressmaking, and embroidery. Like Letchworth, Ariel Colony believed in healthful work rather than healthful recreation, which was the usual way of solving the problems of industry's monotonous labour. Chown, *The Stairway*, 156

49 See the following articles in the *Toronto Daily Star*: 'Paris Sets Toronto a Fine Example of City Beautification that Will Pay,' 20 Oct. 1911, p 5; 'A Utopia Come True, England's Model Garden City, an Example to the World,' 27 Oct. 1911, p 12; 'The Real Garden Suburb Idea,' 4 Nov. 1911, p 1; 'Britain's Great Awakening to the Advantages of Co-operative Building,' 10 Nov. 1911, p 9. Other unidentified articles which could have been written by her appear in the same newspaper.

50 Chown, 'Some Criticisms of the Deaconess Movement,' *Christian Guardian*, 15 Nov. 1911. I wish to thank Ruth Compton Brouwer for bringing these articles to my attention.

51 Chown, 'Will the Deaconess Society Adopt Modern Social Methods?' *Christian Guardian*, 29 Nov. 1911

52 John D. Thomas, 'Servants of the Church: Canadian Methodist Deaconess Work, 1890-1926,' *Canadian Historical Review* LXV, no 3 (Sept. 1984) 388

53 Chown, 'Not Deaconesses, but Deaconess Training,' *Christian Guardian*, 6 Dec. 1911. Florence Kelley was, in 1911, the general-secretary of the National Consumers' League and a resi-

dent of the Henry Street Settlement, New York, where Alice may
have stayed during a recent visit when she met with Kelley.
Chown, 'Some Criticisms'

54 Chown, 'Not Deaconesses'; Woodsworth to the editor, *Christian
Guardian*, 6 Dec. 1911; Thomas, 'Servants of the Church,' 388

55 Harry Chown to Stanley Chown, 15 April 1928, collection of
Stanley Chown descendants

56 Chown Pierce Papers

57 Membership list, 'The Suffrage Club,' Flora MacDonald Denison
Papers, Thomas Fisher Library, University of Toronto

58 'Denied "Votes" in Women's Suffrage Association, New Society
Was Formed,' *Toronto Star Weekly*, 9 March 1912, p 12

59 Unidentified newspaper clipping, Reference Department, Toronto
Public Library

60 'Denied "Votes" '; *Mail* 8? Dec. 1913, newspaper clipping,
Reference Department, Toronto Public Library. Other activities
of the league apparently included bringing Colorado senator
Helen Ray Robinson to Toronto where she spoke on 'Where
Women Legislate.'

61 Wayne Roberts, *Honest Womanhood: Feminism, Femininity and
Class Consciousness among Toronto Working Women* (Toronto:
New Hogtown Press 1976) 40

62 Although Alice referred to the group as the 'Women's Political
League,' it was almost certainly either the Equal Franchise League
or the Political Equality League which, according to Flora Mac-
Donald Denison, was founded in February 1912 and, oddly
enough, was also headed by Constance Hamilton. Flora Mac-
Donald Denison, 'Woman Suffrage: A Retrospect and a
Prophecy,' *Toronto Sunday World*, Editorial Section, 3 May 1912

63 During the strike, J.C. Eaton was reported to have described all
unions as being 'run by one or two men who are engaged in
making poor people earn their living for them.' *Star*, 15 Feb.
1912, p 5

64 Nancy Schrom Dye, *As Equals and as Sisters: Feminism, the
Labor Movement, and the Women's Trade Union League of New
York* (Columbia, Missouri: University of Missouri Press 1980) 100

65 Chown to Edith Chown, n.d., Chown Pierce Papers

66 Chown to Edith Chown, 22 March [1914], *ibid.*

67 Chown to Edith Chown, 20 June [1914], *ibid.*

68 See Jane Addams, *Peace and Bread in Time of War* (1922;
reprint Silver Spring, Maryland: NASW Series 1983); Barbara J.

Steinson, *American Women's Activism in World War I* (New York: Garland 1982)

69 'Canadian Women Oppose Congress,' *Mail and Empire*, 23 April 1915

70 *World*, 26 Oct. 1915, p 4; 4 Nov. 1915

71 'Canadian Women Oppose Congress.' In the summer of 1915 Laura Hughes and Elsie Charlton formed a Toronto branch of the International Committee for a Permanent Peace, the organization that was founded at The Hague congress. Donald M. Page claims that Alice Chown was also a founder. Page, 'Canadians and the League of Nations before the Manchurian Crisis,' unpublished Ph.D. thesis, University of Toronto, 1972, p 30

72 *World*, 4 Nov. 1915, p 6

73 *Ibid.*, 10 Nov. 1915, p 6. A third and final letter from Alice appeared on 17 Nov. p 6. It further defined her anti-militarism.

74 Chown, 'Open Letter to Pacifists,' *Christian Guardian*, 1 March 1916; *World*, 10 Nov. 1915, p 6; Thomas P. Socknat, *Witness against War: Pacifism in Canada, 1900–1945* (Toronto: University of Toronto Press 1987) 52

75 Socknat, *ibid.*, 69

76 Chown to Edith Chown, 29 Oct. [1915], Chown Pierce Papers. Unfortunately, Alice does not name the paper.

77 Chown to Lorne Pierce, 3 May 1920, *ibid.*; Chown to Dwight Chown, 17 Dec. [1918], S.D. Chown Papers, United Church Archives, Toronto

78 Chown, 'Open Letter'

79 Chown to Edith Pierce, 4 July [1916], Chown to Lorne Pierce, 28 June 1916, Chown to Edith Pierce, 26 Aug. 1916, Chown Pierce Papers

80 Chown to Lorne Pierce, 1 March 1919, collection of Beth Pierce Robinson

81 Chown to Lorne Pierce, May [1918], Chown Pierce Papers. At Croton-on-Hudson she was staying with H.R. Mussey, managing editor of *The Nation*, and his wife. Other members of this weekend retreat for journalists, artists, and Bohemians included Crystal Eastman, well-known socialist feminist and co-editor of *The Liberator*. See Blanche Wiesen Cook, ed., *Crystal Eastman on Women and Revolution* (New York: Oxford University Press 1978) 26–7

82 Chown to Edith and Lorne Pierce, 28 Aug. 1919, Chown Pierce Papers

83 *Ibid.*

84 Chown to Lorne Pierce, 3 May 1920, *ibid.* At this time Alice was unable to visit Russia because her criticism of the Canadian government prevented her from obtaining a passport.

85 Chown Pierce Papers

86 Fred M. Goodhue, 'Notes,' c. 1931, Commonwealth College Collection, University of Arkansas, Fayetteville, Arkansas. A note from Alice, apparently written from England, was enclosed in Lorne Pierce's Diary, 1920–3. Beth Robinson, letter to author, Nov. 1987. This suggests a trip abroad during that period.

87 Chown to Edith Pierce, 16 Nov. 1922, collection of Beth Pierce Robinson

88 'Land and Craft Guild, Germonds, N.Y.,' c. 1923, Chown Pierce Papers

89 William H. Cobb, "Commonwealth College Comes to Arkansas, 1923–1925,' *Arkansas Historical Quarterly* XXIII (summer 1964) 99. The students at the college worked in exchange for their tuition. They had a choice of a two- or three-year program in which subjects included mathematics, English composition, literature, physical and biological sciences, and economic history. Students who qualified for third year could take accounting, history, economic theory, psychology, journalism, labour history, or law.

90 Goodhue, Transcript of a meeting, Commonwealth College, c. 1924, Commonwealth College Collection

91 Cobb, 'Commonwealth College,' 116. Unfortunately, little information about Alice's connection with Socialist party circles has been located.

92 *The American Fund for Public Service, Report for 1925–1928*, American Civil Liberties Archives, Princeton University

93 Chown to Murray Chown, 17 Oct. 1925, collection of Stanley Chown descendants

94 Chown to Lorne Pierce, 29 Nov. 1926, Chown Pierce Papers; Goodhue, 'Notes.' Alice's fundraising attempts and efforts to obtain basic necessities were remembered by others. A local woman recalls her mother receiving gifts such as a soup tureen and chafing dishes from Alice in exchange for supplying the college with chickens and vegetables. Mrs O.J. Washburn to author, Sept. 1987

95 *Commonwealth College Fortnightly* (Mena, Arkansas), 14 March 1926

96 Socknat, *Witness against War*, 91

97 Veronica Strong-Boag, 'Peace-Making Women: Canada 1919–1939,' in Ruth Roach Pierson, ed., *Women and Peace: Theoretical, Historical and Practical Perspectives* (London: Croom Helm; New York: Methuen 1987) 176; see also Frances Early, 'The Historic Roots of the Women's Peace Movement in North America,' *Canadian Woman Studies* 7, no 4 (winter 1986)

98 About 1929, for example, she and Mrs Eisman (who was likely the Mrs J. Eisman who became vice-president of the Women's League of Nations Association), as representatives of the Women's Interdenominational Committee of the LNS, attended a joint meeting of the WIL. 'Minutes of a Joint Committee meeting held November 13 to discuss co-operation,' III-4-13, Women's International League for Peace and Freedom Collection, University of Colorado at Boulder. Professor Barbara Roberts thinks it is likely that Alice had been a member of the WIL for years. Letter to author, 10 Dec. 1987

99 'Minutes,' *ibid.*, Page, 'Canadians and the League of Nations,' 186; Strong-Boag, 'Peace-Making Women,' 176

100 Chown to Madeleine Doty, 9 Feb. 1929, II-7-4, Women's International League for Peace and Freedom Collection. The purpose of the letter was to renew her International WIL membership and to book a room at the Maison Internationale. With thanks to Professor Barbara Roberts for sending me a copy of this letter.

101 Chown to Edith Pierce, 7 July 1929, collection of Beth Pierce Robinson; Chown to Elizabeth Shortt, 27 June 1929, Smith Shortt Papers

102 Violet McNaughton to Irene Parlby, 15 Aug. 1930, vol. 18, file 54, McNaughton Papers, Saskatchewan Archives Board, Saskatoon, as quoted in Strong-Boag, 'Peace-Making Women,' 183

103 W.L. Grant to C.P. Meredith, 10 Feb., Meredith to Grant, 13 Feb. 1930, MG28 I20, League of Nations Society in Canada Papers, 1927–32, Toronto Branch, Public Archives of Canada

104 Chown to R.B. Inch, 14 June 1935, R.B. Inch Papers, Public Archives of Canada

105 Violet McNaughton to Chown, 11 Dec. 1931, A1 E52 (1), McNaughton Papers; Chown to Lady Aberdeen, 20 Nov. [1931], MG28 I245, vol. 34, file 505, International Council of Women Records, Public Archives of Canada. Unfortunately, none of the plays has been located.

106 Chown to Dr [H.M.] Tory, 29 June 1933, MG30 C187, vol. 5, file
     125, Inch Papers; Chown to R.B. Inch, 12 Nov. [1933], *ibid.*
107 Chown to Inch, 5 Oct. 1933, *ibid.*
108 Chown to Mrs (Elizabeth) Shortt, 22 Dec. 1935, Smith Shortt
     Papers. Likely related to her doubts about the possibility of pre-
     venting war was a strange request she made to Lorne Pierce on
     the eve of the Second World War. In a letter of 29 Aug. 1939,
     she asked him to 'recapture' her book *The Stairway* from 'the
     Canadian Dept. of Queen's University and burn it.' Chown Pierce
     Papers.
109 Jean Woodsworth, telephone conversation with author, 4 March
     1988. Mrs Woodsworth and her husband, Kenneth Woodsworth,
     later lived in Alice's house while attending the University of
     Toronto.
110 Sylvia Woodsworth Campbell, conversation with author, Nov.
     1986, recalled that Alice's teas also included Canadian communist
     party leader Tim Buck. Other invitees were University of Toron-
     to history professors Richard Preston and Richard Saunders.
     Terry Crowley, Guelph University, letter to author, 14 Jan. 1987
111 That year she travelled to Baltimore to speak to the Mothers for
     Peace Union. 'League of Nations Society in Canada, Monthly
     Bulletin,' March 1936, League of Nations Society in Canada
     Papers
112 M. Conway Turton, 'An Outrageous Idealist,' *Canadian Com-
     ment*, Oct. 1935, p 8. The author also reported that Alice had
     recently talked to Ghandi, Ramsay Macdonald, and Stuart Chase.
113 Chown to Lorne Pierce, n.d., Chown Pierce Papers. In 1934 or
     1935 she attended the first conference of the Canadian League
     against War and Fascism. Thanks to Professor Joan Sangster for
     providing me with this information.
114 Chown Pierce Papers
115 Chown to Mrs (Elizabeth) Shortt, 3 Aug., c. 1941, Smith Shortt
     Papers
116 Beryl Truax, past president of the Canadian Teacher's Federation,
     'Women's Role in Building the Peace,' *United Church Observer*,
     15 Jan. 1945
117 Chown, 'Adventures in Christian Jewish Understanding,' *ibid.*, 1
     Jan. 1942, p 11
118 Sylvia Woodsworth Campbell, Toronto, and Beth Pierce Robin-
     son, Delta, Ontario, shared these recollections with me.
119 Chown to Mrs (Elizabeth) Shortt, n.d., Smith Shortt Papers

Alice Chown about 1886

Alice Chown and nieces, about 1907. Edith Chown is seated
on the floor to the left of her aunt.

Alice Chown with an infant niece, about 1911

Commonwealth College faculty at Mena, Arkansas, March
1925. Alice Chown is third from left in the back row.

OPPOSITE

Edith Chown Pierce, Alice Chown, and Bruce Pierce, 1934
or 1935

My wish for each and all of us.

LOVE IS ETERNAL
God is love and they who love dwell in God and
God in them, therefore, we will seek to love
beginning with those near us and flowing out in ever
widening circles until the whole world is bound
about the feet of God.

LOVE IS CREATIVE
We can transform this world through putting love in
the place of self seeking and profit. Earthly wisdom
has failed. We must return to the commandment

LOVE THY NEIGHBOR AS THYSELF
Let us as members of this League of Nations Society
express love in every relationship that we may bring
peace and good will, unity and co-operation in all the
world.
My love and my faith that we shall become a Society
of lovers.

ALICE A. CHOWN, February 3rd, 1866–1941
53 Howland Avenue. MIdway 5302

At her seventy-fifth birthday reception in 1941, Alice gave
guests a card with the above words and photograph (taken in
1935 or earlier).

Alice Chown, early 1940s

THE STAIRWAY

To Norman
who opened many doors for me
in my climb to freedom
To live,

'Rather consists in opening out a way
Whence the imprisoned splendor may escape,
Than in effecting entry for a light
Supposed to be without.'

Adapted from Robert Browning.

PREFACE

In this book I have tried to tell how freedom has to be gained through very simple experiences by constantly choosing to do the free act which, no matter how infinitesimal it seems at the moment, often takes the courage necessary to remove mountains.

Personal relations have taught me that there is a life force in every individual urging to order, harmony, beauty. We may set this wonderful force for righteousness free by granting to all freedom to live out the truths inherent in them. Society makes an institution and thinks it a permanent dwelling, instead of a tent in which to abide for a night before passing to the next stage in its journey. Man creates a God, then makes an image of Him, a stone image, dead and lifeless. God is not fetish but Spirit.

When I read novels, I am always impatient because life is neither so simple nor so unified as the artist pictures it. To me it is a great hodge podge of all kinds of experiences of which one does not perceive the significance nor the relations except in perspective. While there may be one main key, there are many parts written in subsidiary ones. I wanted freedom, my own individual freedom, to discover what I was. I had to find my freedom in my relations to labor, to sex, to education, to the State.

If I were an artist I should tell simply the story of my experiences among the trade unionists or my re-action to the experiences of my friends who were seeking truth in sex relations, or my growing faith in the potency of ideas that cannot be hurried by propaganda or war. The varied experiences of a seeker for freedom cannot be compressed into any one phase of the universal struggle for liberty. They make a composite picture. Because I want to know life as it is I am hoping that there are people who want truth, not fiction.

I discovered within myself all sorts of impulses at war with inherited inhibitions. Because I followed the light of my conscience despite what the crowd might say I was repaid by ecstasy more keen than had ever come to me in the travelled roads of custom, by a deep satisfaction that gave zest to living. I met all sorts of people, rich and poor, deep and shallow, who were craving freedom too and suppressing their desires through fear of the prejudice and dictum of the herd. For that reason I have hoped that these chapters from the life of a stranger might give individuals faith in themselves. Because I learned that the expression of the impulse to love and beauty must be one's own, and ceased to ask people to measure up to my ideal for them, I saw that simple acts which spring from sincerity are more valuable than great deeds whose motive is fear or expediency, lacking the inspiration of faith in the might of the spirit.

For every individual soul the condition of growth is truth.

CHAPTER I

Lakeside, Canada,
May 28th, 1906

Today I am free. My first day of freedom! It is my new birth!

Life begins for me today.

Forty years old, forty and a few months, but neither years nor months count. Today, let me write the date down, May 28, 1906, I commence to live. During the next few months I shall have all the struggle for life and breath that an infant has, for I shall be breaking away from all the old walls that have surrounded me, from all the old environments that have enfolded me, that have kept me hidden from life and have forced me to live only through others. Yes, I shall be emerging from all the wrappings of this home, of this city. Downstairs my mother lies sleeping; rest has come to her at last.

How can a daughter realize all the struggle, the imprisonment of life and activity, which came to her mother, and fail to rejoice when she ceases to struggle against the prison bars that have shut her in? I have shed my tears, for I am human and death is mysterious. It seems impossible that all that was beautiful in her life shall perish. How I wish I could go back to the faith of my childhood and believe that death is only the gateway to a larger life. I like to think what mother might have been had she had freedom here. She was confined, imprisoned by the conventions of the world in which she lived; by her church, her limited education, her uncertain health. Was her lack of strength simply nature's penalty for the other limitations that life had imposed on her? Was it that she could not stand the constant doing of the thing prescribed, being shut out from large activities, from large deeds, so that her spirit beat itself against the cage of her environment until it bruised her body?

She had fallen from a step-ladder and broken her ankle when she was only thirty, and had never been able to take a step afterwards without pain. For years after the accident, she had managed, with the help of one maid, to board my father's apprentices and to care for his father's family. Often there were eighteen in the family, and she had washed and ironed, baked her own bread, cooked all the food (for there were no canned goods fifty years ago), made her boys' clothes with the help of the trusted family tailoress, and even ironed their shirts and collars, for there were few public laundries. She had entertained all the travelling ministers and social and religious propagandists. The returned missionaries were always welcome at our home, and after school the boys would gather all their chums into the living room to listen to the tales of trips with dogs through the cold North lands or of the strange habits of the Japanese. We were forbidden to read Hans Andersen, but our imagination was fed by heroic tales of real life pursued for high purposes. She had always had time for the church work required of the women of those days. No wonder she had had no time for education. Her father, a farmer, wealthy for his time, had refused to allow her to go to school because he did not think it was necessary for girls to know more than how to read and write. She had made the best of the circumstances that had been hers, but had always cried out for a larger life and had had visions, long before votes for women or even secondary education were considered, of the time when women should have opportunities equal with men.

What she failed to gain in daily, concrete experience, she made for herself in her spiritual life. Owing to the meagreness of her education she did not write often to her children, her pride not permitting her to send a letter full of mistakes, bad spelling, poor writing, to the children for whom she had made such heavy sacrifices in order that they might have the opportunities that had been denied her. She knew very few books except her Bible: her only reading was her church paper and a few religious works. 'The Christian's Secret of a Happy Life,' and Miss Havergal's books always lay beside her Bible on the window-sill near her chair.

Her religion was the poetry of her life. When each child was old enough to go to school, he was taken into her bedroom and she poured out her heart to God who alone could give the son all that had been denied to the mother. Every Sunday night, she gathered her children around her chair and showed them the pictures in the big family Bible, and told them the stories. Then she knelt with them and taught each of them to pray aloud. As she watched each child go off to Sunday school, she would pray that God would make him good. She could be content if he were not great, but good he must be.

The early struggles of the Methodists, in which mother and father had taken their part, to create a church in which individuals should express their religious aspirations, instead of accepting solely the voice of the clergy and bishops, had bred a community feeling in the old members. To them the church was one big family. They bought their dry goods and groceries from church members, always fraternized with Methodists. They retained all the simplicity and kindliness of earlier days.

Next to her church and family, my mother loved her neighbor, especially the struggling one. The widow with three or four children was her peculiar care. She always had several families that she was mothering and for whom she planned with all the solicitude and foreseeing care that she gave to the future of her own children. We were brought up to consider people less fortunate than ourselves, and many a week did we go without sugar in our tea in order to get money for the missionaries. There was always an orphan child in some foreign orphanage to be supported and a box of goods being prepared to send to some missionary on a desolate station. The boys always laughingly told mother that as soon as they got new clothes she saw visions of the time when she would be cutting them up into small pants for some Indian boy. It was a family joke that when a boy came downstairs in a new suit he would say teasingly, 'Well, mother, how many pairs of pants this time? I have grown a lot since you had the last pair.'

'Yes, indeed you have. I am proud of the way my boys grow,' she would reply.

'How long before you expect this pair, mother?' the happy owner would ask.

'Oh, you ought to wear that pair one year for best and one for every day,' she would answer quite seriously.

'Well, if I stand up so as not to wear out the seat of the pants, you could get another pair for some Indian cub. Will you get me a new suit each year, all the same?'

The teasing generally ended with a kiss and a 'Go 'long with you, you are quite likely to tear the legs of the pants climbing trees before I ever lay hands on them.'

Dancing, cards and all such wordly amusements were great sins, but she had all the wisdom of the modern pedagogue in circumventing temptation. She always heard first of the parties where there were to be the forbidden amusements, and quietly planned something so much nicer that her children never thought that they were being denied coveted fruit.

After eight sons (five living), I came, her only girl, then another son, my chum and defender. She was resolved that I should have all the opportunities she had missed. Her boys should go to high school and college, so should her girl, if it were possible. She was too simple and un-sophisticated to know how to agitate for the opportunities she wanted for me, but she was determined that I should have everything available. When the first high school for girls was opened in our city, my name was the first to go down, although I was only ten and had to go to a prepara-tory school before admission. But I was to go to high school, if all the devils and gossips of the city stood in the way. To the women of her church, her social group, her relatives and friends, who met her daily, she was doing a most dangerous, outrageous thing in sending me to high school. I started then my career of breaking precedents for women and later for individuals. If all the nice dames who shook their heads knowingly over my mother's temerity in sending me to high school could know my career they would say very solemnly, 'I told you so!' They could not understand that I have been simply a pioneer.

Dear old mother! How full of ambition you were for your only daughter! Can you see her today? Has the veil fallen from your eyes? Do you see that the spirit that fought and struggled for expression in you, you have bequeathed to your daughter? Although you did not recognize or approve of the struggles in which it embroiled her, now that you are free from earth's limitations, do you recognize that it is the same spirit that seeks ever more liberty for humanity?

For the last twenty years of her life, mother was an invalid, with periodic nervous break-downs. Sometimes I used to think that her later illnesses came from forced inaction. With an active brain, she had not sufficient outlet. If she had had education, if she had had strength – but to be denied both mental and physical outlet – her spirit chafed, until, at last, death has come to set her free! She is free, free from the limitations that have cramped and fettered her soul.

I am alone, all alone, in the house – no one but my mother's body, from which the spirit has fled – the shell which I have dressed in all her dainty lace as she loved to be dressed. Downstairs, she lies at rest.

Up and down I paced the lawn this evening, trying to realize what freedom would mean to me. How far shall I use it? How far must I still be bound by the desires of my family? My sisters-in-law have been here to ask me to wear black – I who want to don my brightest gown because, at last, mother is free – I, who feel that she is being born again!

I know that with her death will come new valuations; new comprehensions of all she was, all she had struggled to be, all she had desired, all she was not and could never be, but to which she had aspired! Death will tear the veil from all our eyes; we shall see her, not as our blinded eyes have glimpsed her, but with the open vision that death alone gives. Why should I put on the trappings of mourning? Why should I yield to the wishes of my sisters-in-law?

I have compromised. I am to wear a white waist and black skirt, gloves and hat. I hate the compromise. I feel that it is untruthful, but I am not yet free.

As I continued my restless walk, wearing a path in the lawn, my thoughts went back to the step I took towards freedom when I ceased to go to church after my father's death. How I wish tonight I could hear him say, 'Your duty to your mother is finished.'

He was such a dear, good man, wonderfully simple and beautiful. When he died one of the city merchants called upon me to express his regret that he had not been at home to attend the funeral, adding, 'I feel as if a Christ has gone out of the city.' Dear father, how surprised he would have been in his simplicity and humility, if he could have known any one would say such words of him – father, whose favorite saying was the one from Micah, 'Do justly, love mercy, and walk humbly with thy God!' That was the real keynote to his life.

I once repeated that merchant's remark to a zealous Socialist and he indignantly asked, 'Did not your father die well off?'

'Comfortably; for him it was wealth, but not according to the standards of to-day,' I replied.

'And any man could think that he was like Christ when he died owning money?'

I assured him that the conscience of my father's time had not felt private property to be a crime. I could not make him see that his simple kindliness and good will to every one was Christ-like. I spoke quietly, but inside me raged fierce indignation at the blindness of the zealot who pinned his faith to some system and failed to see that

'Our little systems have their day;
   They have their day and cease to be;'

...

'And thou, O Man, art more than they;'

as I paraphrased it. Imagine my father, whose simplicity and kindness had freed him from so many of the limitations of a faithless age, being judged by a doctrinaire! My father, who could meet a chance stranger on the street, listen to his tale of woe, look him up and down, and supply his need. When he would tell us the story we would be incredulous, but father, unperturbed, would answer us, 'Why, he said he would repay it.' Days later, with the returned loan, he would come home exultingly to convince us of the unreasonableness of our unbelief.

My father was the poet of our city, who wandered up and down in his guilelessness and sincerity, creating standards. He did not criticize, he did not see the faults of those around him, but his unwavering faith in their good intentions inspired them to answer his expectations. Many a time have I changed my plans through his unconscious influence, with scarcely a spoken word. I recalled that when, six years ago, after a serious illness, I went down to New Jersey to live in a social settlement, I was offered a position and came home to persuade my father to acquiesce in my acceptance. For the two hours crossing the lake I had paced the boat from end to end, saying emphatically, 'I must go back; I *will* go back. It is my opportunity. If I allow this to pass, I may never have a similar one. I shall arrange things to be comfortable at home, and then I will return.'

The boat neared the wharf and my father, bent with age, stood there waiting for me. The scars of the years were on him, the long, hard years when he had borne the burden of his father's family as well as his own. The tears came to my eyes. He was nature's nobleman.

When he kissed me and said, 'I am glad you are here, daughter; your mother needs you,' all my determination to return quietly vanished. I could wait a little longer.

He had a father's care for the men who worked for him. He was too simple and unsophisticated to have any of the attitude of a boss. 'God had crowned his efforts with success,' he said, 'as far as possible, his men must share it with him.' Nor did he ever forget the people who had been good to him in his early days of struggle. The widow of the man with whom he had learnt his trade received her annual turkey at Christmas for more than fifty years. As long as he lived, I went to church with him once every Sunday. My mother knew how I chafed at going, so when he died she said,

'I cannot understand you. You talk as if you wanted to do right, but you cannot get any good out of going to church when you dislike going.'

And so I stopped.

I have gone through all the stages. I have led prayer meetings, been zealous in all the good works of the church; I have visited the sick and the poor; I have spoken to the stranger within the gates. Every church activity has some time in my life found in me an earnest exponent. Three or four services with an occasional committee meeting on Sunday was once quite customary. I used to laugh and say that my past was a graveyard of buried enthusiasms. I had mounted on each grave to a broader outlook. Little by little, I had come to feel that the church had crystallized. The truths that once meant life and growth, force and virility, having been accepted as an end instead of a beginning, had killed the life of the spirit. It seemed to me a dead organism existing by augmentations of number and institutions – a faith in external things. It said, 'This is the path bounded on every side by the dead trees of precept, custom and authority, walk ye therein.' I care for no path, am keen to live, to grow in harmony with principles inherent in me, and, I hope, in all people; but whether they are universal or not, this is my one chance to live, and I do not want to throw it away for dead formulas which have little but a narrowing and blinding influence on the lives of the people who profess them. To live in a world of reality is for me the great adventure.

My lessening attendance at church was gradual, but during my father's later years I went only to the Sunday morning service, and to that one service because it was the greatest pleasure that I could give him. My conscience hurt me because I was consenting to something that was not true for me, but I salved it with the thought that it would be only for a few years, and there was nothing else that I could do that would give my parents equal happiness.

When I finally ceased to go, all the leaders of the church shook their heads, muttering, 'Some bad end! Some bad end!'

Now I am going to add to the sum of my wickedness by refusing to wear entire black for my mother. The height of enormity will lurk in my white waist. My white waist! It will be an emblem of truce to me and a flag of rebellion to my neighbors. My father and mother have conquered death. They live, live forever, in the lives of their children and their grandchildren and the great-grandchildren yet unborn. We shall carry on their message to further heights. They shall not die. And yet, my neighbors will not understand; they will think me failing in respect to my mother. They will forget the lessening yards of crepe from which the mourners of the past have gradually emancipated themselves, until it will not be long before the wearing of black will be numbered among outgrown customs. But today I dread to make my first appearance on the street without the traditional black garb, to face the criticism and censure of the public. It is my next step to be true to the higher significance of immortality. Of what slight texture are the rungs in the ladder of freedom! If we do not mount each one in its turn we must remain forever in the valley of the commonplace, losing all the grand and glorious views from the mountain top.

In many of the explorations that women have made during the last quarter of a century, I have been one of the party. Convinced my family that it was no more unwomanly to ride a bicycle than a horse, which I rode astride instead of in the traditional lady-like way; argued with my brothers for permission or whatever would evince their willingness that I should go to college (after they had tried to render me immune by two years at a Girls' Boarding School!) shortly after it had opened its doors to women; and we were a mere handful in the crowd of men students. To college I went. It was only partially satisfying. Even my college, noted for its breadth of spirit and forward looking outlook, seemed sadly lacking in a perspective of the needs of all humanity. The professor who held the chair of economics, in the late eighties, assured me that the colleges and the churches were wise conservative forces lest new untried impulses should endanger society. He took me for a long walk to try to convince me of the dangers of socialism, which I did not have sufficient self-confidence to accept as a complete solution; but the enthusiasm of its adherents for a new society appealed to me. I hoped their spirit would arouse humanity to find suitable institutions to embody the awakened desire. I was eager that the colleges should clear away the obstacles, in order that neither cold logic nor religious inertia should hinder the humanitarian expansion. I hungered for inspiration to social creation. His affirmation that his conclusions were never final, that he continually revised them as he gained new light, was his greatest gift to me. I have met a few professors who, despite the educational restrictions of the day, exercised constructive thought, but the majority were sponges inflated with knowledge but without life. Their function was one of criticism, rarely of inspiration for today. I would never send a daughter of mine to an ordinary college, because I am interested in the past only as it throws light on the present and is interpreted in the light of a desire for a larger future for the whole race.

It was worth while for me to go to college, because it was the next step toward freedom. My nieces went, as a matter of course. Their fathers, who strenuously opposed me, questioned their going no more than their advancing from one form to another in the high school.

In their early days, when social settlements were regarded as fads, I was a resident in one. Woman suffrage was the next lion in my path. I had to struggle for my opinions. I had to brave the displeasure of my family because I expressed them. Alas, alas, I was always braving the displeasure of my six brothers! They always thought me erratic; yet, despite their disapproval of my pioneering, never ceased to give me love and loyalty. I smile when I see my nieces and nephews, one after another, sponsoring causes that cost me many a hard-fought battle and gave me an unacknowledged triumph, because I was determined to think things out for myself. They calmly accept all the results of my fights, and shrug their shoulders over the latest conflict in which I happen to be engaged.

Now I am to begin life. How often have mother and I talked it over! From the moment I stepped on the train, to leave our small city to go to a larger one, I felt as if each turn of the car wheels tore off a wrapping, that gradually I was being released from all the cruel bindings that cramped my spirit. And when I was returning, the process was reversed; each foot nearer home meant the tightening of a bond. I was going back to a place where there was little thought newer than twenty-five years ago, where nothing was ever done until some other place had proved it was desirable. How I suffocated in that mental atmosphere! Mother could not understand why, but she understood the feeling. She had rarely travelled, never had had any outlet beyond that small place, but she felt it. I knew as I walked, rejoicing that now my duties were at an end, my mother would rejoice with me. She had chafed because her ill health had necessitated my remaining with her. I knew she would rejoice now. She, at least, would understand.

CHAPTER II

Lakeside
September 21st, 1906

The summer is gone. At last, the furniture is divided, the balance that no one wants is sold, and I have turned the key on the old home. One does not do that without a pang. All the old memories cling to the rooms. All the griefs and sorrows, all the joys and gayeties, seem to crowd the door and refuse to be shut away. I have had three happy months. I have entertained all my friends in the garden. Everyone who came to me with a mournful face I have met with the pleasantest smile and the assurance that mother is not dead. I have refused to grieve and they have thought me heartless. Once more I have insulted all the traditions of my native place. Is it worth while?

Yesterday my old boarding school friend came from Ayrdale to spend the day with me. She is a fine-looking woman, small and fair, with striking blue eyes and auburn hair fast turning gray. Often we had walked together in the school procession. As we sat in the garden yesterday laughing over our adventures in escaping the surveillance of the school teachers, I could not but think of the fascination she had had for us, her schoolmates, who were much younger than she. There was an air of mystery, a hint of romance which piqued our curiosity, and her attractiveness completed the spell she cast around us. Her reticence and aloofness augmented the charm, but she discouraged all school girl 'crushes.'

I recalled my dismay when, on a visit to my aunt who lives at Ayrdale, I heard the reason for Mary's cold restraint. She had loved a dashing young stranger who had sung in the church choir, but her family's pride would not listen to an alliance between her and a man whose ancestors were unknown. Mary was sent away to school in the hope that she might forget him, and during her absence he married.

The years passed, during which Mary met Charley occasionally at church festivals. There were whispers of secret meetings, too. She made friends with his wife; with her seeming acquiescence, she renewed her friendship with Charley. All the gossips in the church shook their heads over this great evil. A friendship between a man and a woman other than his wife was utterly taboo. Somehow, nature was stronger than criticism.

One day, Mary went to a neighboring town to visit; a few days later Charley went likewise on business. A good member of the church happened to be in the same town and saw them together at the hotel. Mary came back an outcast, although there was no proof that she had done anything less innocent than dine at a hotel with a married man! On her was vented all the malice and ill will the 'unco guid' could devise. She proudly held her head high and refused to make any explanations. On my visits to my aunt, it took a great deal of courage to speak to Mary. I felt as if I were doing a very heroic act, perhaps jeopardizing my own salvation by countenancing her wickedness. Society would be threatened if any illicit relation were condoned. She lived as solitary a life as if she were interned. The women in the church were afraid they might be contaminated if they spoke to her kindly, and she had too much spirit to be patronized. There was something in me that could not bear to see her snubbed by every one when she had been the victim of her father's pride. I thought that she was wrong, very wrong; my self-righteousness was not much less than her average old schoolmates', but I was too weak to punish her as they did. Pharisee as I was, I could not help feeling that she had some secret of strength that we did not grasp which caused her to carry herself so proudly. I pitied her, but I marvelled at her poise, at her strength of character, that made it possible for her quietly to live her own life unmoved by the ostracism. Gradually I drifted into calling on her occasionally when in Ayrdale. Whenever I met her on the street, I would walk with her as far as our paths lay together. I dreaded meeting any one. Every merchant on Front Street knew when I walked a block with her. My aunt wrote to my mother that I was compromising my good name. Mother replied that the little kindness that I could show Mary would not seriously endanger me or the institution of the family, and, after all, Mary was a human being. It is difficult to understand how a woman can be persecuted so long for one slip. Yet I am afraid that I was very little different from the rest of her town's people in my judgment of her sin.

The years passed, her father died and she went to Pratt Institute and studied institutional housekeeping. She was a capable, successful manager of the various institutions where she held positions. Her dignity and quiet strength, gained through the years of her endurance of the punishment meted to her, won her the esteem of the strangers around her. She saved money and built an apartment house in a university city in the west. Under freedom and prosperity, all the latent qualities which had been suppressed blossomed out and she gained the admiration that had

been denied her earlier in life. When she was at the pin-
nacle of her success, Charley, who had suffered for his in-
discretion by losing his business, all the respectable people
in the community refusing to trade in his store, fell ill. His
wife had died; he had two delicate children; his spirit was
thoroughly broken.

Mary sent east for him and his children, married him and
took care of him through a lingering illness – tuberculosis
contracted from his first wife. He had died recently and she
had brought the body home to Ayrdale and was resting
before returning to her western home. His children were
with her, being mothered and cared for as if they were her
own.

As we sat in the garden, I rejoiced that her long years of
penance were at an end. No person should suffer forever. It
had been a dreadful tragedy, and I, even at forty, felt her
punishment had been heavy, but not too heavy to retard
other women from taking a similar mis-step.

The serene way in which she has worn her scarlet letter,
her gentle dignity and the sweetness of her spirit, all attract
me. She has paid a bitter price for giving way to her love,
and she has paid it with no mark on her face or her spirit.

George Dean came to see me this summer. We went for a
walk together and every little urchin I met saluted me. I
think they must have sensed that George grew impatient of
lifting his hat, for I am sure they must have run around the
block to meet me a second time.

'You might as well mother the whole city,' George said
impatiently.

'Why, so I do, and in return they take good care of me. If
I get caught in a storm, some cabman picks me up and
brings me home; if I am out late, a policeman walks home
with me. Once when the citizens thought I had been un-
justly criticized at a public meeting, every workingman I

met the next day took off his hat to me. It was the most beautiful experience I ever had – their indignation at the unjust criticism of me and their quick rally to show me respect to atone for what they deemed an injustice.'

'That is all very well, but it is a great nuisance to be interrupted when I want to talk to you,' he growled.

'I wish I could mother the universe! My heart is big enough to take them all in, if I only knew how,' I relentlessly affirmed.

One morning this summer, when I was collecting for the City Charitable Society, the minute a woman opened the door she said, 'Good morning,' and called me by my name.

'Why, how do you know me?' I asked.

'Oh, I know you; I watch the paper every day to see if your name is mentioned and to find out what you are doing. You know you belong to us. You are ours.'

I laughed. It was nice to feel that they wanted me. It is some compensation for all the years when I had felt imprisoned in this city, to learn that the people feel that I belong to them.

Tomorrow, I leave all that behind me. I shall win more freedom, but I shall miss their kindly, friendly greetings, the goodwill of the humble people of my native place. They are not bothered by my opinions. They know me only as a human being who smiles when I meet them. A smile – what my smiles have brought me! – all sorts of opportunities for sympathy and a big return in goodwill. The stories I have heard, and the people who have sought to unburden their woes, all because I smiled! Well, it is all over now. I shall be a stranger in a big city where people have not time for interest in individuals.

CHAPTER III

New York
September 25th, 1906

New York at last, and my desired work in sight!

New York, with its extremes of riches and poverty, the poverty so far outbalancing the wealth that for every comfortable looking person you see five miserable, and for every wealthy one, a hundred making a struggle for a livelihood, uncertain and insufficient. It is always the poor that I see. People may talk about the poor not feeling their poverty. I do not believe it, but if it should be so, it is because they are so sunken in misery and wretchedness that they are deadened to it, and this but adds further to our disgrace. In a world where there should be enough for all, the existence of the poor is a great blot on our characters. Imagine loving others as oneself and then being content that they should sleep in rooms without windows, herded, many together, in a few square feet of space. Here in this big city are myriads of people, capable of being intelligent human beings, probably with gifts and possibilities equal to mine, yet starved and stunted so that all ambition is destroyed. They are devitalized by lack of food and fresh air, so that they will never show what they might be, a vast multitude who will never be at their best. They are robbed of their chance to attain their full stature as men and women, and society is robbed in consequence. All the talents that are wasted, all the possibilities that are crushed – all through bad management! Why, oh why, do we tolerate this?

The first few days of New York are always a nightmare. Every time I sweep past the crowded tenements in the elevated cars I am sick to think that human beings live in such conditions. How can you explain the self-complacency of the few rich? What kind of souls can we have to appropriate calmly much more than we need and leave the mass so far short of the bare necessities for healthy, happy living?

I walk the streets tortured by all the evidences of want. I am ill at ease with every luxury I allow myself. What joy can there be in living in a world like this? Everywhere I meet the people who do consciously suffer, the men and women who have lacked opportunity. Their souls are awake, they are hungry for better surroundings and more leisure for real living. They go to the woods each year for two weeks, and shut themselves off from everybody. They feel that they must drink long draughts of beauty to keep their souls alive when they return to their sordid surroundings in the city. For men and women choked by civilization I have unbounded sympathy.

With every visit to New York I repeat the same experience – I feel that I must flee the city. If I am helpless to contend with such conditions, I will not, at least, grow hardened to them; but I do not flee and they lose their power to hurt me so poignantly.

This time it is the same. I thought I could never stay and hear the constant tales of misery, never remain to see the spiritually stunted and dwarfed specimens of humanity. They might have been gods and our present age is making them pigmies.

But I do not flee, and I become hardened; at least, I suffer less. I am staying in a settlement where the wife of the head worker has very little sympathy with the ordinary social worker. She suffers as keenly all the time as I do temporarily. She is the real democrat, whose heart makes her one with all the women with whom she comes in contact. She understands their needs. She started handicrafts for the poor, sick and aged on Blackwell's island, to beguile the tedium of their long days. She has gained the co-operation of the mothers of her neighbourhood and together they have organized a crèche which is managed by themselves. She has very little patience with charitable effort. 'Cold as stone,' she terms it, 'and distant as the stars from the people.' The average settlement worker salves her conscience with a great deal of talk about sharing the life of the poor. She rarely has any real conception of unity with them patronizing them only less in degree than the Lady Bountiful of the past, for whose gifts she substitutes diversions, to drug the people, to keep them pacified, while their Rome is burning. They need no opiates, they need stimulants. They need to be aroused to combat unequal conditions. My new friend feels and suffers with the people and out of her sufferings grows work with the people. Her work with them is a means of growth to herself and her co-workers, while mere work for them would weaken those who accepted. Only suffering which finds no relief in charity brings us to the place where there is any real burden bearing.

When I was a girl I was ill and spent most of four years on my back. Then I dreamed that the ideal thing to do would be to live among the poor, share the life of the people, earn my own living and quietly become part of their life. I wanted to see how much personality, robbed of all its externals, might accomplish. When I went to the World's Fair and visited Hull House, I thought that my dream had come true. I was very happy in the thought that people were doing what I had dreamed about. As I have visited other settlements and felt the spirit of patronage, the consciousness of 'I am holier than thou,' I have learned that settlements are just one step in advance of organized charities. They are still putting their faith in institutions and organizations. They are deluding themselves when they talk of being democratic, of sharing the life of the people. To live in every comfort, even luxury, is not to share. I still cherish my dream that there will be men and women who will strip themselves of all extraneous advantages and take upon themselves the burden of the poor.

During the weeks I have been in New York all my friends have been discussing Gorky. With his wife, he arrived in the country early in the spring. They had incurred the enmity of the newspaper world by promising to write exclusively for the Hearst papers, and accordingly the other papers had stimulated a persecution which had finally resulted in their being ejected from the hotel in which they were staying. Gorky and his wife did not believe in the authority of church or state, and had refused to have a legal or religious marriage in Russia.

The hypocrisy of the American people in their treatment of Gorky, the utter absurdity of sanctioning free divorces and then refusing to recognize a relationship as public as that of Mr and Mrs Gorky were being discussed by Mr and Mrs John Martin, of Staten Island, and their dinner guest, Mr H.G. Wells, when the telephone rang. Mr Martin was called to the 'phone. He came back to tell Mrs Martin that a New York friend was asking if they would take Gorky and his wife into their home.

Mrs Martin instantly replied, 'If the Shah of Turkey were to come to America, and desire to visit me, I should not ask what the customs were in Turkey. Of course we will take them in.'

The heroism of the Martins, and the wisdom and un-wisdom of a marriage that has no legal sanction were being debated by every one I met.

This is a new idea to me. I have never heard before of people to whom it is a matter of principle not to have a legal sanction for their marriage. I feel as if the supports of society are falling. What will become of our civilization if they undermine the family?

My friends not only discuss the Gorky alliance, but calmly wonder if Mr and Mrs James and Mr and Mrs Harvard ever had a legal marriage, and how long it will be before self-supporting women will refuse to have any legal bonds. They think me a provincial country woman because I am opposed to such disgraceful unions. I argue against their theories. Of course my plea is, what about the family?

I cannot rid myself of the idea that the sole reason for a man and woman to marry is the creation of a family. If there is no legal marriage, how can any woman be sure that the man will stay with her after their children are born? I rehearse all the stories of desertion that I have ever heard, but my friends listen to me smilingly. The only thing on their horizon now is the necessity for women to gain their freedom and they are positive that no woman is free who is supported by one man. There must be no families, at present, where the woman is not capable of supporting herself, and ultimately the state must support all children. I, who have glorified the ideal of self-sacrifice and am quite willing to immolate all women on the altar of the good of the family, am sadly bewildered. They say they do not believe in self-sacrifice, that it is all rot (more forcible than elegant) to make saints out of women who have simply not had strength to resist the demands that bad economic conditions and past traditions have made on them.

I quote, 'Whoso shall lose his life shall find it,' and they disdainfully retort, 'Not if she loses it because she is too weak to assert herself.'

Puzzled, I recall for them all the fine women I have known who have sacrificed themselves for their families and have been rewarded by having sons and daughters of whom they were proud. Surely, that was ample recompense for the sacrifices they have made.

They protest, 'But consider all the men and women who have been stultified because their mothers stultified themselves first through mistaken self-sacrifice.'

I cannot see it as they do. Ten years ago one of my friends who married a stupid dolt of a man when she was only sixteen was obliged to support both herself and him. She worked strenuously, but was finally forced to leave him because he treated her so cruelly. I sympathized with her, but utterly refused to encourage her in her desire for a divorce.

'You must suffer for the sake of preserving the integrity of the family. It is better for you to suffer than to do anything that will tend to strengthen the custom of divorce,' I had assured her.

Poor Harriet! I was advanced in being willing to countenance the separation, which was anathema to all the good dames of the town. Once a woman who had been divorced and married again settled there and nobody would call on her. It was not respectable to associate with a divorced woman. The tradition that a woman should be loyal to her husband, no matter how he offended, was still strong.

It is incomprehensible to me that any one who has any claim to good morals should consider, for one moment, the possibility of a man and woman living together without a formal ceremony of marriage.

Mrs James took me to call on Mrs Martin who is enthusiastic about the Gorkys. She told me 'their philosophy of

life may be condensed into four words, 'the sin of possession.' No one has any right to anything, material or spiritual, no goods, no relations, except as the ownership satisfies a real need better than it could satisfy that of any one
else. One must not continue to own one's house, one's
horse, one's wife, or mother or child, if some one else can
love and understand and have a finer relationship with the
desired possession. One may possess only what belongs to
one spiritually, not formally.'

I do not know whether Gorky is a prophet of a new
order or an impossible dreamer, a dangerous thinker who
may tumble us all into the ditch. Poor me! I cannot glimpse
how such great changes in society will ever be brought
about without disaster to all I hold dear.

My interest in the Gorkys is accentuated because, from
all accounts that I have heard of them, they are really sharing the burden of the revolution in Russia. All the money
he made in America was devoted to it. Everything they did
was secondary to their interest in the revolutionary cause. I
have never heard before of the unstinted devotion of the
intellectual Russian men and women to the cause of freedom. They give up their own people, frequently marrying
one of their own group, espousing a mate whose traditions, habits, point of view in everything except the revolution, are different. They identify themselves with their
party by adopting the peasant blouse. They acknowledge
no class in society. For them society is one, there is no high
or low. The common people will listen only to the people
who have become one of them. In this country they still
listen abjectly to those who represent privilege. They are
still bowing to the aristocracy and have not yet gained faith
in their own class. Here democracy is only a name.

On Sunday four of us went for a trip to Helicon Hall, an
experiment in co-operative, democratic housekeeping. We
took the ferry and street car as far as necessary and then

trusted to our feet for the last three miles. We found Helicon Hall a joy and a prophecy. We were all four more interested in the most crude attempt to break a path through the woods to a new goal, than in the most successful following of an old, outgrown road. We saw only the successes and did not discuss the failures. The court, with its pond and fountain, around which the Hall was built, might be somewhat damp, but it was beautiful, and the four-sided fireplace might be extravagant of fuel, but it was reminiscent of the stories of our childhood. Our enthusiasm was unabated even when we had to wait for lunch because some of the women co-operators had not yet discovered the necessity for skilled service in the kitchen and the wisdom of the old adage, 'Shoemaker, stick to your last.' We were all inclined to think that, whatever initial mistakes were being made, the people who had sufficient courage and virility to make the experiment of creating a home where co-operation would make possible better opportunities for the educated woman to follow her profession and at the same time have her family needs satisfied, would eventually correct any blunders made in starting. We sincerely prayed that no misfortune might come until all the preliminary mistakes were rectified.

As we waited for lunch, we played a game devised by one of the members of our group. We each wrote down a question on a piece of paper and then passed it to our neighbor. The paper was folded to hide the answer but leave the question exposed and passed until each one had written an answer to the four questions, and then we read aloud the questions and answers. One of the questions was, 'Do you think we shall have new forms of religious organizations, or will religion become a personal matter?' I think I can foretell the future of each member of the group from the answers given to that question.

I have not the strength to do the work for which I came to New York. The long years of caring for my mother have exacted their toll, and I shall have to be quiet for a few months before I can undertake regular work. I am going to make some visits before I return to my brother.

CHAPTER IV

Philadelphia
October 31st, 1906

From New York I have come to Philadelphia to stay with
Lucy Manning. In New York, I bought some material, as I
desire to fashion a dress for myself that will be individual,
have long lines, and fulfill Ruskin's demand for artistic
building. It must be truthful, no false lines anywhere; it
shall be of good material; and its ornamentation shall grow
out of its lines and not be superadded to it. I want to em-
broider it, for that always seems an enrichment of the
material and not mere added decoration. I am delighted to
find that Lucy has a similar ideal and has begun to work it
out. Away down in a corner of my mind, for many years,
has been the conviction that women must fight the tyranny
of clothes. It takes too much time to keep them up to the
latest change of style. Unless one has a long purse one cannot afford good materials for such fleeting fashions. I want
styles that suit me. I never know when I buy a dress
whether it will be becoming or not. If I could once solve
the problem of suitable clothes, if I could always be well
dressed in suitable garments for whatever work or play I
was indulging in, I could have a much calmer existence. I
have heard very little of dress reform. As usual, from my

own personal experience and not from any knowledge of a popular movement, I have been feeling my way alone. Imagine my delight when I found Lucy not only having the same feeling, but actually with some dresses worked out. I do not care for her styles; they are modelled too much after the Greek, and I am too modern to wish to adopt styles that are not suitable to our more active life; but despite my criticism of her styles, I care tremendously for the motive and effort that lie behind them.

November 10

My dress is complete, and I think I shall take genuine pleasure in it. It is made of copper-colored rajah silk that I found on a bargain counter in Wanamaker's. It has a metallic sheen and despite the small cost, for it had been reduced to twenty-five cents a yard, I think it satisfies my demand for good material. Time will tell if I shall be comfortable wearing it among conventionally dressed people.

I am hearing spirited discussions on feminism, or rather the principles involved. Lucy's husband is as ardent as any woman in his belief in equal freedom for man and woman. It is my first meeting with a man who has these opinions. He shares the work of the house so that Lucy shall have equal time with him for literary work. The home, even the sweeping and dusting, are the joint product of their labor. They have simplified their physical needs so that they can have lives as full as possible of the essentials. Their house is simple, no bric-a-brac, no draperies, no needless furniture to demand care. They have plenty of books and pictures, they spend a large part of their income on travel and entertaining interesting people, or people who need what they can give either spiritually or physically. My constant moan has been that much of our lives is sacrificed to the external, that fashion and custom lay on us such unnecessary burdens. Here are two people who have freed themselves from all the non-essentials, who are not waiting for society to break their bonds.

Buffalo
November 24

When I arrived in Buffalo, Norman met me at the train. I had seen him once before. Five years ago, when I had two of my nieces with me here, my friend Marion had just been married to him. She invited us for dinner, and we sat over our coffee discussing affairs in general. Her husband kept me gasping at the cool way in which he accepted the changes necessary, in my opinion, to a better world. In my home town, 'Whatever is, is right.' I had never dared to mention the radical movements in which I believed. Indeed, I did not know that any one believed in them as reforms for which to work immediately. I thought they were the theories of visionaries like myself, who rebelled against conditions as they were, and clutched at these methods as possible panaceas. Here everything I said was a commonplace. They believed in woman's suffrage, anticipated women taking their seats in Parliament, believed in State control of wealth, did not go to church. It was an old, old story to them. They had outgrown everything that I had merely thought desirable. When I asked them why they were not working to bring about these changes which they deemed necessary, he had said, 'Oh, the changes are coming fast enough.'

I cannot understand such a laconic acceptance of things as they are, this present bad adjustment of goods and opportunities. I always want to get out and shove as soon as I can discern a way in which this old civilization can be hoisted out of the rut in which it is travelling. How I hate having special privileges, having more goods, more opportunities than the mass of the people. Yet I never know either how to escape from my privileges or to share them with people who need them.

After I left Buffalo, five years ago, I wrote Marion a letter, thanking her for their hospitality and saying, 'While Norman did not give me a stone when I asked for bread, he at least gave me only half a loaf.'

Immediately came a reply from him, 'Unsatisfied hunger is the very best provocative to further search for truth. You will find all your questions answered in the list of books I subjoin.'

Despite that very unsatisfying letter, occasionally through the five years when I have been unusually worried over some problem, I have written to him and he has, at least, told me what to read, if he would not give me any further advice. He evidently believes that each individual must work out his own salvation and, if with fear and trembling, so much deeper the salvation.

All that wonderful experience of meeting for the first time a man, a scholar and a gentleman, who had radical opinions, is still a delightful memory. I had grown in five years and I was eager to meet him again and to know where he was standing to-day on other social questions. Expectations beat high as I neared Buffalo. I was going to renew an acquaintance that had meant so much five years ago; what would it mean to-day?

Norman was waiting for me at the station. He brought me home and served afternoon tea. Still Marion did not appear. I had my artistic frock in my travelling bag, and when I told him about it, he was very much interested and insisted that I should go upstairs and put it on. Here is another man who feels as I do about women's clothes. I had thought that I was alone in my feeling, and here within the month I have been away from home I have found two men and a woman who share my feeling. Wonder of wonders!

Marion returned in time for dinner, and we had a delightful evening sitting around the fire.

The next morning Norman took me for a long walk and waited on me all day. I scarcely saw Marion. I was made to feel that I was his guest, and, strange, I did not feel a bit uncomfortable. I might have been in the habit of going to visit married men in their own homes.

I have an immense admiration for Marion. She is clever, self-possessed, progressive. Of course, she believes in the economic independence of woman. She gave up her position as professor of economics in a western university to marry a lawyer, and she has not yet found her new economic groove. Undoubtedly, she will find it.

She has no doubt that men and women will learn to adjust their professions, so that they will be able to live together, although it may mean sacrifice for one or the other. At present, she is studying law that she may have this interest in common with her husband.

After dinner to-night, we sat around the grate fire and discussed all the affairs of the world. Marion's great interest is in democracy and the growth of self-respect in people, so that they will not listen gullibly to what they are told. I do not know how the discussion drifted to marriage, but what was my consternation, my horror – I did not believe my own ears when she said, 'I do not believe in monogamic marriages.'

'Why?' I gasped.

'Because we do not have them, and we are only deceiving ourselves when we pretend to believe that we do.'

'But surely you believe in the love of one man for one woman?' I asked.

'Yes, when it happens; but we gain nothing in pretending that it happens when it does not. We are simply untruthful.'

'But do you not think there is a far greater chance of two people being happy together if you emphasize monogamy?'

'Theory does not interfere a great deal with feelings. You cannot convince a man that he is happy if he is not; all you do is cover it over. No, give each one the fullest expression possible for his feelings. There will be plenty of barriers, plenty of duties to intervene, to prevent the expression of love. There is too little of real, genuine love in the world to lessen it in any way.'

'You will have all sorts of promiscuous relations,' I objected.

'We do now, only we hide them and they are a canker destroying all our truthfulness. You cannot be untruthful in one relation and not have a lessened regard for truth in every relation. People are hungry for love; they want real, genuine love; but they fail to gain it because they are hedged in with all sorts of restrictions. I am ready to trust people to find their own way to a real feeling, rather than have them go on starving and cheating themselves with a counterfeit which sometimes, in their innocence, they have thought the real thing.'

They seem to me to be a most devoted couple. I cannot discern any personal reason for their belief in freedom in marriage relations. I am a novice who has been thrown into a sea of undreamt of ideas which buffet me whichever way I turn.

I am returning to my brother's home, ill and sore perplexed. The peaceful atmosphere where such ideas are never breathed, will soon make me forget the dreadful cataclysm that such unexpected theories would portend. If my home life had depth without breadth, this modern life seems so broad it is flat.

CHAPTER V

Lakeside
January 23rd, 1907

A letter from Frances Marshall today carried me back into the past. I met her several years ago, when I was spending my vacation in New York. Her father had been wealthy, and she had graduated from college, but just as she graduated her father met with reverses, and she had to find a position for herself.

'That was my greatest good fortune,' she told me. 'If he had not had business troubles, I should have had to settle down quietly and become a regular home woman. Neither he nor my mother would ever even have considered the possibility of my having any occupation or profession.'

She had been in the business world for thirteen years, and then she was debating whether she would give up the career where she had been successful and throw her energies into forwarding the cause of the colored people.

I happened to come into her life at the time she was weighing the cost with the strong call she felt to espouse the cause. The cost seemed overpoweringly heavy, but the opportunity and the need were correspondingly great. I was simply a quiet listener to her desires and the objections and fears of her family. She would state them and answer them, but I was audience.

Now, fifteen years later, she has sent a letter introducing a young girl of promise, and I am to share in some of the misunderstanding that she faced when she made her decision. It is strange how different theory and practice are. It takes a great deal of courage to face the criticism I shall incur through sponsoring her protegée. I have the right to share what I gave my friend courage to undertake. My share will be infinitesimal compared to the criticism and misunderstanding she has faced.

I have the weak knees of a coward. I constantly affirm my faith that I believe in individuals, not creeds, persons, not colors. I suppose the only way the populace will ever come to respect the colored people is for them to develop a strong respect for themselves, and we who believe in personalities, not in races, must stand behind them in their initial efforts. There is no way of growing except by conquering difficulties. This is to be my next climb, simply to be loyal to a girl who has personality, culture, ability, and who is shut off from many opportunities on account of her skin.

Lakeside
January 29th, 1907

Joy Worthington Bruce arrived to-day. She is all my friend wrote to me, talented, clever, ambitious, good presence, decidedly fine looking and attractive. If it were not for the prejudice of color, I could imagine her playing a great part anywhere circumstances might throw her. She is very sensitive, and her sensitiveness will be a serious drawback to her wordly success. After greeting her this morning, I said, 'I waited to see you before I decided to whom I should introduce you.'

She immediately replied, smilingly and not unpleasantly, although I thought I could detect the bitterness in it, 'Oh, yes, you wanted to see the particular shade of brown I am.'

'No,' I exclaimed quickly, 'you must not say that, you must not think it. Your whole success will depend on your emphasizing your faith in your personality and ignoring for yourself any barriers your color may create.'

'But the color is so much more obvious.'

'But it must not be a detriment in your eyes.'

'Wait; if you are kind enough to go with me to offices to look for work, you will see how little my ability counts and how much my color bars the way.'

'Granted; yet your faith in your personality and your ability will be the ultimate factor in deciding your destiny.'

'Why, oh why, was fate unkind to me? I do not want to agitate for myself or my people; I want only to sing. I will work, work hard to gain the opportunity to earn money that I may live while I take lessons. Why must I have to fight all the difficulties of getting work as well?' she moaned.

I tried to persuade Miss Bruce that her people were going through their time of struggle, that every race and every group of people had to struggle to embody an ideal, and that so long as they struggled they had life. Perhaps the struggle of the colored people and its contribution to civilization was to emphasize personality. As it was later to develop than the other races, she might be sure that in its development it would stand for some higher ideal than any previous race had reached, and she was privileged to have her share in the struggle for the recognition of that ideal.

'But I do not want to be a missionary; I am like any artist, I simply want to sing. I can sing and I know it. They want me to teach; they offer me all sorts of positions, but I want none of them; I must sing.'

I tried to persuade her that there might be more heroism, more ultimate satisfaction, in setting aside her own ambition and doing work for the good of her race, for which she was eminently suited; but she convinced me that it took courage and endurance to be an artist, and she would be serving her race by developing her talent for song.

Lakeside
February 24th, 1907

Margaret Tovell was here to see me to-day. Father learnt his trade with her father, who died shortly afterwards. When her children were small, father looked after the widow's business affairs and went to see her every Sunday. Very often I had gone with him when I was a child. For the last twenty years of her life, she was an invalid and needed care night and day. A year ago, after she died, Margaret came to mother one day.

'I am going to be married,' she told her.

'That is good news,' mother said, 'whom are you going to marry?'

'Mr Royden,' Margaret answered gleefully. 'He wanted me ten years ago and I could not leave mother; she needed so much attention.'

'Will he be good to you?' mother asked, full of interest that Margaret, after so many years of unselfish daughterly service, should be going to have her own home.

'Yes, I am sure he will. He is blind,' she said brightly.

'Oh, Margaret,' mother exclaimed, distressed.

'He wanted me when he was well, and I cannot fail him now he needs me,' Margaret assured her.

'But you have had so many years of waiting on an invalid. I cannot bear to think of your taking that burden again.' Mother was worried at such a prospect.

'Oh, he is not ill; he will not need care, only companionship. You see, a blast went off in his eyes four years ago. He was digging a well. He had been an active man all his life and now he just needs me to be eyes for him and he will be able to do things,' she explained cheerfully.

'Oh, Margaret, when I think of the years that you have been shut into your mother's room my heart fails me,' mother, still unsatisfied, remonstrated.

'Do not worry. I shall be better off than if I remained single. As you know so well, father died without a will fifty years ago, and according to the law of that time all the property goes to the eldest son. My brother is dead, but it passes to his heirs and I have not one cent of my own,' she reminded her.

'Oh, that is very unjust, after all these years of caring for your mother,' exclaimed mother.

'I always knew the Lord would provide for me, that if I did my duty I should be taken care of,' Margaret said cheerfully.

It was useless to expostulate more, but mother spent many a sleepless night worrying over Margaret's hard fate.

How I wish mother could have seen her to-day. She came to borrow a book, and the bride of sixty was as happy as a bride of twenty-one. Her face shone with joy.

'I want to read him all my old favorites. It is good to have some one with whom to share them. He does love me to read to him,' she said.

'You are really happy,' I remarked, quite convinced that it was so.

'Oh, he is good to me. If I go down street, when I return he is listening for me, and he has my slippers all warm, and he puts me into a chair by the stove and takes off my boots and makes me rest. He just thinks all the time of my comfort,' she said enthusiastically.

'I am glad that you are happy,' I repeated.

'Oh, yes, I am very happy. It is good to have some one appreciate you. He thinks that I am a wonderful cook, that no one ever made such biscuits,' she said with girlish glee.

'Does time hang wearily on his hands?' I asked.

'Oh, no, there is so much for us to do together. Last autumn, we dug the garden. I would show him where to put his spade and he was clever about it. He and I built the chicken house together. Then he always wipes the dishes and does the heavy lifting. He will not let me lift anything. He always scolds me, says, "Dear Margaret, why do you tax your strength when I am here to spare you heavy work?" Oh, we are so happy.' Her face beamed.

I rejoice every time I think that the years of unselfish, unappreciated service – for her mother was very selfish and exacting in her demands – should be bringing her such a rich harvest now. In mother's day, many people brought her just such simple human stories as Margaret's. I must create a different atmosphere, for the tales that are poured into my ears have the flavor of doubt and unrest. Margaret carried me back to the simplicity and certainty of belief in the old home. She was like an old landmark which I had forgotten.

Lakeside
March 28th, 1907

Marion and Norman came to see me last week. They are prospecting in Canada to see if they would like to settle here, as Norman has been offered the professorship of international law in Osgoode Hall.

After tea, Marion, who was tired after her journey, lay down and Norman and I went for a walk. We passed Joy Bruce, who is enjoying Canada, and I told him about the struggle she was making to earn her living, and at the same time studying singing. He disappointed me.

'Don't you mix yourself up with the colored people,' he said impatiently. 'I have one friend who is deep in their problem and sufferings, and one is enough.'

'I am interested in Miss Bruce as a person, not as a problem,' I savagely retorted, because I was hurt that he should seem to be unsympathetic to any struggling cause or individual. I have made a great humanitarian garment for him which clothes him with sympathy for every suffering and oppressed people and person. I hate to have the garment seem a misfit in the least particular.

'Oh, it is all right for you to be interested in colored persons, but the race will have to make their own fight for freedom,' he said pertinaciously.

'Yes, that may be true; but there is also our side of the question. Miss Bruce suffers because she must make such an effort to gain an audience for her art, but we suffer too because we make it difficult for her. Her suffering may be more intense, but the evil to us is more insidious, because we allow an external like color to bar us from beauty, from art. I should like to work at the colored problem from the side of the evil re-actions of our indifference on us.'

CHAPTER VI

Steamer Romania
April 20th, 1907

Yesterday, at eight o'clock, I was calmly having breakfast in my youngest brother's home, in a country town, progressive, up-to-date in its institutions, but more conservative, more provincial, in its thought than even my home town. After breakfast, the postman brought me a letter telling me that one of my friends would sail to-day, and by eleven o'clock I was on the train bound for the sea-port. To-night, thirty-six hours later, I am on the ocean, the broad, expansive ocean, that makes me feel that there are no limits to life or thought or action; all things are possible. It is like entering a new world. The sun went down to-night in a ball of fire. I hope it presages a fine day to-morrow. There are only eleven passengers. It is an old, slow boat; we shall probably be two weeks crossing, but the captain assures us that his vessel is quite seaworthy. It was built when sea-going vessels were planned to last several generations.

The captain is a strong, well-built man. He has a virile face and a substantial air, as if contact with all the vicissitudes of the sea had given him sobriety and a quiet consciousness of strength. I think I shall like him.

May 3, 1907

At lunch to-day, we had a spirited argument on woman's suffrage. I hate being a propagandist. I believe that suffrage is the next step for women to take, but I am not at all confident that it will be the cure-all which its advocates claim. However, I marshalled out all the arguments for the delectation of the table and the captain refuted them with skill.

After lunch, he came and sat down beside me on deck. He wanted to continue the argument and when he was alone I could be strictly truthful with him.

'Do you not think that your wife would be more companionable to you if she had larger interests than her household?' I asked.

'My wife could not; we have nothing in common,' he replied vigorously.

'Not even your family?' I asked.

'Yes, my family. My boys and the wretched divorce laws are the only things that keep us together.'

Then followed his story, which I drew from him piece by piece. He had been an illegitimate child and had suffered at the hands of his mother's relatives until, at eleven years of age, he had run away to sea. He had shipped as a stow-away, and when discovered was kicked and cuffed by all the crew.

'The hard life was my good fortune,' he added. 'If I had had an easy life, I should probably have drifted about just like other boys. I resolved not to go back until I could make a home for my mother. I determined to succeed. I had had little education, and I knew that without education I could never be a captain. With every penny I could scrape together, I bought books, and these I studied during my spare minutes. From the first day at sea, I was bound to be a captain.'

He spoke many languages and was versed in higher mathematics, of which he had made a hobby.

'How did you feel about your mother?' I asked.

'She was treated so badly by her friends and relatives that I forgave her everything, and as the years went on, I came to feel that to have been born an illegitimate child was my greatest good luck,' he answered with feeling. A smile illuminated his face. Evidently his thoughts of his mother were pleasant.

'What about your father?'

'I never forgave him. I met him once. If duels had been in fashion, I should have challenged him, but I have never found any expression for my desire for revenge.' His voice was brusque.

'Would you be willing to start a child of yours along the same road?' I questioned.

'No, I would not. Knowing all the kicks and blows I got, I would not be brave enough for that. Long ago, I would have deserted my wife and married another woman, but I would not subject the woman I love to such hardship as my mother suffered; and whatever good my name is to my boys, they must have it. I see my wife two or three times a year. The woman I love I see at the end of every voyage. We have loved each other for eight years, and no evil must come to her through me.'

I talked with him for a long time about his feeling that it had been an advantage to him to be an illegitimate child. To me it seemed abnormal, even when I explained it as the feeling that being thrown on his own responsibility, having to make good despite the world's cruelty, had been a great spur. He thought the various restrictions of society rotten, but he could not openly fight them where it entailed suffering on others.

Millthorpe, England
August 1907

My travelling companion is a thoroughly conventional woman. She loves nature and beauty, but she has been standardized by the schools and society of to-day into the well-known type. I have done all the usual sight-seeing stunts with her, have admired the stately buildings, visited all points of interest and the common haunts of tourists; we have followed our Baedecker religiously. She returned to London to see her brother, who had come over unexpectedly, and I was left alone. Three days of solitude! I was within thirty miles of Edward Carpenter's home and at once decided that I would come over to Millthorpe and see him. I coached to Haddon Hall as an excuse to myself for my erratic pilgrimage, and then I started to walk to Millthorpe. I had a good deal of difficulty in finding the way, as the bucolic guides constantly gave me wrong directions and I had to retrace my steps many times; but finally I came to a most wonderful lane, bordered with high trees and carpeted with grass and flowers, through which a track, evidently rarely used, made its way. It was the delightful English lane of story books and I lingered along it, enjoying every minute.

Arrived at my destination, I sought a room at the village inn. The proprietor was an old-fashioned hostess. In the kitchen of her house, with its slated floor well sanded, on benches running around the wall, I found men drinking their nightly pint of ale. It was such a simple, home-like scene that I did not feel that her big mother heart would allow them to drink too much or give them anything unwholesome. I was literally her guest, and she busied herself over my welfare and interests as if she were my dearest friend. She assured me that Edward Carpenter was her dear friend and that he would be delighted to see me. When I found that he had gone for his evening walk, I went to bed, despairing of meeting him that day; but she kept watch for me, and when he returned at nine o'clock came and routed me out of bed and escorted me to his door, returning for me an hour later, when she felt that the proprieties would be outraged if I prolonged my evening call.

In the morning she woke me in time to go and have breakfast with Mr Carpenter – a breakfast of bread and butter and honey and tea, but the presence of the prophet turned the homely viands into a repast of the gods. I cared not what I ate; I scarcely knew that I ate. All the time I was conscious of but one thing – I had met my master, the man who had chosen to live simply, sincerely, to be truthful, not only to himself, but to the men who shall be, who saw clearly the coming time when men shall all be brothers, and who chose to live in the coming democracy here and now. I remembered Walt Whitman's advice to the man who desires to write poems and thought how well Carpenter realized it.

'Love the earth and the sun and animals, despise riches, give alms to every one who asks you, stand up for the stupid and crazy, devote your income and labor to others, hate tyrants, argue not concerning God, have patience and indulgence towards all people, take off your hat to nothing known or unknown, to no man or number of them, ... re-examine all you have been told in school or church or in any book and dismiss whatever insults your own soul; and your very flesh shall be a great poem, and have the richest fluency not only in words but in the silent lines of your lips and face, between the lashes of your eyes and in every motion and joint of your body.'

Here was a man who was content to be, who needed no pictures on his walls because Nature spread a changing scene of beauty before his lowly cottage door. He held no theories, so far as I discovered, to which he had not applied the acid test of practice, and the rest was a serenity, a quiet dignity that needed not assertion.

We shall do less preaching when we do more practising.

This glimpse of a great personality was the one significant event of this summer. I have buzzed around and shall talk glibly of other sights and other experiences; but I shall build a little shrine in my memory upon which I shall keep a constant light burning to a simple man who is content to be, and throws aside all appearances, all customs, all artificial needs, all false relations with people, all conventions which men deem necessary, and which in return choke their souls.

The conviction which I have gained from him is, that to be true to oneself is the great achievement, the only permanent reality; all thoughts and acts based on the delusion of expediency or immediate gain are transitory. This is my vaulting pole, which will carry me up my stairs according to the clearness of vision and tenacity of purpose with which I grasp it.

CHAPTER VII

Lakeside
September 29th, 1907

The voyage is over and I am on land once more. An interesting woman, Mrs Cameron, was on board. She had been a school teacher before she married, and when her fourth child was born she had come to the conclusion that they would never succeed in Britain. She had secured a school at a salary of two hundred and sixty dollars a year, with a house and garden attached, and had sent her husband to Alberta to stake out a homestead. He had been there for three years, and she had supported the children and saved one hundred and sixty dollars out of her meagre salary, towards the expense of going out to him. She had kept a maid to look after the baby while she taught. How had she done it? By her thrift and by utilizing every penny. Her children's clothes were all made from some friends' castoff clothing. The farmers around her had brought her wood. The spirit that overflowed in helpful service to others had made it possible for her to take as freely as she gave. She creates the feeling of good comradeship in you and you feel that you are her partner. It is a wonderful spirit of motherliness that transcends the bounds of her immediate family. She mothers every one with whom she comes in contact, rich and poor; she knows no distinction; people are just human beings with the same needs as herself. She overflows with goodwill and sympathy.

A man whom she met the night before she sailed looked after her oldest boy all through the voyage and passed her baggage through the custom as if he had been a genuine son. A young girl whom she met on the steamer took care of her children as no hired maid would have done. These two, her four children and myself, used to meet in Mrs Cameron's stateroom every afternoon for tea. We were perched in all sorts of positions on the upper and lower berths, but we had our tea and a merry time, all seasoned with Mrs Cameron's abundant goodwill. I was more interested in her than in any other passenger. She is the artist mother who serves every one unstintedly and gives herself so freely that she attracts all kinds of service from others. The young man and woman, who had just met her on this voyage, changed their destination to go to that part of the country where she will have her home, that they may be near her. It is the big-hearted people, often with little means, who will make this a better world. It is not money, but love, that counts. I shall remember her after I have forgotten every other person on the steamer.

I do hope that she will succeed. I do not imagine that her husband is her equal, either in ambition or energy. She will be a wonderful godsend to the lone bachelors on the prairie working on their isolated homesteads. I can see a steady procession of them going to her house.

There was an old Irish lady on the steamer and, when I was saying good-bye, she took my hand in both of hers, and shaking it warmly, said, 'God bless you; you have acted as if you were one of us.'

'And am I not one of you?' I asked.

I prize the compliment. I must have got the shove upward from Mrs Cameron.

Lakeside
October 25th, 1907

A letter from George Dean a few days ago, in which he told me of his desire to find some woman, economically independent, who would live with him without a legal marriage, arrived when Leonora Saunders was here, and I allowed her to read it. She was very enthusiastic about the letter and delighted to hear, even through a third party, of a man who really desired women to be free. I laughingly suggested that they should be friends. He is altogether too advanced for me, and I do not believe in playing with ideas that I am not willing to practice.

I told George, when I answered his letter, that I thought it would be a good idea if he and Leonora Saunders should be friends; that she shared his ideas and both of them suffered from too much isolation from their kind. Leonora lives on an island in a small village – two blacksmiths, several general stores, three churches, a school and a cluster of houses. No one in the vicinity reads anything, or thinks of anything but 'What shall we eat? How shall we be clothed? How many kinds of cake shall I bake to-day? Can I remodel last year's skirt?' I cannot imagine being able to breathe in that community. Leonora lives such a solitary life that she is deemed peculiar. She has never been away from her environment and has never discovered that there are people in the world who are holding ideas similar to hers.

George is a scientist and has various hobbies and ideas that shut him off from his community. He is a vegetarian, believes in all sorts of natural living, that the public have not yet thought about. Even his sleeping out of doors is a new fad that they cannot understand. As one of his neighbors said to him, 'Why, you must be crazy to sleep out of doors when you have plenty of room inside.' To go barefoot is a mark of erraticism that bars him from his community. It is a typical bourgeois neighborhood. He is a dreamer and a poet and has no common ground with the people whom he meets every day, and is in danger of becoming what they regard him – eccentric. One pays a very heavy price for being too far in advance of one's time. It may be well for society to have pioneers, but the pioneer is well scarred while blazing a new path.

I received a telegram the next day from George, to say that he would be here for dinner the following day. It is all very well to tell people that they ought not to have ideas that they are not willing to put into practice, but I can foresee all sorts of sufferings that will come to George and Leonora, if they attempt to carry out theirs.

I invited quite a group of people to meet them, so that he should not know which one had the sentiments, which I had credited only to a friend. Fortunately, I had not told him her name.

Such a jolly dinner we had! George defended his dreams and theories, his food, his out-of-door sleeping, his simple living, and this thoughts. Margaret Eaton is very conservative, but a great wit. She led him on and gave him a very gay time, evidently the kind of jollying and teasing from which his fads shut him off, and George fell in love with Margaret, was willing to give up all his ideas, become a common-place citizen, if she would marry him; but alas, alas for him – I am not sure whether the fates did not keep a kindly eye on Margaret – she would have none of him. He never even remembered why he came to Lakeside. I never told Leonora why I had so urgently telegraphed for her to come up for dinner.

Lakeside
May 1, 1909

Two years have sped by. When I returned from the Old
Country, I came back to my home city to take charge of my
brother's orphan family. I had a small house, so small that
often I used to feel as if the walls were closing on me. After
the spacious rooms of the old home, I felt very much caged
and often went out of doors to fill my lungs and spirit with
free air. My days have been filled with household duties
and my leisure time has been spent in darning socks and
teaching the children their lessons. I have been guilty of
only one piece of audacity. My little house had a small
reception room and dining room, but a large kitchen. I
decided to throw my front cubby holes into one living
room and screen off a corner of the kitchen for the gasplate
and the sink and to use the rest of the room for a dining
room. I invited all the dignitaries of the city for dinner,
doctor, lawyer, merchant, chief, rich man, poor man, beg-
gar man, thief, all had their turn, and of course (I must add
for the good of my proper friends) their wives accompanied them; and I provided dinners that cost only twelve
and a half cents per head, and served them in the kitchen.
The kitchen! I doubt if any of them would have confessed
to taking a meal in a kitchen before.

My niece used to say to me when mother was living, 'Oh,
it is all very well for you to keep open house now, when
you have a maid and grandmother's purse, but wait until
you are dependent on your own limited income and exertions, and you will soon cease to have such a constant procession of people for meals.'

I had only replied, 'Wait and see. I shall share my crust, if
necessary.' Because of her prophecy, I kept a register of
every one who came for a meal, including the nieces and

nephews and their chums who adopted me as aunt, and all the lonely people whose paths crossed mine, as well as the old friends and comrades. The list totalled eight hundred extra meals in eight months, but, as I explained to Louise when I sent her the account of my feat, I counted every one to whom I gave a cup of tea and cracker in the afternoon or a cup of cocoa and piece of cake in the evening when the children had a dance.

Such mild audacity! Now I am going to leave all duties behind me and once more I am going to cross the ocean in search of adventure. I am going first to the Garden City to see for myself if the fabled accounts of this place are true. Oh, I forgot my most audacious exploit!

Two or three times every summer a group of seven women with varying additions to swell the party to some multiple of four, have gone for a drive. We take as many double-seated carriages as the party requires, leave the city at half-past eight, drive eight or nine miles and rest our horses, eat our lunch that we have brought with us, drive five or six miles more, again rest our horses and go walking or boating. Then we turn our steps toward home, stopping for supper and arriving about half past eight. Twelve hours in the open, drives, walks, sometimes boating and bathing, a day full of outdoor life. I organized the trip some years ago, to get in contact with a group of women whom I rarely met. They are among the broadest of the town's women, but they are so hide-bound by convention that only on an outdoor jaunt would they dare express their opinions.

The original seven who have been on all our picnics were here for lunch during the winter. I am not a society woman. It is not worth while for me to spend my time that way. These women like me, envy me my freedom and pity me for it. In my home they feel the atmosphere of freedom.

At lunch time, the conversation turned to Elinor Glynn's 'Three Weeks.' I never read books of that kind. I am perfectly willing to know all the underlying facts of sex, and to face them, no matter how distasteful they may be, but I am not willing to read books that think they are wrong and yet exploit them, that rather glory in doing the forbidden thing. I expressed my opinion very strongly and then I told them of a letter that I had received, to which I was not ready to assent, but as I had great faith in the author I was willing to study it from every point of view to see if there were any basis for the opinions he held. They all begged me to read the letter. I did so.

'The sex question is changing on account of economic changes. So long as pestilence, famine, war, bad sanitary conditions, caused a high death rate, all the moral demands were for large families. When better industrial development gave women leisure for study and increased medical knowledge aided the physician in securing better conditions for children, the high birth rate ceased to be necessary to overcome a high death rate. The growing economic independence of women has changed the whole moral value of sex relations. The sex functions must adapt themselves to the economic changes, just as other functions in life have done. Man depended solely on his eye for hunting game, but as civilization developed other means of supplying food the eye was used more and more for aesthetic pleasures. The sex relation becoming less and less necessary for the creation of life will become more and more a spiritual relation. As we have chained the lightning, prevented its doing the harm it formerly did, so shall we chain sex. To-day men and women, especially women, are suffering from the suppression of feeling. There are women who realize that sex is a natural function and are seeking their own expression for it without regard to marriage. Ultimately, the number of self-supporting women who will do so will increase.'

They were ready to discuss any novel, any romantic treatment of the sex question simply as a product of the author's imagination, but the actual question was as unreal for them as any child's fairy tale. The one criterion by which they disposed of every phase of the sex problem was, 'That would be immoral.'

It is a great disadvantage to be always a lady. I did want to swear. Nothing makes me so cross as to have any idea answered by, 'It would be immoral,' in a tone of infallibility, ignorant that the basis of morality is custom.

They were my guests. With conventional people, I conform to conventional standards! But I laugh about it afterwards.

'Does the author of the letter believe in God?' one of them asked me.

'He believes in God as a principle in the universe, not as an autocratic being,' I tried to explain.

'Oh, that explains it,' she retorted quickly, 'God would not approve of such ideas.'

I was inclined to ask, 'Who told you so?' but refrained. May the good angel who keeps the Social Record place one mark to my credit!

We had a long argument.

They did not seem a bit disturbed, but the door had hardly closed on them before the news began to fly about town that I was advocating free love. One evening an old friend of my mother's came to me with tears in her eyes, to beg me for my mother's sake not to discuss such questions. It was useless to try to explain to her. She had only one standard, the ten commandments, and I could not convince her that it was hypocrisy for us to say that we obeyed any one of them. It is futile to try to make these women understand that there are truths deeper in life than in the Bible; at least, in their interpretation of the Bible.

I am divided between my inability to form an opinion on the sex question and my consternation that those women who read Elinor Glynn, Robert Chambers and their like, who are quite tolerant of men in society whose moral standards are shaky according to their theories, are shocked the minute you attempt to awaken questions concerning economic and social conditions that lie at the bottom of our moral code and the necessity for re-organizing it in harmony with the needs of individuals to-day.

Every one of them would assent, for they have all travelled broadly, that there are different codes of morality, according to the social and economic conditions of the various countries; but when you endeavor to explain that the same country changes its code according to economic changes they are frightened.

Never mind, everything I told them to-day will be an old story ten years from now, and they will wonder how they ever questioned it, but I shall probably be promulgating something just as startling.

In the meantime, I am going to investigate some social experiments in England.

CHAPTER VIII

The Garden City
June 25th, 1909

My Utopia exists! Not in dreams, not in books, not in the 'Land of Nowhere,' but bodied forth in bricks and wood – principally wood – plaster and mortar, trees and gardens and real people living in them – real flesh-and-blood people, who are just ordinary every-day people, but different. It is the difference that makes the Utopia. Moreover, Utopia has been in existence for five years and is growing healthily. If John Bull could step from Morris's 'Land of Nowhere,' he would find many of his dreams actualized here. Yes, I have arrived in Utopia, and I am hastening to send word to my friends. Of course, they will not believe me; but then I can say, 'Come and see.'

To start with, this is a bona fide attempt to create an ideal city of homes. The Englishman cherishes his home even more closely than his religion. When the British workmen began to lose strength and vigor, and to decrease in stature, as the volunteers for the Boer War brought forcibly to the attention of the British public, the cause was sought in the conditions under which they were obliged to live, and a movement for improved housing conditions led to many experiments. One of the most ambitious was the Garden

City. Perhaps the desire to improve the condition of the workingmen's homes might not have blossomed into Utopia, if the reformers had not felt that it would be good business policy to secure permanently whatever gains they had fought to establish. So they made this a sort of Single Tax city. It has been modified by the exigencies of the object they wished to attain. A joint stock company bought the land and laid it out as a city, planned ultimately for thirty thousand people. They constructed the gas and water mains, made roads, provided all the municipal buildings for education and civic purposes. They lease the land for a ninety-nine-year term, and when a sufficient amount has been realized from these leases to recoup the company for the money they have expended, according to its charter, the city will pass into the hands of the citizens and all further income derived from the leasing of land will be applied to reducing taxes and increasing the civic wealth and the bettering of municipal conditions.

Each house must have at least one-eighth of an acre of land. At present, in 1909, there are about five thousand people, with promise of more coming.

The people who came here first were all idealists. The material wisdom of the world values one according to his worldly success and scoffs at poets and idealists, but you cannot too often assure this same doubting public that it takes 'the ideal to blow a hair's breadth of dust off the actual,' and that schemes of barley feeding and material ease will accomplish little without the spirit that gives them joy and life.

I feel quite inclined to be poetical and rhapsodize this morning. This is the place for poets, first, because it is so beautiful to look at. Every vacant lot blooms with flowers and every house has its garden. It is literally a garden city, a city of gardens – and such gardens! Here are roses that you dream about. Here are wall flowers and blue forget-me-nots such as one finds in the farm laborers' cottages everywhere in England. All flowers are here, and shrubs. The gardens are as dear to the inhabitants as some rare collection of pictures is to a wealthy man with a mania for collecting; dearer, because the gardens have been planned and made and worked over. Each is its owner's own creation. When you meet people they do not talk about their aches and pains, but about the condition of the various plants in their gardens. The special flowers and experiments in gardening are all asked after; they are known by name and their progress enquired about as if they were of real human interest.

The gardens are the background, but the people are the real interest of the place. They have come from all parts of the world. They were brave enough to dare the chances of living in Utopia, with other cranks. I am sure that each one who came was warned by his friends that he would find only cranks. But they came with their trunks packed full of tolerance for their neighbors' idiosyncrasies. They had probably discovered that they themselves were regarded in the world as faddists and, knowing themselves to be harmless, they were less inclined to regard the hobbies, faiths or beliefs of their neighbors as dubious possessions.

How did the Garden City people, coming from all parts of Britain, and even the continent, and the colonies, bring the same spirit of brotherhood and goodwill, of willingness for each individual to follow his own bent? Every one you meet seems animated by the same spirit of love. It is like living among people who really believe that Christ was a teacher to be followed, that it was possible to follow him, that he had enunciated living truths, truths which could be tested in actual life. A society of people who love, who are helpful to one another, makes a heaven on earth. When you are here you wonder why any other place should be different.

Everyone believes in simplicity in dress and house. Many of the women have worked out their own designs for their gowns, designs which they think suitable to them as individuals. Some of them are artistic and some the reverse. I am not concerned half as much with the success as I am with the attempt. Will they be strong enough to live up to their ideals when the world has discovered Garden City and has swept in upon it with its false measuring stick? I hope they will. The earlier residents, who came here to live in peace their own lives, after their own theories, had fought for that right among aliens in the world, and now that they have tasted the stimulation of a place where every one's hobbies are respected, surely they will not give up their individuality for any newcomers. I hope and I fear. The pioneers who adventure for the sake of an idea are always so much more interesting and virile than the people who succeed them. Pray the gods that the imitators of the spirit that brought the pioneers here may not crush out the original spirit.

Even their Sunday is different. It is a full day, starting with a meeting in the Hall where they have, as the opening exercise, extracts read from the works of all the great religious teachers of all countries and creeds. The pertinency of the selection to the subject under discussion is the only ground for its adoption. One grows to feel that religion is just the cry of the universal human spirit. In our need for something that will embody our longing for infinity, all human souls are alike. Even by our needs we belong to one great family. After the reading comes a discussion on some pressing modern readjustment. Non-resistance, cooperation, syndicalism, the substitution of feeling for institutions, all the modern questions that are just commencing to lift their heads in America have their adherents, who eagerly espouse and work for them here.

The unique thing about the evening gathering is its order of service. One feels condemned at its very uniqueness. In the twentieth century, a group of followers of Christ have substituted the commandments of the New Testament for those of the Old. Why should it be remarkable to have a service that discards all the negative commands of Moses and substitutes the positive ones of Christ? 'Thou shalt love thy neighbor as thyself' is the spirit of the New, and it is a command that we have not yet realized can and ought to be obeyed literally.

There are two key-notes to the whole place, freedom and love. It is the linking of the two that makes Garden City unique. You have freedom here, to live your own life. I do not believe that there are any restrictions. Your freedom is limited only by the good of your neighbor. The atmosphere of the place itself creates the spirit that restrains the individual and that directs his efforts in helping his neighbors attain with him their heaven.

It is the personality of the citizens that makes Garden City interesting. It goes without saying that each and all belong to some communistic faith. There are socialists, single taxers, syndicalists, communistic anarchists, Tolstoyans, people who believe it is wrong to own property and people who are seeking ways of assuaging their consciences because they do not know how to live without it.

Next door to where I am staying live a man and his wife who are both artists. She belongs to one of the well-known scholarly families of London. They do not think it right to take interest, so they are living simply, earning their daily bread by manual work in making beautiful sanitary dishes. It requires faith to believe that people will ever return to dishes made of good material, under wholesome conditions for the workers; that they will be content to have a few good dishes, rather than the many cheap abominations made in bad factories, where the workers run the risk of poisoning through lead glaze. They are making the attempt to create a demand for such wares. My faith goes with them that they will succeed.

On the other side is another artist couple. They are weaving and designing their own materials. They have all the social tenets of William Morris, but they are more mystical. They came here, made their experiment, and lost, and lost, and lost. When they had put their last five hundred dollars into the business and faced ultimate ruin, and were ready to go to America and start all over again, fortune took a turn and success, moderate, but sufficient to make a living possible for them, began to come.

Just a little way down the street is a man who had a leather business in London. He hated the commercial methods of salesmanship, so gave it up and came to this place to try his hand on a small holding. He has had a hard struggle. That is true of nearly all the people who are clinging to an ideal in the face of great difficulties, and in opposition to the wisdom of the world. They are sacrificing their own material comfort for the sake of something that is more important to them than physical well-being. There have been many and great hardships. The Garden City has not yet achieved perfection. She has still to climb before she reaches the top of the Hill Difficulty, but at least she is making the attempt, an attempt that is fraught with interest to every one who bemoans present-day conditions and standards.

There are a few factories which have come here for the sake of economic advantages, cheaper water and power and better facilities for transportation, and the workingmen belonging to these came because their work was here. At first, the majority of them (there are a few rare souls in every group) were very discontented. They missed the noise and excitement of the city streets. They were not accustomed to the quieter pleasures of the country. However, before they had been here a year, their children's improved appearance, better health, and greater energy converted them to the place. They caught the spirit and they, too, took to gardening and had a hobby.

The intellectual people, who dominate the spirit of the city, have all reached the state of mind where they are disgusted with our present civilization and feel that if it is to be made endurable it must be changed. Many of them are firm believers that the only way to change it is to do away with private property, to simplify life in both its needs and its pleasures, and to substitute creative work for the mechanical toil of to-day. When it is impossible to change the industry, they would try to lessen the hours of labor and to provide more hours of leisure. They would plan to train all workers for the proper use of that leisure that they need not to be too exhausted mentally and physically to do individual work.

They are taking whatever steps they can to simplify their own lives. They make their houses as simple as possible and have discovered that good lines and harmonious colors are far more effective than are all the modern arts of house building. The same is true of clothes and food. Simplicity means not deprivation but gain, more pleasure in the providing of actual necessities and more leisure for other things that add zest and value to life.

There are all sorts of art and literary societies and an endless variety of clubs: reading, dramatic, painting, open-air sketching, wood-carving, clay-modelling, Greek dancing. Every modern effort to express creative ability has its devotees and its clubs. Almost every person has some art which he practises, and he finds companionship among the congenial members of his own club.

The children dance around the May-pole, and all the residents join in community fêtes. The most interesting is the annual Parody, when all the idiosyncrasies and little peccadilloes of the citizens are laughed over. As long as the Garden City can laugh at itself, it is safe. When it commences to take itself too seriously, it will be spotted. Let us hope that there will be ever new infusions of the spirit of laughter and of innovation to keep the Garden City fresh and growing.

CHAPTER IX

Steamer Freedonia
September 23rd, 1909

I am on my homeward way, after one of the most wonderful experiences in Garden City. The day after I arrived I went to the book-store and bought all the literature about the Garden City I could find. In the back of a little pamphlet called Brotherhood, there was an advertisement of a library of books on philosophy, psychology and other psychic subjects, open Tuesday from twelve to one. I waited impatiently for the opening of that library Tuesday and was there betimes. A very charming lady was in charge; the regular librarian was out of the city for the day. We soon were in the midst of an exciting conversation. It began to rain. The water poured down in torrents and we prolonged our talk long past the hour for closing. She invited me to come to her house for afternoon tea the following Thursday and I gladly accepted her invitation.

Another delightful hour resulted. I had told her of my lack of strength, and without any comment, she asked me if I had ever heard of magnetic healing.

'No,' I replied, but was very little interested.

'I would like you to meet Mrs Tolive, who lives a few doors from here,' she said. 'I will take you there when you leave me.'

The words 'magnetic healing' had meant very little to me, and I paid little attention to her intimation, but when I rose she rose also and came with me to her neighbor's door. Just before the maid opened it, my new friend said, 'Mrs Tolive believes in magnetic healing. Good-bye.' She left me on the door-step.

If I had been told that she believed in any cult, known or unknown, I would have desired to embrace my opportunity to learn about it at first hand.

As quickly as I could do so, courteously, I introduced the subject and Mrs Tolive tried to explain to me that magnetism, life, was everywhere in the universe and we drew it into ourselves through concentrating our thoughts and our desires on it. The final direction she gave me was to seat myself, at the same hour every day, taking the position of the sphinx, hands on my knees, body held upright, facing the east, and take ten deep breaths; and then hold my thoughts on God for ten minutes.

I irreverently asked, 'But what if I do not believe in God?'

'Then take the first high thought that comes to you and hold your mind and spirit to that,' she replied sincerely. 'Very soon you will contact yourself with the energy, magnetism, life, in the universe. It will flow through you like an electric current.'

'It is a very easy river of Jordan,' I said, almost as serious as she was, because I could not be flippant in the face of her earnestness.

I soon discovered that Garden City was imbued with a faith in love's being the actual life force of the world, that life and love were synonymous.

Either because of a natural state of scepticism, or that my reason is stronger just now than my faith and chokes my mysticism, I could not hypnotize myself into an attitude of mind that brought the healing current up and down my spine.

However, before I had been in Garden City three weeks I was ill and unable to move. I was rooming with Mr and Mrs Adams. They had been co-workers with Edward Carpenter in some of his social experiments and were most stimulating hosts. Mrs Adams fell ill, too. She was in one bedroom and I in another when my librarian friend found me and took me to a boarding house near her home, where she could watch me closely. I named her Pippa then, because as she passes she brings hope and help and inspiration to all. She is one of the most delightful women I know, a strange commingling of the old and the new, new in her sympathies, in her need to find expression for love and fellow feeling, old in her aristocratic traditions, from which her desire for democracy has not yet freed her. Friendless and unknown, and ill in that boarding house, I might have been some stray star dropped from the firmament, because I was absolutely without connections known to the good Garden City people. Yet Pippa, as soon as her maid returned, took me into her home and kept me there for a week, arranging for her friends to do likewise. After my visit with Pippa, Mrs Herth, a life-long friend of John Ruskin's, and her charming daughter invited me for a week; then I went to Mrs Bartel's, who had two interesting daughters and a son, all intellectual radicals. Such a delightful time as I had, lying on my back, the guest of charming, cultured people imbued with the new spirit of love.

Dear Mrs Macfail, one of the saints even in the Garden City, met me out driving one day and insisted that I should come to her next. She bought everything I needed for my homeward voyage, packed my trunk and sent me off with all the loving care and solicitude of a mother. Was it some of the love that mother had shed so broadcast come back to me in my need?

To crown all, Pippa is taking me home, and will be followed by Bruce Wallace, who has been the prophet of the new faith in brotherhood in Garden City, where there are many people who are seeking freedom to express their craving for beauty, for truth, for love; they are conscious that there is for them a 'quest of a new Holy Grail,' and this quest brings to them new life, new zest, new joy. All the words in the vocabulary would not exhaust, words cannot utter, the charm and glory of living when one is controlled by a new idea, an idea that has joy and virility and life for one. Their quest is the substitution of service for profit in business, the creation of beauty in all one's surroundings and of fellowship in all one's relations. It is the faith that the spiritual life is more than possessions or power or success or any external institution or form in which we seek to confine it. Among the leaders in the quest is Bruce Wallace. I am hoping that Canada will hear his message, but I am afraid that she is not yet ready to cast aside her utilitarian aims and idols of material success.

One is never tired of remarking on the coincidences in life. A very charming girl, with all the wit and vivacity of the warm-hearted Irish, shared my cabin on the way over. She was a great friend of Mrs William Vaughan Moody's. I found her with Mr and Mrs Moody, passengers on this ship. They are intensely interested in questioning Pippa about the experiment at Garden City and we have had various arguments whether we had to work for the spread of the spirit or for the institution of Garden Cities.

Marion and Norman are abroad this summer. They are studying international law, Marion taking the course at the Sorbonne and Norman in Berlin. They will spend the winter comparing notes. They are preparing to specialize in international law and are debating moving from Buffalo to New York or to Boston. They had planned to sail on the same steamer with us, but at the last moment had to postpone their sailing. We were very disappointed. Pippa is very anxious to meet them. I have told her a great deal about them.

CHAPTER X

Lakeside
October 25th, 1909

Pippa has kept some of the atmosphere of the Garden City for me here. She is leaving for home next month and I am disconsolate. It has been interesting to me to watch her trouble with her vocabulary when she tried to explain the Garden City ideals to the citizens. Things that seem quite a matter of course there are too Utopian here to seem rational. She has had the same trouble I have always had in trying to explain new ideas. Mr Wallace also has had a similar experience, but he has faith that the 'Kingdom of God cometh not by might nor by force, but by the spirit' to those who are ready to receive it, and is more patient than we are. He believes that men, having once gained the vision of a land where love and service prevail, will ultimately realize it.

A few days ago I went to call on a friend and found one of her boys very ill. His father came downstairs to meet me and told me the doctor held out no hope, that they scarcely thought he could live out the hour.

I hesitated a moment; then I told them about the faith of the good Garden City people that there was a life force present in the universe which we could capture through concentration of desire, purpose, and thought, and suggested that as they had no hope he should allow me to go up and sit by his boy and see if I could help him. As a drowning man clutches at a straw, he clutched at my suggestion. I went up the stairs slowly, torn between my desire to serve my friends in their dire distress and my fear that my lack of faith might prevent my doing so.

I sat down by his bedside, clasped each of the boy's hands in one of mine and took the ten deep breaths as Mrs Tolive had directed. Almost immediately the thought came, 'In Him was life and the life was the light of men.'

I sat there, his hands tightly held in mine, concentrating every faculty on that one thought. Slowly the electric current, of which I had heard so much, but which I had never been able to summon through concentration for myself, began to run down my arms, and I could feel it pass into his hands. I sat there, not daring to reason, scarcely daring to feel, but tensely holding to that one thought.

In about fifteen minutes, his father came up to say that the doctor was downstairs and would I go into another room. I retired. The doctor came up and reported the crisis past. My friends overwhelmed me with gratitude, and I crept home, scarcely able to drag myself there through the deep fatigue that accompanied the intense concentration. As soon as I was undressed and in bed, such a wonderful feeling of exaltation came over me. It seemed as if the exaltation of saving a life must be as great as the exaltation of giving birth, an exaltation that passes beyond words into the mystery of silence.

The next day, still tired and spent from those few minutes, I went back to see my friends. They wanted to ignore everything but the doctor's skill in saving their son. They go to church regularly and pray both night and morning, but for them the age of miracles had passed.

For me, I do not know. There was the need and I tried to meet it. Some day I shall understand.

March 21st, 1910

Gertrude has been to see me to-day. At last she seems to be settled. It is eighteen years since a policeman brought her to me. All these years I have watched over her, and yet I have never understood her or known how to do what she needed. She was just sixteen when the policeman found her wandering about the streets and asked her where her home was. She told him she had none.

She had been one of Dr Barnardo's children, had been sent to this country and placed with a farmer. Even then the daintiness and delicacy of taste which has always been her strong point rebelled against the rough surroundings on that farm, and she had run away to escape the ugliness and coarseness of the life there. After I had known her for years, I decided that she was probably the child of some gentleman and a woman of the streets. She had inherited refined tastes, the love of beauty both in nature and in clothes and surroundings, and nice habits about the care of her body. When I enquired in England at the Home, they could only tell me that she had come into the orphanage as a baby and had been sent to Canada at three years of age, to one of the Homes there. While all the surroundings of the Barnardo homes are clean and wholesome, there was nothing, as far as I could discern to give Gertrude her supersensitiveness to beauty.

When the policeman brought her to me, I took her in for the night and found her a home with a bright, wholesome, whole-hearted woman. As usual, Gertrude won her love at first and they were very happy together. When she had been there about ten weeks, she had a burst of uncontrollable temper. She wanted to go to Toronto, to a place where there would be children, so I secured her a situation in the larger city. I went to see her every time I visited Toronto. It was a constant repetition of her first experience. She would win the love of everyone in the house at first, but after a time she had a few days of ungovernable rage, or, as I later came to believe, nerves.

Finally, I placed her in a reformatory for girls, but the matron, although a very wise and tactful woman, was baffled by her. Coming out of the reformatory, she went to live at a gentleman's house where there was an only son. He fell in love with her. There are few more attractive girls than Gertrude, and, added to her prettiness, are her romantic temperament and her strong emotionalism. No wonder the young boy fell in love, and these two children trod forbidden paths.

When the child was born, Gertrude spent the days in the hospital full of terrors.

'Every night, I wondered what would become of me. How could I care for the baby; how could I care for myself?' she told me. 'I used to cry myself to sleep. When I was discharged from the hospital I had nowhere to go, no friends, no one to give me a meal, and I was desperate. I just went and left the baby on the father's door-step. I had not gone very far, when my courage returned and I went back. Some way or other, I was sure I would find the way to take care of my baby.'

'They had found the baby and taken her into the house, and when I rang the bell they asked me to come in, and kept me until a policeman came. When the baby's father saw them take me to jail, his manhood awoke and he followed me. He offered to marry me and he succeeded in getting me released from prison. He planned for us to go

West, where nobody would know anything about us. But I loved him; I could not sacrifice his future. He had been brought up a gentleman; I could not satisfy him very long. I would not go with him and see him humiliated by me, because I did not know what a lady ought to know. The baby died, and he went West without me. But I love him still.'

That is her story as she told it to me, with its pain and its heroism. All through the years she has kept her hold on me, craving love, hoarding the few crumbs I gave her. I have never known how to give to her all she needed, and yet, little as I have given, she has clung to me. She wrote to me that she wanted to come and live in the country near where I am, so that she could have the beauty of the country and see me occasionally. I arranged with one of my friends to take her. She came down a month ago and now she seems happy with Bessie Field, who is giving her the love she needs. I am glad for my poor little stray bird, who seems at last to have found her right nest.

London
May 20th, 1910

This summer I decided to spend in England and France, and to bring my niece Agnes with me, for the sake of her French, which she needed to brush up for her college course.

To-day's mail brought me a letter from Marion. With her husband, she has gone into partnership with a law firm in New York whose members are life-long friends of them both. She enclosed a picture of the woman suffrage parade down Fifth Avenue, with the small, brave handful of men who were hardy enough to walk with the women. Norman was almost in the first line, and I could plainly distinguish him. I can understand how he hated the parade, for he shuns publicity. He hates fuss and wishes mankind would do the rational thing without the noise and propaganda that seem necessary to induce it to take the right path. Knowing his disposition, I appreciate his heroism in marching.

We landed in England the day after the King's death. Agnes was eager to see his funeral, so we rose at five in the morning and went to a side street. The main thoroughfares through which the procession would pass were all crowded before we arrived, but we took our places near the corner. We sat on two boxes which we had bought from an enterprising pedlar, but which the police soon confiscated. I hated being there; I hated the spectacle; I hated the interest of the masses in an institution that enslaved them. The procession swept by with pomp and circumstance. It was a magnificent display of national wealth, military glory, and hereditary honors – the celebration of a past relation out of which all power was gone, but whose symbol the people continue to worship.

We waited in London for three weeks for another procession. It also swept through the city streets, a blaze of color, with brilliant dresses and uniforms, not of war but of peace, with flying banners proclaiming the aspirations of half of the nation and bearing portraits of leaders in civic and artistic movements of the past, this procession was pulsating with life and devotion to the coming idea – the rule of democracy.

It was a glorious day when the Woman's League for Social and Political Equality, with its fraternal organizations, marched through London. It was the procession of the great democracy – the democracy that includes women as well as men. In this pageant were represented every in-

terest and activity of women, from the great ones of the
past who, like Queen Elizabeth, bore their share in government, to the sweated worker of to-day, who, on account of
bad industrial conditions, earns a bare subsistence. Thou-
sands strong they marched, full of the new interpretation
of democracy in its demand for the extension of the franchise to include more than half the race.

Agnes and I had desired to be included in this procession. We had gone to headquarters and had seen the banners that the various organizations were going to carry.
Our purse was light, so we could not aspire to any such
magnificent banners, but we wanted Canada represented.
For eighteen cents we bought a couple of yards of cheap
yellow cambric and a box of crayons. On this cotton we
stencilled Canada on a background of Maple Leaves and
petitioned the Canadian Commission for a sheaf of wheat.
We found some compatriots who were glad to march with
us and with them we divided our grain. The papers said
next day that a Canadian wheat field marched through London. We shall gain the suffrage in Canada with almost no
effort when other countries have granted it to their
women. Canada has never had to struggle for her ideals.
Her fight lies in the future when she becomes self-con-
scious. We wanted, at least, to have an infinitesimal share
in the struggle of the British women, because we shall reap
such rich harvest from their labors.

Steamer Urania
September 21st, 1910

There is a charming young woman sharing our stateroom.
She seems about thirty. Her face is very fresh and her manner bright and frank. Her husband, who is in a stateroom

with men, seems much older and more serious. The fourth member of our cabin is an elderly woman. She has been a schoolteacher and has written some books, and is now too old to teach any longer. She is on her way to California to spend the rest of her days with an old friend whom she has not seen for twenty years, and who has offered her a home. The small income she has from her savings will be sufficient for only a little pocket money. She is such a charming old lady. I do hope that she will be happy with her friend; but to me the risk of living with anyone not seen for twenty years is tremendous. I cannot imagine living with any of my friends of twenty or even of ten years ago. We have travelled along such different paths. Life now seems almost directly opposed to what I thought it then. What I condemned then I now allow, and many things that I upheld, I denounce. For me, good and evil have often changed their values. I am quite inclined to think that I may change many of my present judgments, because the things for which in the past I made the greatest sacrifices have all been outgrown. Why, then, should not my present standards be superseded by some other? I know it is not so with my old friends. The majority of them have continued along the same road on which they were then travelling. I do hope that my *companion de voyage* will not be disappointed.

Steamer Urania
September 28th, 1910

A week ago, I had a long talk with my married room-mate, or rather the room-mate I supposed was married. I wonder why people tell me their secrets, as if they were glad to find relief in confiding in some one. On Wednesday, as we walked up and down the deck, she said to me, 'The man with whom I am travelling is not my husband. He had been married twenty years. His wife and he are firm friends. They happily understand each other, and she is big enough to see that he needs more than she can give him. She knew that he loved me, and she sent for me to come to visit her and then urged me to accompany him on this trip. It would be impossible for them to get a divorce in Canada, without Parliamentary proceedings, which are both costly and annoying in their publicity. Neither of them desire to face the public disapproval that would accompany their effort to get a divorce, so I have come on this holiday with him.'

'But what about the future? How can you, after three months of intimacy, return to a separate existence?' I asked.

'I do not know. It is a case of taking a half loaf rather than having no bread, with him. I have a happy disposition. No matter how much I may suffer, I shall always have these three months to look back upon. It is not ideal to separate, but sometimes I think we shall keep our love better because we shall never have it associated with the common phases of life. We shall never be so familiar that we shall take each other for granted. The few occasions on which we can be together will always be red-letter days. As his wife is keen that he shall have every experience that will enrich his life, so we are keen that she shall not suffer because we have each other's love.'

I have watched them closely all through the voyage. They have almost convinced me that the compromise, the accepting what was possible to them, was better than to go through life starving and hungry for each other, with no opportunity of satisfying the frightful loneliness for a comprehending spirit.

Among the interesting passengers on board is a scientist. He has specialized in Germany and each year he goes to London to work in the laboratory of one of the most famous biologists. His experiences have been interesting and his point of view has been well defended. He is very delightful. I had a long walk on deck with him to-day, and found him a strong feminist. He is prepared to go even further than I am. It is interesting to meet a man who is more liberal than myself in his opinions of freedom for woman. I have had to fight so hard for my ideas that I thought that I was advanced, and now he laughs at my conservatism. Ah me, if my brother could only hear a man, a scientist, call me conservative, how I would rejoice!

September 29th, 1910

This is the last night on the steamer. It is strange how the night brings such a general feeling of good fellowship. Friendships grow with mushroom rapidity the last day, and everywhere one meets regret that the pleasant acquaintances of the past week will soon be separated, with slight probability of ever again meeting. Always the last night at sea is a wonderful emotional experience. It is so full of memories of the previous weeks' wandering in foreign lands. It is crowded with anticipations of the home-coming and over all is the wonderful *esprit de corps* of the passengers. I always love its thrill, its vibrations, but to-night it has had its climax for me. The scientist has asked me to marry him. He offers me wealth, social position, a share in his work, everything that head could desire – and I like him. I like him as I have liked few men. Surely, on that foundation we could build love. I want love, I want companionship, I want to be needed. I want my own home, to be shared by some one with whom I am in sympathy. He seems to offer me everything, and, knowing my love of truthfulness, he has told me his past history. I am confused. What shall I do? He offers me everything I desire, more than I desire; but in his frankness he has told me his theories of sex relations. Perhaps I might not be strong enough to stand against all the temptations he places in my way. I might give way to my longing for companionship and forgive him his past, but how can I go back on my principles?

He is to come for my answer in six weeks' time.

CHAPTER XI

Lakeside
October 1, 1910

Home! Home! No one to meet me, no one to care whether
I live or die! True, I might have sent word for some one to
come to the station, but I do not want mere people, not
even friendly people. I want friends. I want to belong to
some one, to have some one who belongs to me. I agree
with Gorky, at least so far, that mere relationships do not
satisfy me; relationships of blood but not of spirit do not
content me. I want some one who understands me, who
believes in me.

I have six weeks in which to decide whether I shall
marry the scientist, Mr Hayes. He bombarded me with
arguments. He tried to show me that there was a relationship between men and women that they disregarded at
their cost. He assured me that once I gave up my life of repression I would be strong. I want to be strong; God
knows how I want to be strong! Life is so full of things
I want to do, and I have tried to do some of them, only to
start brilliantly, to work enthusiastically and suddenly
to find myself against a blank wall. At such times I could
not think, the pressure on my head was so great I could
scarcely understand what was said to me. This, he assured

me, would all disappear, and I would go from strength to strength. I would do brilliant things. I know if there were some one who had faith in me I could accomplish much more. If I had not always to fight my environment alone I might succeed. He is strong, and a fighter. We could work together for a better world. He has strength and brains and purpose. Was ever a woman offered so much?

I was pacing the floor when the door-bell rang. It was my neighbor, come to welcome me home and tell me the news of the summer.

Ruth Wood had died. It was a happy release, as she has been in an insane asylum for ten years.

Poor Ruth! When she was young, an enterprising young man wanted to marry her. He was not a member of the church, and Ruth felt she must obey the Biblical injunction, 'Be ye not unequally yoked with unbelievers.' She refused to marry him. He went to another city, became one of the wealthiest men in the country. She and her mother continued to live simply, to scrape along as meagerly as possible in order to save money for her when the mother should be called away and her income cease. They denied themselves all the things that would have enriched their lives. Ruth had never been fitted to earn her living. Indeed, in her youth, such a thing as a woman in her position being self-supporting was not thought of. When her mother died and Ruth was left absolutely alone, she had no interests, no object in life, and slowly she became a nervous invalid, and finally a maniac, spending the last ten years of her life in an asylum, where she ate nothing but eggs, whose shells she broke herself, for fear of poison.

If one could do heroic deeds and not pay such a price!

I came upstairs again, saddened. Poor Ruth! She made her sacrifice for her principles, and she has paid a tremendous price. What gain has there been? Was there some moral fibre added to the race consciousness by such a tremendous sacrifice?

October 20th, 1910

To-day I start to get my clothes ready for his coming. I have never cared about dress. I have rather discounted it, because I wanted to appeal to men on their intellectual side. I did not want to attract men by externals, but now that Prince Charming is to appear I am like all women; I want to be correctly apparelled.

I have had men friends all my life, strong platonic friends, friends who never mistook friendship for love. I have been simply my ideal – a human being. I have not known how to make men love me, how to attract them. As a girl, I was content not to go to dances because I was sure I would have been a wall-flower. Of course, I had the usual feminine longing for children of my own; but, somehow or other there never was a man on the horizon with whom I wanted to live. Many were the days when I have walked the streets in agony, because there was no way for me to have my own children without marriage. To marry any man I knew seemed an awful price to pay for a child. They were all good men; I did not question their morality, or their intelligence, or their ability, but they were men who believed in the sovereignty of the man, and, without ever having come into contact with the feminist movement, I was born an individualist. I wanted to work out my own salvation, in harmony and comradeship with some one if possible, but if not, alone. Freedom meant more to me than marriage. It had taken scant consideration for me to reject the various men who had come to me with proposals of marriage, but this one was different. He knew of my admiration for Norman, my friendship for Daniel; he was quite content that these men should always remain in my life, and he was equally glad that I should accept it that he loved deeply and sincerely a woman whose memory he must always cherish. For neither of us was there to be any denial of our feelings, or attempt to negate real feeling that did exist; all love was precious to him, as well as to me. All that had been beautiful about our loves should remain.

But, and the 'but' is so tremendous, he believes the sex relations are natural and inevitable. He maintains there is no security for a lasting relation between men and women unless there is a real spiritual relation, and only time can tell whether the love that draws a man and woman together is lasting.

I am almost ready; three weeks more and he will be here. I am as restless as I can be.

November 9th, 1910

When I was a child I was an invalid for four years at the adolescent age. I was too weak to walk and had to spend most of my time on my back, dreaming.

One day, as I lay quietly, all at once, as if some sudden, blinding light shone round about me, as if the very brightness and glory had stilled every noise, out of the silence came a voice, insistent, clear, strong, with its message for me. 'You must be true.' All the rapture of a lifetime was crowded into a minute, all the joy and pain of an eternity were compressed into a few seconds. It was as if I had received a great mission and had been shown at the same time what it would cost to fulfill it – all the suffering and misunderstanding, the perplexity; and I had seen it all and accepted it and said, 'I will be true.' With the vow the vision passed. When I saw Bastien Le Page's picture of Joan of Arc in the Metropolitan Museum, New York, I understood the glory she perceived and also all the pain it entailed. If the angels were in the dim horizon, she also apprehended the demons that would lurk in her way. It was the one moment worth a lifetime, the one moment that gave meaning, dignity, and value to life.

I can never recall the feeling of that moment, never glimpse the glory again, but the memory of it has always remained.

Two weeks ago, I rose restless and with the persistent haunting memory of that childish vision. I am forty-five, and yet that one moment was with me through the day.

'Will you be truthful if you marry Mr Hayes?' an inner voice kept asking.

Remember, the one thing to which you thought worth while consecrating your life was the emancipation of women. How can you accept his ideas about sex freedom, when you believe that sex relations must be limited to reproduction? When you fear that so long as woman accepts indiscriminate sex relations, so long as her physical relation to man is stronger than her intellectual or spiritual, so long will she be subject to him?

All day my head seethed. First I saw one side, then I saw the other. I was very human and I wanted his love. I could not give up all he offered to me. The next moment I was back, repeating the vow of my childish vision, 'I will be true.'

It was a day of torture, of uncertainty. I went to bed restless and perplexed. I was worn out with the conflict of the day and soon fell asleep. In the morning I woke, calm and decided. I would be true, and so I sent him word.

It has not been quite two weeks. There have been days when I felt I must recall the word I sent, but I have not.

'I am willing to pay the price, but grant me vision,' I pray. I go on from day to day blindly, unable to see my way, not knowing what is right, only following my feelings. 'Oh, God, if God there be, grant me vision.'

How I pray and hope against hope that I shall see more clearly! The way is dark.

December 30th, 1910

My landlord, a man of forty, suddenly took it into his head to marry. 'God bless him,' I said, 'even if it does mean that I have to move so he may have my house.'

I did not move far, only a block, but it was a larger house, and I thought I would take Mr and Mrs Fair, a high schoolteacher and his wife, to board.

'Shades of the family will haunt me when I keep a boarding house,' I feared, but I decided to risk it.

I had just finished settling the last week in September, when one morning there was a ring at the door and when I answered it a father and daughter were standing there.

'I am looking for a room for my daughter. She is going to business college. Do you rent rooms?' the father asked.

'Oh, no,' I replied, quite decidedly.

'Have you a spare room?' he asked.

'Yes,' I said hesitatingly, 'perhaps I have.'

'Please, may we come in and talk to you?' he said.

Most people would think I was out of my head to allow a strange man to question me that way, but I said, 'Why, yes, come in and I will see if I can help you to find a room for your daughter. I will telephone the business college and they will give me some names of people near here who have rooms to rent.'

I telephoned and brought him back a list.

'Would you not consider taking Annie into your house? She is a nice, quiet girl, and you look like the kind of woman with whom I would like her to be,' he insisted.

Subtle compliment.

'Well, you had better go and see where she could get meals, and I will consider a room and tell you when you return, if you do not find some other satisfactory place.'

I put on my thinking cap. If I rented the room that I had planned for the maid, I could pay a maid that much more wages. I ran down to my charwoman, who lived three doors away.

'Would you be willing to give me all your time, if I were to pay you the same wage as you are earning by the day now, and get your own meals at home?' I asked her eagerly.

We talked it over and she decided that she would try the experiment. She was to come at seven o'clock, to prepare breakfast. When it was on the table, she was to go home and get her own. Then she was to do my morning's work and go for her own lunch when ours was ready, not returning until time to get dinner. There was a schedule of hours worked out, whereby she gave me the weekly factory hours distributed over the seven days.

When Annie and her father returned, I showed them the room and Annie said, 'I would stay here in any kind of a room.'

'You will give her meals, will you not? She is such a nice girl, once you have her in the house you will like her,' he assured me.

'Well, I will give her meals for a few days until she gets accustomed to the city,' I agreed.

The father left quite sure that he had found a home for his daughter for the college session. I had a family of seven, two nephews, a niece, Annie, and Mr and Mrs Fair. I had solved my service question for the year. My maid did everything I required, even to darning stockings, as long as I did not ask her to overstep the prescribed number of hours. Renting the room a maid would occupy and having no meals to provide for her more than balanced the increased wages. She was very competent.

Three years before, she and her husband had sold matches on the streets of London because they could not get work. They had decided to come to America. They borrowed the money from one of the societies that furthers immigration, and during two years they had both worked and had paid back their passage money, had furnished their house and sent to England for her sister, who did their housework and took in washing. Before Christmas they had bought eight houses and made a first payment on the row. The rent would pay the interest on the mortgage and would gradually eliminate the principal. That was not a bad record for a penniless couple in three years in Canada.

One morning, when she was dusting my nephews' rooms, she came across some botanical specimens and I explained to her what the boys studied. Then she said. 'I want Will (her husband) to go to college. I am too busy to study now. I will some day, but in the meantime, he could get ready to go when we have our money made.'

That tickled me immensely, and I offered to teach him the elementary subjects, but he did not appear for the lessons.

Another day she said, 'If Will does not go to college, I will be sure that little Will (a dear little curly-head of four) goes.'

'What is he going to be?' I asked.

'He is going to be a gentleman.'

Blessed faith and ambition! I do not doubt that you will be wealthy before little Will's college days come.

CHAPTER XII

Toronto
November 15th, 1911

In August I accepted a position on the *Daily Herald*. I am writing on the various experiments for civic betterment and their practicability for Toronto. The managing editor and proprietor is a very broad-minded man, but he blue pencils every reference to woman suffrage that I smuggle into my articles. Some day I shall have my revenge on him. The world does move and we will have woman suffrage in Canada. I smile to-day in anticipation.

On the first day of September, when I came up to see about a home, I met two women, Nancy and Betty. We had never heard of each other, had no connections in any way, but we were rash enough to decide to keep house together. It was the most venturesome jump I ever took, after two or three chance meetings, to move my furniture two hundred miles and furnish a house on the mere hope that we three might prove congenial. It was a great success. We all three look back on that year as the most momentous of our lives, and a great deal of its significance is due to the constant play and interplay of ideas and criticisms among us. We were the center of a changing group. We were strong personalities with three strong hobbies, and each of us was a most enthusiastic supporter of her particular nostrum for the betterment of social conditions, and had only a polite interest in the others.

We were as divergent in our opinions and our outlook on life as well could be. We belonged to three different nationalities, religions and political creeds, but we agreed in being tolerant of each others' peccadilloes. We were not propagandists of our respective remedies for the woes of the world but when any one of us became a bore to the rest of the group she was promptly silenced. We were frank egotists, but we had a saving sense of humor and nothing was sacred from the slings and darts of the passing joke. We gathered around us a continuous succession of guests of all classes and conditions and had many an amusing experience. We invited a number of guests for lunch one day, and forgot to include in our count the one for whom the lunch was given. When the twelfth guest arrived, we sat down at the table and, lo and behold, a thirteenth came late and the members of the family had to sacrifice a knife, a fork, a glass, an entree, and so forth, to fill up the needs of the uncounted guest.

Nor were we embarrassed when one of our wealthy visitors, unaccustomed to dining without finger-bowls, made use of her goblet.

Oh, those parties! If only we had kept a diary of the ones when we had the proletarians and the aristocrats, who had never heard of such mixing with their 'inferiors'! The proletarians were often the most courteous.

I went to the hairdresser's one afternoon. Such an interesting young girl did my hair. She came from England, was the daughter of a well-to-do farmer, but was born with the desire to travel and see the world. She knew that there was no hope of doing so if she had to depend on what she could earn ordinarily. Accordingly, she planned to learn dressmaking and hairdressing, that she might go as a lady's maid with families who were in the habit of travelling. She told me her various experiences, and how, starting as a maid, she became the trusted friend and adviser of her employer. She had been in the employment of one widow, an artist, for three years, and had travelled all over Europe. Her mistress became her friend and together they had enjoyed the beauty of the many places which they had visited.

She had grown tired of being under even such pleasant authority, and had given up her last position and come to Canada, to see a new world which she had hoped to find more virile and more spontaneous in its various expressions. She had been disappointed, because it seemed conventional and more limited in its freedom and thought than the old world.

I went home brimming over with enthusiasm for my afternoon's meeting. When I told the family group, Nancy at once said, 'I, too, went to a hairdresser's this afternoon. I sat and wondered what your hairdresser was telling you, and I thanked the Lord that mine was holding her tongue.'

'But, you see, earth is crammed with interesting people, and I am forever turning them up, while you have to go to theatres and read novels to discover caricatures of them,' I replied egotistically.

April 10th, 1912

When we had lived five months in a poor part of the city on account of Betty's social work, we moved to a more respectable street three blocks away. We were now eight women in the larger house. We had been there three weeks, when one night, we were awakened about two o'clock by a persistent ringing of the bell.

'Let me come in,' we heard a voice say.

I rushed to the front window and poked my head out. 'Who are you? We know no man in the city who has the right to come in.'

'Oh, I am Mr —. I have been here before.'

'No, not since we lived here.'

'Oh! Have the people who lived here moved?'

'Yes.'

'Oh!' An expressive grunt, but even then we were not enlightened. In the morning, we were inclined to take our nocturnal visitor as a joke; we did not realize what his visit portended.

The next night, three other men woke us after twelve and thrice more I had to hold a dialogue from the front window.

Then we realized what had happened.

Night after night we had callers, and night after night we had to listen to their plea that they were respectable, that Mr S., who came here regularly, had told him that we would take him in.

The electric light shone right on the door-step. We could see these men were respectable, well dressed, nicely spoken, intelligent looking men. They gave us no trouble, once we had convinced them that the previous tenant had moved. But they influenced us. One might theorize as one would about the social evil, but all our theories were jolted by the calls of these would-be visiting gentlemen.

One day, we were giving a luncheon in honor of a prominent woman speaker who had been lecturing in the city. One of the guests was late in arriving. Suddenly the telephone bell rang. It was our guest, wanting to know where we lived. We gave her our address. She answered, 'The cabman refuses to take me to that number.'

May 13th, 1912

This morning I went down to the station to meet a friend. All the passengers left the street car at the upper entrance to the depot. A minute later, I heard a voice.

'Good morning.'

I looked around. There was no one but myself and the conductor in the car. I looked enquiringly at him, but he gave no sign.

'Good morning,' again came the voice.

I looked around, still more puzzled.

'I hear you, but where are you?' I said.

'Oh, right out here. It is the motorman. Don't you remember Bob Norris, the bad boy you had in your Sunday school class?'

'Oh, yes,' I said, 'I had lots of bad boys in my Sunday school class, but he was the worst.' I remembered the desire of the bad boy to outshine all competitors in the new devices he sprung upon the innocent teacher and over which she would steadily refuse to get angry.

'Well, I am Bob Norris. I sure was your bad boy, but then, I have remembered everything you told me.'

'How is your mother?' I asked. I had not yet placed the boy, but would not disturb his self-respect by letting him think I had forgotten him.

'Oh, she is still living. I went to Lakeside last month and brought her up here. My Jiminy! Wouldn't she like to see you smile?'

'Well, Bob, how are you getting on?'

'Oh, I have done well. I roved around and had a good time until I married and the kids came. Then I had to settle down and work hard. You bet they go to Sunday school, and they know about all you taught me and how you laughed when I pinned your dress to the rung of the chair with a clothes pin.'

'Oh, you boys were a handful,' I laughed.

'I go to church on Sundays because you taught me. My! I was a bad boy, but you would only laugh at all my mischief.'

Loyal Bob! Cherishing the Sunday school lessons twenty years!

And I go to church no more!

CHAPTER XIII

Toronto
December 15th, 1911

Soon after my arrival in the city, I was asked to write a series of articles on the life of the working girl. I began to investigate and was immediately horrified and troubled by the prevalence of the social evil. Often a factory girl's job or, if she did piece work, the kind and amount of work given to her, depended on her courting the favor of the foreman. There were numerous accounts of the advantage that foremen had taken of the girls under them. Then the constant nasty jokes, continuous insinuations of clandestine relations, the talk of the shops and the stories the girls told me, worried me very much. I could not accept the old attitude and simply denounce them. I suppose it is my open-mindedness, the willingness to hear a story and to judge it, not by any standard of morality or custom, but purely on its merits, that has always brought me so many recitals of human need. I have seldom forgotten Burns' advice:

> 'Then at the balances let's be mute,
>   We never can adjust it;
> What's done we partly can compute,
>   But know not what's resisted.'

Here were girls, young, full of life, attractive, with the natural instinct to mate. I could not see that the instinct that led to marriage under other economic circumstances was more impure now, when conditions prevented marriage. I could not condemn, I must know what could be done for these girls, and not only for those who, full of life and energy, were being betrayed by their natural impulses, but also for those who were still held in bond by the traditions of the past. I went to see the leading physician in the city, and told him my experiences, and my problem about these girls who were gaining economic freedom, but not losing the feeling that had led to marriage in the past and from which present economic conditions debarred them. He advised me to see Dr Barnes, who had spent many years abroad studying the Freudian psychology. The university had arranged for him to give a three years' course of lectures on psycho-analysis. He spent his winters in Toronto, his summers in London. This was my first intimation of the existence of Freud. I went to see Dr Barnes, and found him a most enthusiastic disciple and co-worker with the Viennese doctor.

It is always strange to me, how I come into touch with a new idea. Perhaps I discuss it as a theory, but never until it comes into my own experience does it seem to form part of my consciousness. Ten years ago I had thought a great deal about the desirability of women being able to have their own children without marriage. I had accepted it as a fact that the economic conditions which made the child dependent on the father were at the base of the present monogamic marriage, and that as women grew more capable of supporting themselves and their children they would naturally refuse to remain partners in a marriage without common sympathy and aims. I had thought about the wisdom of unmarried women being free to have their own children, but now I was face to face with the fact that they were having them.

When I talked to a doctor who was dealing with these unmarried mothers when left to their own resources, he said, 'The young girl who has been betrayed into a relation from which a child results gains immensely in character by caring for the child. Indeed, it is often the making of the girl. She is turned from a thoughtless, careless girl into a mature, unselfish woman when she faces the result of her own act.'

One old, respected doctor, who had a great deal to do with the city charities and who was too old and too conservative to uphold openly a radical idea, was very frank.

'A woman ought to have children; it is her natural work. If she is not mothering some one, she has natural instincts and aptitudes going to waste. Much as these girls suffer, I believe that they suffer less with a baby in their arms than they do without.'

'Society has no right to inflict such a heavy penalty on them, then,' I quietly retorted.

He was not ready to admit that.

When I went to see Dr Barnes, I was searching for light on the question, 'Ought we, as people interested in human welfare, to fight illicit relations by penalties or should we find some other way? Was it to be liberty or prohibition? If we took the barriers down, would all sorts of license creep in, endangering our social life? Were there new motives, new instincts, to be developed?'

My reply rather startled the doctor, after the misunderstanding and abuse he had met, when he asked me, 'Do you want to establish a single standard for men and women?'

'Yes,' I answered, 'but I want to know what that standard should be. I want a standard that is true to nature. I am tired of all the hypocrisy, the untruthfulness, the secret relations. If nature ordains sex relations for men and women, let us know what is natural and not found our conduct on some economic or religious decree.'

I gasped myself. Despite all my previous experiences, I was surprised that I had arrived there.

Dr Barnes discussed theories less than the contingencies I was facing, stressed less the Freudian doctrines of the evils of suppression than his equally important message, the necessity for the sublimation of desires. Perhaps he followed my mood. After the stories of the girls who had not suppressed but had followed their instincts, and who were now suffering pangs of conscience, I questioned whether these pangs were due simply to the reflection of the mental and moral atmosphere around them, or had some real basis in the nature of the relation and its offspring. If they could be free from the incubus of public opinion, would they be better mothers? Would they have no misgivings? I, who had so often fought for tendencies in advance of the crowd, did not know whether they were unconscious instruments of the next step in human progress – the right of every woman who desired it to have her own child. Knowledge of the facts of life and sublimation of desire in all sorts of creative work was the remedy he gave me for the present emergency. He opened a new field of thought in psychology, in education, in life.

Perhaps the most valuable thing he said to me was, 'I have long ceased to pronounce judgment. I know what things are. I do not close my eyes to facts any longer, but I do not profess to know how things ought to be.'

He supplied me with books to read and I had my usual experience of being able to accept only what interpreted my own experience. In the numerous conferences I had with him, the kernel of truth that I gleaned from the Freudian doctrine was very simple. Freud makes sex the main-spring of life and action. I have contended that sex was too narrow a term even in its broadest interpretations. Even should some of its original significance be restored to the world so that it covered all human relations, it would be well to call the incentive to desire 'creative activity.' That would cover work, action, relations.

I was quite content to accept Freud if I were allowed to take him in my own way. When the individual cannot pursue a straight line in his attempt to realize a desire for creative activity, he is led into suppression and denial of his desire. All sorts of physical and mental evils result. I was sure that Freud had caught a glimpse of a great idea, the evil of thwarting nature. He had overstressed the sex desire as the cause of the thwarting. The crudity of the herd, which exalts conventions and standards of conduct above life; which puts faith in men, but not in man; which believes that public opinion may be right, but private opinion wrong; which believes in masses, not individuals; which says, 'Thou shalt not,' without regard to circumstances and persons, seems to me the fundamental cause of the suppression of self-expression in individuals.

Freud was invaluable because he emphasized the necessity for the life of the individual. Love in its broadest significance is the cause of life. We have narrowed the words sex and love, and we have deprived them of their virility. We have exalted laws, conventions, reason, knowledge, science, and organization, all the forces that standardize life and make it mechanical. It is essential that we return to some living source of action, that we revive our faith in imagination, spontaneity, emotion, all the spiritual elements that nourish the little plant of life in the soul of each one of us.

Freud and Dr Barnes gave me a new comprehension of

freedom and truth. Even when disagreeing with them, I felt that my very disagreement gained strength from their interpretation of life.

Sublimation was their word of hope and counsel. Overcome evil with good – not condemnation, but understanding and direction, of the creative impulses. A student in Dr Barnes' class told me about one of his boy scouts, a healthy lad of eighteen, with strong sex impulses, whom he had advised to seek outlet for his energy in open-air creative work, or in enjoyment of nature. The boy returned to him some months later, saying, 'I thought you were kidding me, but it is true. Often I have found relief through doing some special work in my garden or in going out to watch a beautiful sunset.'

I felt that once society had ceased to say, 'Thou shalt not,' and had begun to busy itself with all the delightful possibilities of human nature and talent, the sex question would take care of itself. I began to speculate as to whether the monotony of the daily toil, the parasitical amusements, the absence of opportunity for individual work and play, had not their share in the social evil. The social reformer must find all sorts of opportunities for creative ability, the impulse to expression in work and play. I rejoiced in every evidence of the new efforts to express creative ability in recreation, in pageants, the new spirit in dancing and the drama.

My first step was to encourage one of my girls who is studying dancing in New York. I hope she will, through her studio, add to the possibilities of creative recreation. Dancing in any form makes for grace, poise, and self-control. The new dances give scope for spontaneity and originality. The few steps in each dance, which are very simple, are but the skein from which the dancer weaves his own fabric of figures and postures, adding here a graceful curve, there a flowing line, until the whole is a work of individual character. Dancing is essentially a democratic art, because it is open to all people who are denied extensive training in other arts, and affords them a means of expression for their sense of beauty, harmony, and rhythm.

I watch with joy all the developments of modern dancing, the aesthetic, the Greek, the folk dances, everything that opens up new avenues for individual expression of beauty. It is only a little step to take to encourage an amusement that opens possibilities for self-expression, but I hope other developments of the same spirit may follow.

I persuaded Dr Barnes to give a talk on the Freudian psychology to a group of women whom I previously pledged that whether they agreed or not they would not discuss the lecture with unsympathetic people. I was afraid they would increase the misunderstanding sure to follow any attempt to discuss the Freudian idea, if they should try to explain it to people who had no knowledge or comprehension of it. I want to know what people are thinking. I am never afraid to encounter new ideas, but I do not want to be held responsible for ideas until I have accepted them myself, though I am no coward in sponsoring unpopular ones, once I am convinced of their truth.

The whole sex question is largely woman's question. It is we who have suffered in the past, who are always bearing the penalty of any falls from established standards, and ultimately the decision rests with us whether the present system of clandestine relations and the inability of women to have children and acknowledge them outside of marriage, shall persist.

My friend, Mr Beveridge, came to me after the lecture and said, 'You are doing a daring thing to meddle in the sex question.'

'I am simply trying to understand it. I do not see that

there is anything in life which cannot be investigated, and opinions of it built on knowledge instead of prejudice,' I replied.

'The world is not ready for it yet,' he insisted.

'But the world will never be ready until there are pioneers,' I said.

'Well, it is getting ready fast, with all the books that are being written. They will do the work,' he argued.

'No, they will not do it until people face it out frankly, either through their own experience or experiences that they may learn from others,' I affirmed.

'You will find yourself ostracized, if you go any further,' he warned me.

'It is the same old story. There have always been lions in my path, and somehow or other, I have managed to elude them,' I said to reassure him.

'But you throw away your influence,' he pleaded.

'Well, there are others ready to do the work I have been doing, if this is the next piece of work for me to do.'

'But you run risks of being misunderstood,' he remonstrated.

'Very well. If I refuse to face the risks and turn from this problem because of its dangers, I shall lose my ability to discern truth.'

'Do you not think that you can gain your knowledge of truth through other channels?'

'No,' I said very strenuously. 'I have fought shy of all sex questions; I have refused to read problem novels or see problem plays; I have had no morbid curiosity about it; but the subject has been forced on me. I shall forfeit my freedom and my truthfulness if I refuse to face the facts now.'

'Sex and religion are the two subjects on which the public will not allow you to disturb its beliefs,' he reminded me.

'I accept the dangers, but one does not win freedom by avoiding difficulties.'

'There is much work to be done. We need your help badly and you will make yourself unwelcome on our committees if your name gets associated with the discussion of sex questions,' was his answer.

'The question of sex is to me much broader than mere relations between men and women. It is the one question that the world has never faced dispassionately, without prejudice, and with open mind. You cannot have people equivocal, even openly untruthful with themselves, you cannot have all the clandestine relations openly condemned, yet flourishing in every corner, without having a canker that eats at truthfulness and real relations among people,' I said.

'But people are thinking; you do not need to injure yourself.'

'I want to know things as they are. When I was a child I used to think that I would like to stand naked before people and say, "Here I am; you may like me or dislike me, but at least there is no untruthfulness in me." Now, I feel that I do not know how the sex question is going to be solved, but it must be solved in some manner that is open and above board. There must be an end to secret relations, and there must be something substituted as a controlling motive in place of present prohibitions.'

He laughed. 'You are incorrigible,' he said, and the conversation drifted to other matters.

If Freud is right, not until we recognize the unity of life and give sex its right place shall we outgrow it and eliminate its evils. We must first say it is clean before we can direct it. It is the old Pauline doctrine, 'All things are lawful, but all things are not expedient.' Not denial of desire, but the choosing of a higher good, will solve the sex problems. When we have rid ourselves of adherence to arbitrary commands, we shall discover living principles of growth within us. Constantly I repeat the same words with new content. I look back from some new conception of an old truth and wonder what significance it had formerly. Dr Barnes pulled me up a big step to where I was willing to know the facts of sex as they are, to face the evils of suppression with no reservations in my own mind. I want truth. I have thought that I always wanted to know it, but I am continually discovering new lands from which my cowardice has first excluded me and then blinded me to their existence. I am convinced that, once we are willing to be frank and truthful, we shall find our way out of this morass of falsehood, hypocrisy, and illicit relations, with their heart-breaking results. Henceforth I hope I shall be brave and not try to cover over my own or any other person's sex experience with some moral platitudes.

CHAPTER XIV

Toronto
April 30th, 1912

When I was a young girl I used to have periodic fits of wanting to be friends with my world, the whole of it. I used to go out in the morning feeling, 'I am alive and so are you; let us be friends.' It is fun to look back now and see the various receptions my friendliness met. The hide-bound society women, who arrogated to themselves special privileges because they had been born or forced themselves into a certain social set, used to eye me with amazement. The working people, who felt that I was their friend, smiled back. I responded with the same feeling that my friendliness evoked, for I had not outgrown my environment. I have long since burst that shell. One day I was going to entertain some distinguished guests at lunch and I was telling my friend about them.

'Why,' she said, 'people are just people to you, and why should they not be?'

It took years of groping amid all sorts of social traditions, the going ahead and trying things out – for I am not a thinker (I feel my way slowly, follow some instinct – not a very clear one to-day, then judge my action and grow a little more to-morrow) before I decided to become a democrat in my relations with people. It is amusing to recall my feeling of consternation the first time I sat at the breakfast table with the maid. She was a very nice girl, intelligent, and quiet in her manners. Around the house, I used to talk with her a great deal, and yet, when I had occasion to sit at the table and talk to her, the force of habit was so strong that I felt that I was doing something daring. I had a similar feeling the first time I took a meal with my washerwoman. I can laugh now at the barriers we erect between ourselves and other human beings, but the barriers were there, and they represented an authority and fear of endangering my social prestige that seems not understandable now.

One morning some years ago, I received a very mysterious letter in my mail, 'The Seamen's Union would be very much obliged if you would come to their meeting, Wednesday evening, at half past eight.' It was a bolt out of a clear sky. I had never been conscious that there was a Seamen's Union; indeed, I knew very little about trades unionism and thought that the working people were not so thrifty as they might be. Economy was the saving virtue for working people. I could not understand why they had asked me to attend a meeting. I asked my friends tentative questions about the sailors. Everyone condemned them as a very rough lot, drinking up their wages at the end of each voyage, quarrelling, and spending their time with rough women. I did not dare tell my brothers, for fear they would object to my going to the hall, and I debated very timidly whether I should take a chaperone or a man friend with me. Finally, I decided to be brave and go alone. I climbed two rickety flights of dark, dirty stairs to their hall, pausing many times to wonder if discretion would be the better part of valor.

'What could those men want of me?' I asked myself over and over. I did not think they would do me harm when they had sent for me, but despite my reasoning I was trembling when I knocked at their door.

A little hole in the door was uncovered and a voice asked, 'Who's there?'

My voice shook as I gave my name.

I heard the president say, 'show her in,' and two men opened the door. The room was thick with smoke, a pungent, cheap tobacco. Thirty men immediately stood to receive me. Their faces were rough, their clothes, for the most part, pretty battered, although a few were as neatly apparelled as any thrifty man after his day's work. I walked with beating heart across the room between my escorts, who presented me to the president. As soon as he had shaken hands with me, he introduced me to the Union and placed a chair for me. When I had seated myself, the men took their chairs. Underneath their rough exteriors, I knew they were gentlemen. My fears vanished, and I waited with interest to learn why they had summoned me.

The room was small and poorly lighted. The men had resumed their pipes. Despite the numerous cuspidors, the floors were badly stained with tobacco. They were a hard-looking lot of men, all nationalities, all ages, some bent and worn by their years as well as by hard usage, others young boys who had not lost their desire for adventure. Their courtesy surprised me and transfigured them in my eyes.

The president, a tall, powerful man with a face which exposure to the weather and the hard life of a sailor had lined until he looked more like forty than thirty, a strong voice and the inborn genius for leadership which had placed him so early in the chairman's position, seemed like an old-time Viking as he stood among them, only he was not there as commander, but as comrade of the men with whom he had won the rights they now possessed. He called on the secretary to read the minutes of the last meeting.

'Whereas, the Sailors' Home is appealing to the churches for donations to support it, and in so doing is telling stories of the misdeeds of the sailors which are not true, thus tending to give a bad impression, it is hereby moved that we ask a member of one of the churches to come to our next meeting and hear our side of the story, and then to ask the churches not to allow the sailors' missionary to speak among them or collect money from them.'

At once I was interested, although I could not understand why they had selected me.

The president asked one of the younger men, with a fine, open face, to explain the resolution. With an earnestness that made him eloquent, he told of the old days when sailors were indentured and treated almost like prisoners on shipboard. Their hard lives, with poor food and crowded accommodations in the forecastle, made them desire drink as soon as they went on shore, that they might forget the misery of the sea. Often, while sunk in drunkenness, the sailor was entrapped and signed up for another voyage. In those days, he was often a most forlorn, despicable creature, the victim of bad conditions, and the Sailors' Home, which pitied them, but never sought to change the conditions which created the poor wretches, may have sometimes been a refuge. But to-day, the sailors themselves, through their unions, were gradually remedying the bad conditions. They wanted no more charity; they wanted justice. They would take care of all the weak members of their craft. The missionaries, with their stories and appeals to the pity of the churches, lessened the respect of the people for their calling. They were men, and wanted to be treated like self-respecting individuals.

I had little understanding of trades unionism, but I was able to comprehend their desire for respect, and to be interested in their struggle to improve the conditions under which they must work.

Yet, despite my sympathy with the men, I had many misgivings in sponsoring the Seamen's Union. They gave me a glimpse of the perseverance with which they had worked for the amelioration of the conditions of their calling. Their human craving I could understand, but I was full of the prejudices against trades unions which were as common then as prejudices against the IWW [Industrial Workers of the World] today. All my past experiences would have led me to seek to reform the men and to put the blame for their excesses on weak human nature rather than on the conditions which had caused them. I had more faith in God's converting them than in the men's working out their own salvation by winning proper conditions for work and living.

It was a strange, unfamiliar world. I knew I should have to face a great deal of misunderstanding in mothering their cause, and I was afraid that I might be ostracized socially. I had been a Lady Bountiful, an agent of organized charity. I had taken part in all sorts of perfectly respectable reform work, but to speak for a union as if I believed in it, to attest my faith that these men were capable of becoming respected citizens if they were given the economic opportunity, required bravery.

I could not, however, go back on the men when they had appealed to me. I acceded to their request, and went to the various churches to try to interest them in the sailors' desires for respect. The general attitude of both ministers and people was that a little missionary work would do the sailors no harm. They could not grasp the sailors' viewpoint.

Having sponsored one union, I made friends with the

others, until the central council dubbed me their honorary president, more because of my interest in them as human beings than for my understanding of the Trades Union movement. On the mast of the Seamen's Union, I had been hoisted to a comprehension of the similarity of desires in all people.

CHAPTER XV

Toronto
April 30th, 1912

Last month I had my first participation in genuine trades
union activities. Nancy and I went down one morning to
get our new spring gowns. As we got off the street car, we
noticed a crowd in front of a large clothing store. There
were several policemen driving the people along. We could
hear the constantly reiterated, 'move on.' We were soon in
the midst of the surging mass, and a policeman attempted
to shove me. I asked indignantly, 'Why do you push me?'

He looked surprised at me a moment, and then said
quietly, 'Are you not a striker?'

Immediately incensed by the change of tone of the
policeman and aroused because of his roughness to the
young girls who were evidently making their fight for liberty, I said, 'Yes, I am.'

'Then why do you ask me questions?' he said, in a very
gruff tone. He seized my arm and whistled.

I remonstrated, 'You have no right to touch me.'

But the burly man tightened his hold, and said, in a
growl, 'We will see.'

Immediately the police patrol drove up, and several
other policemen appeared to rise out of the ground, each

holding one or two young girls in his grasp. We were bundled into the wagon and driven off. As I looked around at my companions, young girls, nearly all of them under twenty, I marvelled at the courage that made them face such an ordeal. They, in turn, viewed me in amazement, not expecting to see a woman with gray hair. The young girl next to me broke the silence, 'What floor do you work on?'

I answered quite glibly, determined that, having been thrust into the strike through no volition of my own, I, at least, would be game and not seek exemption from the struggle, 'I am in the millinery department.'

'But the millinery department did not go out on strike,' she objected quickly.

'No, but I was late to work this morning, and when I saw the policeman handling the young girls so roughly, I had to remonstrate with him. The policeman gave me no chance to protest. To what department do you belong?' I asked, questioning her in turn.

'Oh, I am a messenger girl in the garment factory.'

'Why is the factory striking?' I enquired.

'One of the men in the cloak department lost a piece of a garment he was making. He would have to pay for the whole garment, if he did not find it, so he tipped the sweeper, and the next morning the missing piece had been returned. The next day another man had the same experience. So it went on. Every day some man would have to tip the sweeper to get a missing piece. When one worker went to the foreman and complained, he was told, "You must be a grumbler; no one else is complaining." They organized a committee and sent it to the manager of the factory, but he refused to hear it, saying, "It is against the rules of the firm to listen to any committee from the workers." '

'But why are *you* striking?' I asked her, knowing that she could not be involved in the disputes of the adult workers.

'Oh, they got some new machinery last week and threw a lot of operators out without any warning, and my father was one of them to be discharged Friday night. Of course, when each man makes an application for work, he signs an agreement that he can be discharged without notice; but it is hard on them. They want work so badly they sign, hoping they will escape.'

I know the rule of the house. One of the head officials had told me some time ago that every man, from the highest paid manager to the youngest cash girl, signs that agreement.

'It is not fair,' the little girl added. 'Father did not get very good wages. The firm says that they pay less wages than trade union wages because the work is more regular, but I do not think it is the same. Father has to work more hours, and the firm gets more work out of him.'

'Do not the people object to the wages?' I asked.

'Oh, the firm puts it all over them with their welfare work and their charity stunts; but my brother will not work for it. He says he will get a fair wage and look after his own welfare.'

'Is your brother a trade unionist?' I asked.

'Oh, yes, and he hates the big firm, because he says that they dominate the wage scale all over Canada. Sometimes he gets very angry at it and calls it a heartless, lying autocracy.'

'Do you know what that means?' I asked her amusedly. She was evidently very proud of her big brother. Her eyes shone as she talked of him, so I drew her on.

'Oh, yes, Morris reads a lot. He had a book called a "Benevolent Despotism," and he said that was what the big store was. The intentions of the managers were all right, but they ought to trust their workers and let them have committees who would curb the abuses.'

'Where does Morris learn so much?' I enquired, interested in the little sisterly parrot.

'Morris goes to night school, and he gets books out of the libraries. He knows all about the big co-operative stores in England, and he says that some day the state will own our big store and all the system that the bosses work out to make money for themselves will be used to benefit the workers, but it is a long time to wait.'

The patrol stopped at the station, and we went into the court room. Nancy, who had been very much excited over my arrest, had taken a taxi and arrived before us. She whispered to me, 'You surely will tell the judge who you are, and he will discharge you at once with an apology,' but I only smiled and warned her to be quiet. No, I was not going to lose my opportunity to share the experiences of the workers, even if I were only playing at what, to them, was a very serious problem, on which their bread and butter depended.

My little messenger girl was called first.

'What is your name?' the judge asked.

'Rebecca Ralinsky.'

'Where were you born?'

'In Russia.'

'How long in this country?'

'Ten years.'

'How old are you?'

The child was growing frightened. 'Fourteen years,' she barely whispered.

'How long have you been at work? Speak up,' the judge added, rather crossly.

'Two years,' she said, a little louder, in a trembling voice.

'Why are you working?'

'We are a large family, there are six children younger than I, and father does not earn enough money to keep us all.'

'What were you doing when you were arrested?'

'I just changed off with father. He was picketing since six o'clock. He went home and I was watching the door so no scab would go in.'

The crowd gathered in the court room laughed. Such a little mite to be substituting for her father! Poor little child! The tears came to my eyes. The judge ordered silence in the court.

I fancied I detected a little pity in his face. 'Step down,' he said, and then beckoned to me.

'Are you a striker?' he asked, but before I could answer Nancy came forward. 'Your honor, she is not,' she said, and then stepped to his side and told him who I was and that he was a classmate of my brother's; also about our shopping expedition and my arrest because my attitude betokened sympathy with the strikers.

'The case is dismissed,' the judge declared, without hearing further evidence, 'you may all go.'

The young girls gathered around me and poured out their stories incoherently.

'Oh, miss, if you only knew! My foreman will not give me enough work some weeks to keep me going,' one shabby girl of eighteen said. Some one at my elbow whispered, 'And she has no home, either.'

'The foreman favors girls and keeps others waiting. It is well seen who gets the best jobs, but I'd starve first, before I'd go out with him,' another emphatically remarked.

'My father's foreman made him lend him twenty-five dollars, and do you think we will ever see it again? We need it to pay the doctor's bills,' chipped in another young girl.

'My uncle had to give his foreman twenty-five dollars to get a job,' another one added.

I knew that the members of the firm would be aghast at the extortions of the foremen. They were sincere in their desire to treat their workers squarely, according to their proprietors' ideas, but in refusing to have committees of the workers they let in all sorts of abuses which they were impotent to know and to curb.

'Will you come over to the Hall with us?' the girls asked me. 'We are going over to the Labor Temple, where the strikers are meeting.'

Very soon after my entering the hall, I was sought by one of the leaders and asked to go on the publicity committee. It was my business to interview the various papers, who were all afraid to publish any account of the strike, because the firm carried a large amount of advertising matter.

I tried to interest the various women's clubs, but I was amazed because they had no sympathy with the strikers, unless I had some tale of hardship to tell. The common, everyday longings for better conditions, for a life that would provide more than food, clothes and shelter, were not recognized as justifying a strike. I had to tell over and over the old, old story of the bosses who favored the girls whom they could take out evenings, girls who had to sell themselves as well as their labor to get sufficient work to earn a living.

I shared in endless discussions on how to reach the head of the firm and lay the facts before him, but the benevolent autocrat was so sure of his good intentions that he refused to hear anything that would cast a slur on them. He has shifted his responsibility to many managers, whom he held responsible, first and foremost, to make profits, and secondarily, to have as good conditions for the workers as were compatible with that end. The welfare work was a tremendous advertisement and bulwark against the workers' case being judged dispassionately on its merits by the public.

I worked with might and main to interest the employees who had not joined in the strike, to make them class conscious, to arouse some fears that if they accepted autocracy in industry they would be the victims of autocracy in government also. Some of the abuses for which they struck were remedied, but the firm refused to recognize the union. It pulled down the blinds of the big show windows on Sunday, so no one would be tempted to break the Sabbath by gazing on desirable goods. It carried on extensive welfare work for the employees, and gave handsomely to civic causes. The members were rated as good citizens, loyal supporters of the Methodist church and its various causes, were fêted by both church and national authorities. I am sure that the members could have echoed the rich young man's words, 'All these have we kept from our youth up; what lack we yet?' The modern answer would be, 'Go, share your authority with your employees,' and they would have 'gone away sorrowful,' for they had great possessions and power.

During the strike I had to preside at a meeting of the Woman's Political League. I asked Miss Bostwick, who had been sent from New York to conduct the strike, to speak to our association. She made a very wise and illuminating speech. I did not expect an audience who had never considered that justice to working people was a higher virtue than charity, to respond any more cordially than it did. As soon as the discussion started I closed the suffrage meeting, and asked all who were willing to try to awaken interest in the strike to remain. I thought I made it quite clear that with the adjournment of the suffrage meeting a new meeting came into existence, but I aroused a great deal of hard feeling amongst the zealous suffragists, who were afraid that their pet cause would be hurt through being linked with an unpopular one. As usual, I wrote to Norman, my fountain-head of wisdom, and also to another friend, a Professor of Economics, in New York. Their answers were diametrically opposed to each other. Norman said that the suffrage cause would gain strength by allying itself with a real social need; the professor said, on the contrary, that while the suffrage question was not sufficiently alive to be jeopardized by my action, as it became a more vital issue that it would not be wise to mix it up with any other question.

When I showed the letters to one of the members of the committee, I discovered that she had known Norman in Pennsylvania, and his opinion made her support me in the ensuing controversy.

She told me a lot about his early days as a university professor, when he was dismissed for his radical opinions and his support of the printers' union in its strike. His mother and three sisters were dependent on him, and for a short time they all suffered until he gained a commercial position in a distant city. Then his experience in causing his mother to suffer made him more judicious.

'He has such a clear head and such a good judgment that it was a tragedy for the radical movements to lose his leadership,' she said sorrowfully. 'It is the eternal tragedy of all weak causes that revolt is too high an end for us weak mortals.'

'Say, rather, that it is the eternal tragedy for us that the revolt against evil takes more virility than most of us have,' I replied.

'Sometimes we could pay the price for ourselves, but we are not strong enough to pay it in our families' sufferings,' she said, almost reminiscently, as if she too had failed in her high endeavor.

She gave me a new light on Norman's past, for, despite our deep friendship, I knew very little about his history.

CHAPTER XVI

Toronto
May 20th, 1912

Judge Lindsey, who is making a brave fight against special privilege, and has bravely denounced the public utility corporations as the source of municipal corruption, is seeking re-election to-morrow. Marion, who has been restless with the petty reforms, is in Denver campaigning for him. The revelations of graft, corruption, and exploitation of the poor, have made her very indignant, and her speeches have rung with fierce denunciations of the bribes of special privilege which have crept into every nook and cranny of Denver, destroying manhood and transforming high-standing citizens into the enemies of the state. Norman admires her astuteness, her grasp on political questions, and her idealism, and has bidden her 'God speed,' while he drudges away in New York, obtaining justice in the law courts for his clients.

New York
January 15th, 1913

During the strike in Toronto, I promised that when the big strike in the ladies' garment trades should be called I would come to New York to help. Word came that they expected three unions to strike this week. I hastened to obey the summons. I felt like an astronomer, going to watch for the appearance of a new comet. I was seeking to be present at the birth of a new epoch.

As I neared New York, I eagerly scanned the morning papers. Seventy-five thousand women had walked out that morning, Italians, Jews, Russians, Slovak Armenians, Arabians, Greeks, Poles, Germans, French, Americans, eleven nationalities, many different races, and in ages from eleven to the bent women of seventy. I was eager to be in their midst, a learner from them. A new era was dawning, when women, who, it had always been predicted, would never stand together, were coming out a regular army, to take their ranks with men in organized labor, to fight for wages that would make possible for them a better living.

The strikers had marched out like a regiment from their various factories, marching with precision born, not of discipline or drill, but of a great purpose. They sang the Marseillaise and shouted in unison, 'Our day is coming!'

I checked my baggage quickly and rushed down to the lower East Side picket line – the largest picket line that had ever been. The leaders were moving from factory to factory, giving words of encouragement; Pollakoff, with the shrewd, alert mind of a boy, quick to cheer the crowd with a joke or to see an advantage to be gained; Dyche, more mature and determined, but equally alert. They gave the strikers instructions to quietly walk back and forth in front of the factories, no violence, no loitering, to explain to any workers who tried to enter the reasons why they were on strike, and if they should win how all needle workers would benefit. Everywhere I could catch the voices of the officers urging, 'Be patient. Keep your self-control under provocation.' It was different from my expectations. I marvelled at their calm in the face of such powerful opponents.

I was eager to be a partner in the struggle and went to the headquarters for instructions, and will commence my work to-morrow.

January 16th, 1913

Marion, Norman and I went out for dinner last night. She came back from Colorado last spring, despite the over-whelming victory of Judge Lindsey, thoroughly disheart-ened. The revelation of corruption in Denver sapped her vitality, but increased her desire for the election of a pro-gressive who would give sincerity and honesty to politics, thus augmenting the chances for continuous development of justice in Denver. She had hope that the political game which is now played with so much chicanery and duplicity might once more become a real expression of opinion by the American people. When Roosevelt, whom she consi-ders the arch-enemy of democracy, was nominated, her hopes were frustrated, and she has never recovered her buoyancy and courage. She is not well, and has to rest a great deal. Over our coffee, the political question came up, and Marion said with discouragement, 'It will always be so; the men with social spirit will be outwitted by so-called liberals, like Pinchot, who give themselves over to playing the political game.'

'Pinchot was sincere,' Norman interrupted her.

'I do not doubt that he was sincere when he stooped to do what he thought was expedient in supporting Roose-velt, but he destroyed the work of the insurgents for the last three years, and he dragged the Progressive cause down into the muck of the political arena, where it is all a game of grab and influence,' Marion answered warmly.

'He will learn by his mistakes,' Norman replied calmly, trying to stem her indignation.

'The people are honest at heart, if they could only be dealt with honestly, but not until we have a party who will be square and above board in all their dealings as well as public utterances can we hope for right social conditions,' she continued, more hopefully.

'There was no reason to hope for a swift victory,' Norman reminded her. 'We are just at the beginning of our insurgency, and there will be many battles lost before the cause of the people is won.'

'We will never win if we rely on liberals,' Marion said bitterly. 'This campaign in Colorado has made me a radical. It is no use trying to reform present institutions; we shall just have to get rid of them and establish others which will have more hope of fairness in them for working people.'

'I am still a liberal,' Norman affirmed, more optimistically. 'The mass of people are stupid; they have accepted the authority of their masters for so long that they are slow about questioning "what the boss says." We cannot hope for a rapid victory; we shall just have to peg away slowly in a great many directions, trying to make them think, and to awaken them to the necessity of controlling their own political fortunes.'

'Do you not think that it might come more quickly, if you appealed to other motives beside self-interest?' I asked timidly.

'You still have a religious mind,' Norman jested. 'Despite your discontinuance of church going, you are a Christian.'

'But, Norman, you do not believe that the political measures you are keen to gain for them will accomplish a great deal,' I persisted.

'No, the ultimate hope for the people is a right spirit in them,' Norman answered me seriously, 'but we must work through existing channels to create that spirit. It is too slow for me to sit around and wait for some great awakening to come. I must do something.'

'I am not sure that we are not just making a fuss and blinding ourselves with the splutter in all our efforts at changing social conditions through political or economic changes,' Marion said thoughtfully.

'Supposing we put our faith in people, and not in measures, believed that there was in every man a desire for justice and the possibility of awakening his faith in the potency of goodwill to create a new world, might it not be a case of the longest road round was the shortest road home?' I asked, because I am positive that the millenium will never come until faith in man comes.

'Too slow for me,' Norman laughed.

'I do not know where to make the distinction between the power of institutions to shape the man and the ideals of man to create the institution. At present I believe if we could change the institutions of society we might change the man,' Marion said.

We all rose from dinner to work at the problem in our own way – Marion to attend a socialist committee; Norman, to hasten to court to plead the case of some pickets who had been arrested; and I, to return to the halls where the strikers assembled, for whom I felt my greatest service was my goodwill and sympathy.

March 25th, 1913

The strike is over, all the workers are back, I have had an exciting time. I have watched it all with keen interest. It has been the greatest event in my life to see people trying to free themselves, to watch the new birth that has come to many young folks. There were five different unions out on strike. The oldest and best organized was the Waist and Dressmakers' Union. The intelligence and general appearance of the workers increased with the length of time they had been organized, and the terms they had won for themselves. The last to organize was the Wrapper and Kimono workers. They were just emerging from sweat-shop conditions, under which they had had to own their own machines in the shops where they had worked, carrying them from one job to another; had been obliged to pay for their thread and needles, often even for drinking water; had had low wages and long hours; and were consequently underfed, devitalized, and seemingly robbed of ambition and the self-respect that was necessary for demanding their rights. It was essential to lead them to believe in themselves and to overthrow their faith in their bosses.

It was interesting to hear how the tone of the speakers changed, according to the union they were addressing. They unconsciously adapted themselves to the stage of development manifested by their audiences. While at the meeting of the most recently formed unions, they simply denounced the bosses, at the older ones, which had succeeded in winning better conditions for their members, the speakers suggested co-operation and plans for its consummation.

Raising the standard of wages had meant raising the standard of living and intelligence, the possibility of better conditions, not only for the workers, but for the manufacturers as well. If I had needed any proof of the necessity for fair wages and fair hours, that strike would have convinced me. The workers who were the victims of bad labor conditions were a menace, not only to themselves, but, through their lessened vitality and intelligence, to democracy as a whole.

It was interesting to see the eager way in which the young people read, amid the tumult of the halls where the strikers assembled. There were twenty-two halls and every striker had to report to his shop chairwoman at one or other of these at certain hours during the day. There were a great many speeches, plentifully interspersed with music, but in every lull in the proceedings you could see these young people eagerly reading books. Investigation showed that they were usually good English works by authors like Ruskin, Morris, or Carlyle.

At this time I met a Christian Scientist, who denounced the strike as unnecessary. In the course of my defence, he offered to treat anyone I might send to him for prosperity. I told that to a group of girls and tried to explain to them what Christian Science and the various New Thought societies stood for. I said, 'They believe that love is the great creative force in the world. If one aligns oneself with this force, accepts it through faith, and believes that it is working in and through one, it will accomplish for one whatever good is best.'

A girl interrupted me, 'I was sent to jail ten days ago for picketing, and they allowed me to go a day before my sentence expired. When I came back to the hall where the strikers were, they were so surprised and delighted that they all gathered around me. I knew more love in that hour than Christian Scientists will ever know.'

The girls with whom I picketed interested me immensely. They had some of the spirit of revolutionists; they had often come without breakfast; sometimes there was sickness in their homes; they had suffered privation and want and they said persistently, 'It is for the women who will sit in our seats after we are gone. We cannot make up what this strike costs us as individuals, but we will make it better for those who follow us.'

I went around the the various meetings during the strike and watched the people, saw how recently they had emerged, if indeed, they had really emerged, from the influence of those in authority over them. How little faith most of them had in themselves or their own class. How easily they would listen to some one in good clothes! They had not become class conscious, had not gained faith in their own power to create a society that would be a democracy. They had servile minds, ready to worship anyone who had money, power, authority, or social position. How could they ever be emancipated from subservience to their masters? How could their faith in their own leaders, whom they selected, be won and kept?

In England once, when I was visiting my cousin who rented the manor farm, I commented on some new cottages for laborers that were being built, and asked why they were building them when the old cottages were so picturesque. He replied, 'The state inspector had condemned the old cottages and the lord of the manor *sees fit* to build new ones.'

I smiled that the lord of the manor 'sees fit.' In those two words lay a whole volume of acceptance of the authority of the ruling class. I speculated, if submission to the lord of the manor was so strong with the tenant of the largest farm on the estate, what must it be with the farm laborer?

It is that spirit of acceptance of the word of the aristocracy that makes the workers recently arrived in this country so dubious of their own class and so easily influenced by the constant mud-flinging of the newspapers, which preach almost constantly that the labor troubles are due to agitators who are seeking their own profit, that the workers, left to themselves, would be content, and are being victimized for the sake of the leaders. They never give a hint that the lords of the factories also desire their own good. They poison the minds of the public, including the workers, against the leaders. Even I had not escaped the poisoning.

How I watched those leaders for one hint of graft, one suggestion that they were seeking their own good. I never saw a finer, more disinterested lot of men. They were very intelligent, progressive, far-seeing men. They had been laborers in the ranks, and through zeal, enthusiasm, and perseverance for the labor cause, had won their positions.

I was much interested in watching them in the offices of the International Ladies' Garment Works. They were like generals in a battle, thinking only of the victory, not one thought for themselves. They worked long hours and often went without food, sometimes for days scarcely stopping for a bite after they reached the office in the morning. Their organizing ability would have won them large salaries in capitalistic concerns. As I sat and heard their deliberations, I thought that I had scarcely heard fairer or more disinterested discussions of the possibility of gaining advantages for their people. They were like fathers, thinking only of their members' good. What amazed me most was the frequency with which they would throw aside some proposal of gaining an advantage over their sworn enemies, the bosses, by some one protesting, 'That would not be fair; we must give the manufacturers a square deal. We are fighting a righteous battle.'

Never was a saying truer than 'A prophet is not without honor save in his own country, and among his own people.' Yet these men held to their work of freeing their people despite the inherent distrust of the union members and the calumnies of the press.

There are few men with sufficient personality to be

leaders in a large union, or to have advanced to be an officer in an international union, who have not the ability to give them success in the business world. Thank God, the idealists are not all dead yet, and I believe that more of them are to be found in the ranks of the labor leaders than in the churches.

It was touching life, real, genuine life, that stirred me. The suffering and the misery of those brave girls who have to work so hard and under such bad conditions because the world which could remedy them is wrapped in its own comfort and does not heed, made me a strong upholder of trades unions. The comprehension of the necessity for economic freedom for the workers as the basis of opportunity for them to fulfill their destiny, is the next step on my stairway.

The protocol for the adjustment of strikes was the termination of all five strikes. It provided the machinery for settling of disputes through a Board, on which manufacturers and unions were represented, and a Joint Board of Sanitary Control, to maintain satisfactory conditions in the factories, to protect both the health of the employees and standards of labor for both workers and employees. The unions accepted the responsibility for the good conduct of the members. It certainly looked to more democratic control of industry, more co-operation between all interested. It seemed a forward step towards democracy. It meant protection for the girl in the factory who, by herself, must bear all the injustices and insults that the foreman chose to place upon her. It meant a voice by the workers in the conditions under which they must work, and it looked forward to the day when all industries should be controlled by those who worked in them. It was alike protection for to-day and a prophecy for to-morrow.

Among the labor leaders I met, was one who had started life as a poor boy, whose parents were degenerates, and who, somehow or other, had developed not only a great faith in his own classes, but a strong idealism. He had suffered, as a youth, all sorts of privations for the sake of the cause, and had endured them with no sense of sacrifice.

He married, and his earning power began to increase. Little by little, he became prominent in the ranks of the printers, and finally forged to the front and became a leader who could always be called upon in cases of emergency. He was a student, a thinker, doubly valuable in times of crisis, when men's feeling must be swayed to some high ideal, but utterly useless in planning measures or in dealing with the bosses on practical questions. He was the born propagandist, able to catch and hold his people through their emotions.

He might have been a wonderful leader – but for his wife. As he became more valuable to the labor movement and his salary increased, so did her needs for brass bedsteads, fine clothes, and other non-essentials. Like all impracticable men, he had no idea of the value of money and handed it over to her freely. She was simply a spendthrift, who let it slip through her fingers.

Any man who deals with the untutored masses through appealing to their feelings, has many ups and downs. He is to-day the darling of the mob, tomorrow its outcast. It was so with Valinsky. When reverses would come to him in the Printers' Union, there would come also discord at home. Like many a marriage consummated when the parties were young, there was no sympathy between husband and wife, and as they grew older, they grew farther apart. Valinsky never cared what he ate, where he lived, what he wore; but the wife demanded all the luxuries which he disdained.

When the union was at cross-purposes with him, he would have to turn to some good money-producing proposition, and then when they were ready to hail him back, he could go only if they paid him enough money to satisfy his wife. The tragedy of the case was, that while he had to support his wife and family there was no sympathy between them. There was one woman, who had risen from the ranks of the workers to be a leader. She had been won by his enthusiasm for the socialists and labor causes when she was a young girl, and she had never out-grown her love and admiration for him. She would gladly have given up every advantage she had and shared his times of ill favor. She was the one who gave him faith through all the years to make the struggle, and yet their relation had always to be incomplete.

I could never reconcile his enslavement to his wife. She had created for herself a lot of superficial demands, the kind of woman who is of no use to herself, to her family, or to society. There were two people who could have given each other much encouragement and help, yet who were kept apart by a marriage which had taken place when the leader was but twenty. It was seeing this tragedy, not only for them, but more for the cause of the people, which made me feel the need of better divorce laws, protection of children by the state, and a demand for truthful relations between husbands and wives.

New York
April 2nd, 1913

Once a week, I run up to see Marion, who has not recovered her strength. After we have tea, she lies down and Norman and I go for one of our long, silent walks. It is strange how little we have ever talked to each other, and yet I feel that I know him better than many of my loquacious friends.

The wonder of Marion grows on me more and more. She has such a clear head. I stumble along, my only consolation being that I continue 'stumbling on steadily – nothing dreading.' I am beginning to think that Marion did not believe in a legal marriage, and that the fact that she did not have the courage to follow her belief has been a worm gnawing at her soul. It is strange that life exacts from us full penalty if we do not follow the light that we have. We are denied satisfaction in the thing that we choose in its stead. The undivided life is the only satisfying one.

We are a crowd of faithless people, lacking courage to be true to the divine vision in us. We do things, expedient things, deeds that seem desirable, but lacking the courage, the vitality, the force, to do the thing that is true to us, to fulfill to the limit of our powers the intention that was born in us, we lose contentment in lesser things which we substitute.

I cannot understand Marion's feelings about institutions. They seem to me necessary. But what I cannot understand I still sense that she feels. Once when I was visiting her, she quoted the motto on the day's calendar, 'He conquers fate who goes half-way to meet it,' and added, rather sadly, 'If you allow circumstances to destroy your creative desire, you are beaten, not by fate, but by your own cowardice.'

How often I have to learn and re-learn that truthfulness to one's own inner purpose, despite the judgment of the multitude, is the only ascent.

CHAPTER XVII

Lakeside
April 15th, 1913

A friend of my mother's, a woman ten years older than I, who has lived all her life in my home town, has asked to go abroad with me. I have been away from Lakeside for three years, and in that time I have changed so rapidly that I dread to have her come. I cannot constantly recall her mental environment; I cannot always remember that ideas which are commonplace to me will have audacity and a tinge of wickedness for her. But, wisely or not, I have consented to take her. She is a warm-hearted, wholesome woman, a real mother. She mothers her community effectively; her big, warm heart takes in all sorts and conditions of people and gives them the sympathy and uplift they crave. Her emotional nature is so strong that it gives her a genius for mothering.

Steamer Esthomian
May 10th, 1913

We arrived at the steamer in a friend's automobile. We were sailing on a steamer that carried only second-class passengers; consequently, we were the people of distinction and were placed at the captain's right. The captain who has a genius for conversation, is a godsend at sea. We sailed from a Canadian port, and our captain one day said to me, 'I suppose that you are proud to have a member of the Royal Family as Governor General of Canada.'

'No,' I replied, 'I wish they would keep their effete royalty at home.'

He had found a theme that admitted of endless discussion. Every day he tried to draw from me my opinion of aristocracy and monarchial institutions. At lunch, one day, he said, 'Well, you must have a figure-head; why is not King George as good a figure-head as any?'

I had grown tired of the constant harking back to the subject and said laconically, 'we might have some one more efficient.'

My comment instantly offended an English gentleman who sat near me at the table. Immediately he sprang from his chair. 'You cannot expect me to sit at the table with anyone who has such sentiments!' he said excitedly.

I looked at him in surprise, and quietly said, 'If you do not like my ideas, I will keep them to myself,' and went on eating my lunch.

'This is a British ship, and you have no right to speak against a British king.'

After I had finished my meal, I rose from my chair, saying, 'Captain Ross' (the offended gentleman was an ex-captain in the navy), 'I want you to understand that neither on ship board nor anywhere else on British soil' (too sweeping a statement; I forgot Ireland, Egypt, and India) 'is there any curtailment of the right of free specch. While out of courtesy to you I shall refrain from expressing my opinions, I want you to understand that I do so only from courtesy and I still believe in free speech.'

'I have dined with the King.'

'That would not affect my judgment.'

'He is thoroughly proficient in the navy.'

'That may be, but I am not criticizing the King as an individual, but as my hereditary servant. I much prefer to choose the men who will serve me.'

I left the table. At dinner that night Captain Ross's seat was vacant. He had gone to another table rather than be contaminated by my presence.

I have always believed in non-resistance, but never had any chance to practise it. No one ever did me any injury, no evil ever came near me. When I say this to my friends, they always retort, 'Oh, but you would not recognize it, and so do not know whether evil has been done to you or not.'

Here, I thought, is my chance to return good for evil, so I wrote a little note to Captain Ross, telling him I was sorry if I had been obtrusive in my opinions, and that I respected everyone else's loyalty to his own established institutions, even when I did not share it, and expressing my regret if I had heedlessly disturbed him.

Immediately came back a note, 'I am sorry I sat at the table with you so long.'

I laughed at my attempt to return good for evil, to turn the other cheek. Of course, the whole ship was informed of our little controversy, and thinking that if I were radical in one particular I might be in everything, all sorts of stories were poured into my ear.

One young girl, of twenty-five, with a baby about eighteen months old, came to ask my advice. She had been a self-supporting woman even after she married. When she became pregnant, her husband objected to her having a child. She broke off all friendly relations with him, although they continued to live in the same house. Until the baby was five months old, the father would not go into the same room with the child. She was devoted to the baby and indignant with the father. After he began to notice the child, she could not forgive him for his previous neglect. Another man, a musician, came into her life at that time. He had gone to Canada as a travelling artist, and was going to sail from Vancouver for Australia. She had followed him to Canada with the baby. When she reached Quebec, she was intercepted by a cablegram. The father wanted the child, and she was being sent back with the little girl by the Canadian authorities.

'What shall I do?' she asked me. 'I do not want to go back to my husband; I am determined to follow the man I love.'

'Will you not be able to get a separation from your husband?'

'I hope so, I hope that I can make him consent. I am not worrying about him; but what shall I do about the man I love? I have made a failure of one marriage. I do not want to try it again, yet I want to be with him.'

'How radical is the man you love?' I asked her.

'Radical enough to marry me if I separate, but he wants to be married.'

'If he is conservative enough to want to marry, you are wiser to marry him. You cannot fight the world on every side,' I advised.

'I can support myself, I can support my child; why should I not keep my freedom?' she argued.

'Because, if your lover is conservative, you are fighting not only public opinion as it affects you, but, much more dangerous to your peace of mind, you are fighting it as it affects him.'

'But I want to do my bit for freedom for women,' she objected.

'Yes, but do not try to do too much at once. Be self-supporting and keep your own name, and do not wear a wedding ring, but have your marriage lines to flick in their faces when you are questioned. If you do not have a legal marriage, take his name, wear a wedding ring, but do not attempt to fight the world on too many things at once.'

It was her complication of circumstances that drew such advice from me. Where was I, who believed that truthfulness at all costs was the only path through the quagmire of sex falsehood, drifting, when I could give such advice? I hated myself for being an opportunist.

When we reached the dock, the husband was there, waiting, with her mother. He agreed that she could go home with her mother and he would come to see her.

She wrote me later that he would not give up the child. She must either go back and live with him or give up her little baby.

'The law upholds his claim on my little girl. I cannot give her up, and so back I go to a life of misery. My mother has no other idea but the subjection of the woman to her husband; she has aided and abetted him all she could, but I would not give in, if it were not for little Jessie. I cannot give her up.'

When I used to tell the various experiences on shipboard to my travelling companion, she would marvel, and say, 'Why, how do you discover such people? To me they are just average, ordinary people; to you, they reveal ambitions and longings that make them different.'

Seaton, Devonshire
May 11th, 1913

The first letter I received after landing was from Norman. Marion died four months ago, and he had not been able to find me. When they saw her strength failing and the doctors held out no hope of recovery, they took her south to the country, that she might die among the trees and birds. She had been forced to live in the noise and confusion of the city, but she fell asleep in the quiet and peace of the open fields, with the woods in sight of her window.

Norman is coming to England in August. Our long silence will be at an end. Despite all Marion's theories, she clung to the desire for a monogamous marriage. Now she will grow increasingly into his life and become more and more sacred to him, but I hope our deep, long, silent friendship will have its fulfillment. Why do we all limit love? Why, because she has passed from an earthly relation to a spiritual one, although I am sure a much more intensive one, do I feel that I shall have freedom to express my feelings for him that I have never had before?

The long, quiet years of simple faith in him, of the unity between us too deep for words, will now find voice. It has been worth waiting for.

Seaton, Devonshire
June 22nd, 1913

There is only one place in the world for me. If I could choose where I would live for my own pleasure, I would not hesitate a minute. There would be but one choice, and I am going there to-morrow. Devonshire has been lovely – her wonderful hedges, the charm of her sea, her beautiful walks. Nature has treated her with lavish hand, but it is not nature alone that I crave, it is people. I would rather live alone in a beautiful country place, no matter how isolated, than live alone in a city. If I must live with uncongenial people, I would choose to live in the country. I think I must be a pantheist, because I am not so lonely there. To-morrow I shall have both congenial people and beautiful, country-like surroundings. I shall be in the Garden City.

Garden City
June 24th, 1913

To-day, I have been seeing old friends. Pippa is as charming as every. She is the one person I know who has succeeded in her gowning. Her dresses are all cut after one model. They have a varied touch in the embroidery and color, but the model is always the same. She fulfills my ideal in dress. I came at once to Pippa, and she gave me the English welcome. The English are home-makers and you feel the atmosphere the minute you cross the threshold. It is good to be seeing all the Garden City people again. They are the salt of the earth, and they have not lost their savor since they overwhelmed me with kindness when I was ill here four years ago. I shall never forget, never cease to pass on that kindness.

Such a characteristic thing happened this morning! I was sitting at the cross-roads waiting for the bus to take me to the far side of the village. A very dainty lady shared my seat. I was in a state of wild enthusiasm on re-entering my earthly paradise, and I exclaimed on the beautiful rose hedges we could see on all sides.

'I wish that you could see my garden,' she suggested quietly.

'I should love to,' I rejoined enthusiastically. 'There is one garden I am eager to see,' I added impetuously.

'What one is that?' she asked timidly, for she evidently was too old when she arrived in Garden City to catch a spirit of freedom with strangers.

'The rose garden in the Adams place, where I lived five years ago.'

'As this is Garden City,' she said dubiously, 'perhaps it would be all right to ask you to come to tea this afternoon, as the ladies who own that place now are coming too. Perhaps – they might ask you to go to see their garden.'

'Oh, yes, it would be all right to ask me,' I assured her, 'everyone does.'

I always chaffed my Garden City friends that they may have more theory of freedom, but I have more practice. I think even Pippa was a little aghast when I told her how I had invited myself to have tea with my aristocratic friend of the cross-road bench.

To-night, we sat out in the little stretch of woods that has been left in its natural state as a border to Pippa's garden, and I enquired about all my friends and the various happenings since my last visit. I was anxious to know how each one had prospered. Soon I asked about Mabel.

A silence fell over Pippa.

At last she broke it, 'She and Arthur Horsey have been living together without a legal marriage. They simply announced their intention to do so.'

I was interested. Why had they chosen to do that? It did not seem to me worth while to brave all the criticism and disruption that had surely followed the announcement, and to bring a slur on the good name of the Garden City. I was so sure that as the news of their union had gone abroad the good name of the whole community had been assailed. I was not ready to grant the wisdom of doing anything so inexpedient in the early days of this civic experiment. However, Pippa was not nearly so much disturbed about the Horseys as I was. They had announced their intention; they only were concerned; and there had been so much discussion in the Garden City about substituting life for legal institutions that Pippa had made her own application. She passed it over quite lightly.

CHAPTER XVIII

Garden City
June 25th, 1913

The next day I went over to hear the Horseys' story from their own lips. I knew that Mabel would tell me everything that had happened since my last visit to her, two years ago. I found her living in a little workingman's cottage of four rooms, consisting of a kitchen (having a stationary bath with a cover that served as a table), a living room, from which the stairs led to two bedrooms above. It was simple and artistic; the pretty porch and garden made it attractive. I had liked the house three years previously, when I had lived next door. She told me their story.

'Arthur and I had known each other ever since we came to live in the Garden City, but never intimately. He had intended to practise medicine, but gave it up because so large a proportion of the sickness of the world is due to 'nerves,' another name for lives stunted in some way. He felt that he could not give drugs to patients who needed other interests, other faiths, than are common in civilization to-day. He was positive that half the ills of humanity came from wrong valuation of the essentials to happy, healthy living, the imprisonment of the soul by false authorities, and the slavery of life to unsatisfying demands. He felt that the people were selling everything, life, including leisure and freedom, expecting in return gold or popular approval, and finding only ashes. He wanted to carry a message to sick people of love and hope, of the value of work which satisfied their own cravings. He was convinced that freedom was the one thing needful, the freedom that is the utterance of the transcendent life in man from day to day; freedom that must come through following the promptings of truth and can never come from following authority; freedom that is the condition of the growth of the life force in the soul of man, stimulating it to produce flower and fruit. There were few ready to listen; the many were still unconscious of their chains.

'He worked in the Cloisters, a centre where men were studying and working at simple arts and crafts and agriculture, preparing to earn their living and preach the gospel of truth, beauty and love, to whoever would listen. He went out as a speaker, travelling from place to place, preaching simplicity and brotherhood, trying to give people a consciousness of the beauty and glory that lay around them; but he came back convinced that people wanted neither theories nor education, but a spirit that would awaken love in them.

'I had travelled the same road. I had started as a socialist and then had begun to feel that people must free themselves, as individuals, from the burdens that this civilization has laid upon them.

'When we had both reached that point, we were thrown together, and, after talking it over, we decided that we would meet regularly and talk and pray over it to see if we could discern more clearly our path.

'We understood each other, and from that common understanding and purpose grew the idea of a more permanent union. We had come to the place where we felt we could not put our faith in institutions, that so long as we trusted that this or that institution was to improve the condition of men, we would be disappointed.

'We were convinced that no social reform, no change in industrial relations, however desirable, would be of any lasting benefit. So long as men put their faith in any external thing, we shall have misery and unhappiness in the world.

'If there is any remedy for bad conditions, for all the misery of the poor and the indifference and unselfishness of the rich, it must come from a spiritual change in man. We prayed day after day, we agonized over the way we might find help for poor, blind, suffering humanity.

'Finally, the vision came to us, and we saw that new life is to come to the world, not through movements, not through reforms, but through individual relations expressing the inherent principles of love and truth as the source of growth. We must put all our faith, all our efforts, into living love, that we may release the life force which slumbers in every man awaiting the touch of faith and sympathy to awaken him to new relations, new visions of life and service.'

Mabel paused. She is so frail, so intense, it is as if the flame of the vision that has nerved her to face misunderstanding is burning up her body. She is like an old-time prophet, more spirit than flesh. I could only sit and marvel at her courage, and envy her her confidence in the ideal they had elected to follow.

Mabel resumed, 'By this time we were ready to unite, and we were faced at once with this problem. We were going to denounce institutions, going to preach and practise love in place of law, we could not commence by making an exception of our marriage.

'We thought over it a long time. We had to choose,

either we must decide to put our faith in love to bind us together, or we must give up our newly found belief. We decided that we would hold to our belief in the efficacy of love.

'Before we finally decided, we talked to a good many people. We were surprised to find that everyone to whom we talked had friends who had reached a similar conclusion. They could see the point as it referred to our marriage. Their friends had taken their stand privately, that they did not believe in legal bonds for such a personal relation as marriage, but we were going to come out and say that we did not believe in any legal bonds, that love could create durable and just relations between people. We announced our intention.

'Immediately the persecution began. Everyone thought we would injure the Garden City.

'No one was willing to risk any injury to this place. A great deal had crept in to lessen the first spirit of idealism, but still everyone who had made any effort to build this city did not want it marred. They were determined to protect it. Even the strongest advocates of love were afraid, because of their certainty that the public would not distinguish betwen promiscuity, which they associated with free love, and a marriage which trusted to love instead of to law to ensure its permanency.

'In spite of this we took the step. First, Arthur was turned out of the shop where he made sandals, and his equipment, which had been loaned to him by one of the shareholders of the city, was taken from him. Then the shop where I had my business was taken from me. For three nights, no one would take us in and we had to sleep out in the Common among the trees and birds.

'We got down to our last crust. The waters of misunderstanding, condemnation, want, all seemed walled up around us. Everyone was against us, apparently, and we had to say that we were willing to die, if need be, to attest our faith in love as the great regenerating principle for this universe. When we came to the last crust, the way was opened. It was as if our faith were to be tried to test it, and when we firmly determined to abide the consequences, the waters were parted and we came over dry shod, and we have never lacked for bread since.

'Arthur sold papers for a time. This cottage became vacant, and we secured it. Then the shareholders sent word that Arthur might have the tools for sandal-making once more. (Those tools are the descendants of the stock with which Edward Carpenter began to earn his living by making sandals, when he turned to this way of life, in order to "get off the backs of the people.")

'Customers came back to me for dresses, and here we are. If we are to share the life of the people, we must learn to live on the average income of a working man. It is important that we should share his needs, if we are to share his struggle for better life. We have had education, we have had all sorts of experiences to enrich our lives; we cannot divest ourselves of them and if we, with so much, cannot make a life full of joy for us, what can you expect of a workingman with much less?

'We do not believe that we shall ever have right conditions until we have equal conditions. As soon as we have equality of income and opportunity, and the abolition of special privilege, we shall have great diversity in people. Once people are set free to live their own lives, this world will be full of beauty and variety, because each one will be doing the thing that is within him or her.

'We believe if we put service first we shall have opportunity to provide for our simple needs – service first, then livelihood, so we never turn away the people who make

demands on us for love and sympathy. As far as possible,
we are doing away with payment for services and substituting exchange. I give my neighbor some of my vegetables; she gives me fruit; and it is wonderful how many
things come to us in exchange. We are giving something
that is alive, not a cold, dead metal. Ultimately, we can do
that with everything.

'Every week people come from all over the world to see
us. They are hungry for something vital in which to place
their faith. They want to be assured that our belief that
truth and love are present in every man and can be trusted
to inspire right action, has been justified. Our great hope is
that little groups will form around our idea; in each
member of the group the seed-thought will develop into a
plant; fresh seeds will spring from each plant. We trust not
to externals, we do not believe in the clap of any organization, any reform, but we have faith that the new spirit will
come from the contact of life, the silent, almost unnotice-
able touch of love.

'We are willing to strip ourselves of all outward advantages that their faith may be in the spirit within men. We
have no propaganda, we believe in life, ever more life.
Christ said that He came that we might have life; love is the
germ of life; so we want to spread love.'

How I envy her her faith, her clear vision of what was
desirable for them to do! How I wish I could be equally
sure for myself!

Garden City
July 9th, 1913

Neither Mabel's father nor Arthur's mother would have
anything to do with them. When her mother came to see

them, they brought her in to meet me, because she was eager to talk to me. She was full of questionings.

'When Mabel was a little girl, she came home one day wearing a very shabby dress, for which she had exchanged her good one with a poor little girl,' her mother said.

'When I remonstrated with her, she said, "Oh, mamma, doesn't the Bible say that if you have two coats and some one else has none, to give one coat away," and then she added reproachfully, "my Sunday dress is better than this one and I should not have kept the best for myself." '

'It was rather awkward that she should apply the spirit of the gospel so literally,' I remarked amusedly.

'Yes, she was always doing something different from other people and justifying herself by one of Christ's sayings. I have been catching up to her ideas all my life, but I never thought anything so terrible as this would happen,' she said tearfully. I tried to re-assure her.

'Their faith is strong that they have really found the secret of abiding satisfaction. All the words in your vocabulary would not exhaust the charm and glory of living when one is controlled by a new idea that has virility and force for the individual or nation. It is the spiritual renaissance that recurs once in a while.'

'But everyone condemns them; do you think that they can possibly be right?' she asked apprehensively.

'People are blinded by their adherence to precepts, maxims, and rules of conduct. They have worshipped too long the gods of expediency and material profit, are too confined within the limits of approved institutions to be able to discern what is true. One can only keep the divine fire burning on the altar of one's own life by being true to the spirit within you and refusing to practise what seems false,' I repeated the platitudes we all say so glibly, but rarely apply.

'But how can they know whether they are right or not?' she asked, still unconvinced that it was safe for them to follow their own inner light and ignore the voice of the accumulated experience of the world.

'It is only to the few humble, sincere and courageous souls that new ideals come, bidding them forsake all and follow. When the idea for which the pioneers are willing to sacrifice life itself becomes definitely outlined and adopted by the multitudes who proclaim, "This is the only path; walk we therein," the zest which gave vitality to the new thought is destroyed and once more the everlasting element in life must reveal itself in new guise. Mabel and Arthur are convinced that one cannot limit life by any principle less than life itself, without losing one's soul.'

'Mabel was always quoting, "What shall it profit a man if he gain the whole world and lose his own soul," but I hate to see them misunderstood,' her mother continued.

'You must make up your mind what values you will choose. Christ was despised and rejected of men for teaching that God is love,' I reminded her.

'Do you think that they can possibly succeed with all the world against them?' she questioned, with increasing distress.

'It will all depend on what you call success. Christ was crucified for His idea. You thought that was fine. There may need to be more crucifixions before people believe in the possibility of supplanting prudence with love,' I warned her.

July 15th, 1913

When she went home, she wrote back that she was much happier than she had been since they announced their marriage. Both Mabel and Arthur wished that I could talk to his mother.

Without saying a word to them, I went to see her. She lived in a suburb of London, in a house with all the old-fashioned furniture of a previous generation, the bric-a-brac, the embroidered tidies, which this generation has almost forgotten, the crocheted centrepieces, and the heavy carved furniture that takes so much time for dusting. Before I saw her, I knew she would be a Martha, cumbered by her household duties.

'Arthur might have been a doctor. We would have given him an electric brougham and a West End practice, and he has thrown it all away,' the mother complained.

'But Arthur does not believe in the practice of medicine,' I interjected.

'That is all foolishness; there are lots of good men who are doctors,' she replied.

'Yes, but I knew one man who felt about the practice of medicine as Arthur, who went against his conscience and continued to practice when he despised it, and finally he took to drink.'

'That doctor was foolish to do that. Arthur would not be so unwise if it were not for that girl,' she fretfully objected.

'But it is not the girl that has made you cross with him. She is a very nice girl, and I am sure that you would like her,' I said.

'It must be all her fault. Arthur was foolish; he would not go to his uncle's funeral, and his uncle was a good man; but my son was *not* so foolish as to live with a woman without marrying her, if she had not persuaded him to do so,' she said.

'Do you remember that Christ said that you cannot serve God and mannon? Well, Arthur and Mabel believe it is equally true that you must choose whether you will follow authority or love.'

'But they could do both. He could love her and still be married to her,' she said, unmoved by my arguments.

'They think that they must base their marriage either on their love or on the authority of the state, and that love and authority, being two opposed ideas, you cannot follow both, but must choose,' I explained.

'But I did not choose; I did not need to do so,' she said.

'Perhaps if you had understood Christ's meaning a little more clearly you would have chosen too,' I suggested.

'No, indeed, the church knows more than I do. I do not pretend to be wiser than the church.'

'But the church in Christ's day persecuted Him. They did not respect Him any more than people respect Arthur to-day. Christ was despised and rejected of men.'

I accomplished nothing. I did not expect to, however. She was bound with all the traditions of church and society of to-day, a church and society which believe in form, ceremony, and custom for every act of one's life, and which have no faith in life or in individuals. She could not be expected to rise above her environment.

July 24th, 1913

One Sunday I drove over with some friends to a very beautiful country place. It was encircled by a little stream and edged by woods that had been left almost in their primitive wildness. Then came the lawns and a circular drive, a round of grass and last some magnificent oaks grouped in the centre. It was a beautiful day, and after lunch my friend, Mrs Shailer, asked if we would mind if the children danced on the grass. They had been for a bath in the brook and their bodies were all glistering with the water drops, which gleamed in the sunshine like diamonds. They danced before us in beautiful Greek dances. The wonderful trees, the velvety lawns, tended for centuries, all made a wonderful background for the children. Their lithe, naked bodies, as they moved through the graceful mazes of the Greek dance, will be the one unforgettable experience of my trip this summer. The beauty, the freedom, the absence of self-consciousness in the children, and the calm acceptance of the whole beautiful scene by the group, linked me to that little party and opened my eyes to the possibility of a time when once more we should believe in nature, when all conventions that we impose to restrict freedom of thought and action will be seen as chains, cramping the human spirit. Those children, delightfully unconscious of anything in their lack of costume, were completely at one with their surroundings.

When I told my travelling companion about the events of the afternoon, she said, 'That is typical of this summer. I went to church with the Shailers this morning. We had a delightful service, and I enjoyed it; but you go this afternoon and have a fresh and novel experience.'

CHAPTER XIX

London
August 1st, 1913

A group of people who are not content to wait for a change in the structure of society, who, indeed, feel that the new organization, when it comes, may be as futile as past attempts to create an ideal state, have organized a colony to express their desire to improve present social conditions by the return of individuals to simpler, truer methods of living. They hope to stimulate and inspire each other so as to live the principles they wish to see realized in society.

They are frankly idealists who believe that 'There is an inmost centre in us all where truth abides in fullness.' Truth and beauty must be expressed through institutions, but they will be different and constantly growing when we seek them as an expression of a spirit and not as an end in themselves. To-day we exalt the institution, the external form, and we have only a death masque.

I am going down to spend a few days at Ariel Colony, to see how firmly they have grasped their ideal. I like their little pamphlets; I say, 'Amen,' when I read them.

The members of this particular group believe they have two duties to perform: First, to protest against and correct useless, cruel, and extravagant habits and fashions; and, secondly, to advocate and adopt simple, kindly ones.

It is a reaction from the materialism of the day, which insists in regarding science and organization as all-important, and emphasizes intellectual and scientific knowledge, but neglects the unexplainable qualities of imagination, feeling, and religion. This colony is modelled on the group's interpretation of Ruskin. It is a return to the land, with the joy in out-door life and the growth of living things; it is the cry for life, life in work and play; it is the attempt to separate ourselves from dead fashions and dead things which clutter life, the conventions, the rule of Mrs Grundy, and all parasitical amusements.

Besides agriculture, they are attempting to revive peasant arts and crafts in spinning, weaving, and pottery. Many of their clothes are home-spun and generally home-made and home-embroidered.

The wrongs of to-day are due to ignoble labor. The worker has an instinctive need for excitement after his monotonous work. We begin at the wrong end when we endeavor to create healthful recreation instead of healthful work – good institutions instead of good motives. Simplicity will come as the result of healthful, beautiful living.

The Ariel Colony
August 15th, 1913

When I arrived, I was almost immediately told that something dreadful had happened.

'Why, what is it?' I inquired anxiously.

'Mr Harrison, one of the earliest settlers in the colony, is living with a woman who is not his wife,' Muriel said to me with bated breath.

'Where is his wife?' I asked, interested in this mysterious calamity.

'She is living in London. I think that she acted rather well. When she discovered that the woman was pregnant by her husband, she went away and left the house to them. The children are at boarding school.'

'Are the man and woman in love?'

'Yes, they appear very much in love.'

'And they are living together openly?'

'Yes, they are living in the old home,' Muriel replied.

'Then the colony has justified itself,' I said, quite cheerfully.

My friend was shocked. She believed that commerce and government were to be changed through new ideals, but the family was sacred. Individuals might be improved, but the form of the family must be kept inviolate.

'If we are going to trust to the "Kingdom of God within us," to the realization of inherent principles, then why make exceptions?' I asked her impatiently. 'We shall never know truth until we are brave enough to be truthful.'

Everyone I met told me the story of the Harrisons, and I defended them valiantly, until I was forced to face the desirability of strengthening my words by deeds. It is easy to theorize, difficult to translate theories into action.

I fortified myself by the remembrance of a letter that my next older brother had written to me at boarding school, when he was facing the doubts and accusations of wickedness entailed in accepting higher criticism, 'No matter what it costs we must follow the truth.' I smiled sadly as I imagined his consternation at the application I was making of his letter thirty years later. Finally I sent the Harrisons a note, asking if I might call.

It was taking my courage in my hands for me to deliberately step into this complication, but I felt that if there were people brave enough to stand openly for a relation that was true for them, there must be others brave enough to support them.

Until their answer came, I quoted constantly,

'This world's no blot for us,
Nor blank; it means intensely and means good;
To know its meaning is my meat and drink.'

I felt as if I were venturing on a very dangerous precipice. I went over to call with great trepidation. I came away conscious that I had mounted on my stairway.

They had had such a hard time, the scowls and frowns of many of the colonists, who preached love, but were not prepared for it to have full expression, had eaten into their consciousness. They welcomed me warmly, and persuaded me to come and stay a week with them. The week grew to two weeks, and I learned to know them very well.

Mr Harrison was born a radical. He had grown up with a fierce dislike for all the conventions that obstruct free action. He had not found any woman ready to share his desire for freedom. When he was thirty, he had met a young Jewess who was working in a factory and had educated her, and married her. She had grown very quickly, responding to her environment and her opportunities, until she came to the limits of her possibilities in the small community. She pined for other worlds to conquer. She was also impatient with the absence of worldliness in her husband, yet she was not lacking in appreciation of his bigness of soul, and realized that she did not give him the comradeship he needed.

She used to invite Grace, a little girl artist, to come up for week-ends, and often she would go away leaving her there with the children and her husband. The consequence was, that the constant giving of sympathy, the understanding of a man whom Grace felt had one of the most beautiful natures that she knew, and the constant indignation at the wife's neglect, all fed her love for him, and the baby had come.

The wife, when she knew about the expected child, exclaimed, 'Now I am free,' and hoped at once to get a divorce; but the laws of Great Britain do not give a divorce for adultery by the man; it must be accompanied by abuse as well. He would not stoop to knock her down before witnesses and she was powerless to secure the divorce.

Mrs Harrison had never questioned that her husband and Grace would remain together. She arranged for them to go to London and stay until Grace was convalescent and the baby was strong enough to return home. Then she vacated the house and set forth to seek her own fortunes, which she hoped to find in the literary world.

'How did you feel when you knew you were pregnant?' I asked Grace.

'I did not worry,' she answered. 'I had perfect confidence in Douglas. I knew he would look after me until I was able to earn sufficient money to support the baby and myself. I had no regret for any love or sympathy I had given, and I did not feel that any harm would come to me or the child.'

'Were you not afraid to face the world alone?' I asked.

'No! I did not think of it. I had no misgivings. I knew Douglas must be responsible for his wife and children. They were his first duty. Whatever plans he made for me and our child must be secondary, but I knew I could trust him to do the very best he could for us. I felt that I had done nothing wrong and so I could calmly trust in God to look after me and my baby.'

During several years, Grace had been so much with the

children that now they cared for her almost as much as for their own mother. She certainly was much more solicitous for their welfare. They divided their week-ends and holidays equally between their father and mother.

It was a most amicable household. Whenever the husband went to London, Grace sent flowers and fruit to the legal wife. They might have been sisters, and Grace the unselfish, home-keeping one, always considering the welfare of the wanderer.

All the conventional relations had been overturned, and yet here were six people, the husband, wife number two, the separated wife, the two children, and the charming baby, all happier because a truthful relation had been established among them. The old formal relationship, lacking the spirit, had meant only ill feeling and unhappiness to all.

I have enjoyed every moment of my stay because I feel sure of their sincerity and the devotion to each other. It had been tried in the fire of opposition of their little world, they had gone on quietly, and now the people around them were commencing to recognize that they were worth knowing.

Strong as the opposition was in the colony, I suppose there is no similar place of its size where there would be so many people sympathetic with their struggle for free, and at the same time truthful, relations.

CHAPTER XX

London
August 29th, 1913

I wrote Norman to the steamer for fear my courage would
fail me when he arrived, asking him to come away into the
country, where we could think and talk things out.

He has small faith in laws, organizations, governments.
He is quite willing to say that the great tragedy of our days
is that the people are mere puppets, moved by invisible
wires, with no desires of their own, no wants except those
authorized by their group, no feeling, no imagination. He
would emulate Gorky in his denouncement of the evils of
the craving for possessions, and simplifies his life as much
as he can in order to free himself from striving for things.
He is ready to encourage anything that will foster imagination, feeling and spontaneity. I call him 'my old Greek,'
because he keeps the balance between what he deems desirable and considers practical. He believes in evolution
from the old, and I believe in new births, new concepts. I
hate that saying of Shakespeare's, 'Be not the first by whom
the new is tried.' If an idea be true, I care not whether it is
old or new. Norman seeks freedom from convention and
tradition, so far as it is compatible with his profession.

How I wish that I could persuade him to give up his law
practice! I am sure that there are many men ready to do the

work that he is planning, many to tinker at institutions, while there are few with the vision to see that institutions are of little moment, that the real necessity of life is faith in the creative power of truth and love, justice, freedom, beauty, the following of one's own destiny, even if it collides with tradition, custom, all accepted standards of conduct. Life offers one great opportunity simply to test it out and discover for ourselves what is true, true for us, that is our limit. There are many, many worlds, each individual must find himself in his own world and hope that in the multiplicity of fearless followers of ideals we shall find some unity that transcends our differences, something fundamental in all sincere lives.

Norman has been here two days, and I have not mentioned his law practice. If I could only induce him to come into the wilderness for forty days, perhaps we too might come down strong enough to withstand all temptations, the temptation to worldly success, to apparent accomplishment of a high purpose, the temptation to yield to the desire for immediate results, but above all, the temptation to try to make bread from the stones of any material aims.

August 30th, 1913

This morning, while Norman was busy, I went to help the suffrage women, who were picketing Albert Hall, where the International Medical Congress was being held. The banners bore all sorts of appeals in all languages. Mine was in German, urging the German men to protest against the brutality of the British men to the women suffragists. A doctor came up to me, 'You ought to be at home minding your children,' he said gruffly.

'I haven't any,' I replied.

'You ought to have,' he said sternly.

'I never had the opportunity,' I meekly answered.

'You look like an attractive woman, as if you might have married,' he said, a little more kindly.

'Alas, no man has seen me with your eye,' I returned, smiling.

'Go out to the colonies,' he advised.

'I came from Canada, and had no better luck there,' I laughed.

He laughed and I passed on. My friends say that I made the retort equivocal, but I maintain that I only made the retort diplomatic.

I have the most tremendous admiration for the sagacity and the unceasing resourcefulness of the militant suffragists in their efforts to gain publicity for their campaign. I have learnt something of human nature in my various visits to Britain. When I first came over after their campaign was launched, nearly every man to whom I spoke, except the few intellectual radicals, was opposed to woman suffrage, but year after year there was an increasing majority of men who were ready to denounce the militants, and yet wanted to enroll themselves under the suffrage banner. I was firmly convinced that if you want to carry any measure, you must have an advanced guard, who take all the stones of the mob, on whom the unthinking mass can expend their ire, some radical measure that they can denounce when the mass are willing to accept a more moderate measure.

I saw the same thing in the labor strike in the spring in New York. There was an IWW strike going on in New Jersey. We would never have won the good terms for our more conservative strikers, if the manufacturers had not been afraid that unless they gave moderate terms, more might be demanded of them. All hail to the radicals, who carry the advanced banners, who are mistreated and maligned even by those whose cause they aid. They are misunderstood and seldom gain any of the applause which comes with victory to the progressives who join the cause when it is safe and snatch a compromise measure, winning the plaudits of the throng and joining in the denunciation of the real winners. And yet, as my brothers often reminded me, it is quite possible that my sympathy is wasted, and that I shed my tears where they are not needed.

'More true joy Cato, exiled, feels, than Marcus, with a Senate at his heels.'

The joy is in the struggle, the breasting the stormy waves, and not in the half-way goal achieved in calm waters by the latest adherents to the cause.

August 31st, 1913

We have had five happy days together. We have been to the Hampstead Garden Suburb, for Norman is intensely interested in better housing and richer opportunities for community life, which the garden suburb is providing for middle-class people. It is similar in its aims to Garden City, only the houses have less ground. We spent a day at Kew gardens and at Hampton Palace, and have been to the theatres and House of Parliament. Norman has brought letters of introduction to all sorts of interesting people. We have had our long silent hours together, but we have not broached the subject that is nearest my heart. We are working it out without words, quite conscious of each other's thoughts, but dreading to express them, dreading the separation that may ensue.

He must be free to do the thing that is true for him; but oh, must I simply stand and see him go back to the expedient work, to be an opportunist! To-morrow I am going into the wilderness alone. I shall go back to Garden City to think it out. He does not believe in law, he believes that we must establish right relations between people. For him to practise law because it is expedient is a prostitution of intellect which is as wrong as prostitution of sex.

Garden City
September 9th, 1913

I have been ill, with a severe attack of neuritis, unable to stir a finger. Intense pain accompanied even the slightest movement. It is decreasing. Why do we not learn that spiritual pain cannot last forever?

A letter from Norman yesterday said, 'Stop worrying about me. Your sickness is nothing except worry. I am contented with my work. I want to accomplish something before I die. As a lawyer, I can do my share in simplifying the practice of law. It is a little thing, but I shall do thorough, honest work.'

What troubles me is that what separates us is so impalpable. I cannot reconcile his distrust of institutions, his feeling that laws and law courts are a means of injustice rather than justice, with his willingness to practise law. He hopes that honest lawyers can make the people see the futility of law. I put all my faith in new motives, new faiths overcoming evil. He would reform, and I create. My instinct tells me that if he feels the insufficiency of law, he must not practise, and I must not be a partner in what is not true for him. I would be an accusing conscience, always at his elbow. If we cannot see things alike, then we must go on alone. There must be no diversion of his strength from his chosen work, through my lack of sympathy or comprehension.

There is no light on the stairway to-day. I am stumbling on a landing, not knowing whether the next step leads up or down. As soon as I am able, I shall start for home. Norman goes to the Hague to make some investigations.

Steamer Lamentian
September 15th, 1913

On my way to the steamer, I stopped over a few hours to
see Edward Carpenter. He is still the quiet prophet of the
wayside. Men and women come to him from all over the
world, and he sends them away with the quiet benison of
faith in the life in all men. William Lloyd, of Westfield, New
Jersey, was there in June, and hurried south to catch the
song of the nightingale, ere she ceased to sing for this
season. Norman was there early this month, and Carpenter
thought he had grown to be more a man of the world. Has
he? Or has he just accepted the livery of the world, that he
may succeed with his work?

There were trades unionists from Manchester, who interrupted my brief call. A mature woman, who has taken a
cottage near him in order to bring her influence to bear on
him, came to the door. I was amused at the things she
thought good for his soul. I wrote to Norman, 'Pray the
gods that I shall never come to think that I can dictate to
any individual, especially to you, what is good for your
soul. I do not know what is good for my own. How can I
tell what is good for yours?'

Montreal
September 29th, 1913

Once more my homeward voyage is over. The vessel that
carries only second-class passengers always carried such a
living freight of hope and ambition, of courage and ven-
turesomeness. There is always a thrill in talking to people
who are going to an unknown land with all they own in
their pockets, to do or dare. No wonder that Britain, who

sends her children abroad to all her colonies, retains a wonderful spirit of adventure. Everyone I met in Britain has a brother or a son, a daughter or a sister, in some foreign land. It would be impossible for a country who sends her children so broad-cast to keep her insularity. Among the passengers who adopted me as aunt this voyage are two, a young lawyer who had been educated at Oxford, taught in the family of one of the Indian Princes, and had been engaged to a rich girl who was to secure his future by her wealth. But two years ago he had met a charming girl in Switzerland, had fallen in love with her, and his love for the penniless woman had proved stronger than all the glitter of the wealth of his fiancée. He had thrown up his hardly achieved position in Lincoln's Inn, and was going to Manitoba to create a new position for himself, hoping eventually to marry the woman he loved, who had promised to wait for him. He felt it would probably be three years at least before he could send for her. I advised him to send for her at once, and let her be economically independent until he was established and could support the home himself. He was overjoyed at the prospect of an earlier union, and cabled her as soon as he reached land.

There was a charming girl, one of many who were going out to be married. She had not seen her fiancé for two years, and was full of fear and foreboding. Would she love him? Had she done right to cling to her promise? She had never broken her word, and once she had promised him to come, when he was home on his last trip, she felt nothing could absolve her from her duty to keep it. I counselled her to wait until her fears were quieted. She could come to my youngest brother's home, and her fiancé could spend week-ends with her until she was sure that she really loved him. We planned it all, but the moment she saw him again all her fears were at rest, and she was married the day the ship arrived.

Oh, those human stories! How I wish I could follow those passengers who will never reach the goal which drew them all across the Atlantic!

CHAPTER XXI

New York
March 25th, 1914

When I came home from England, after some visits to my brothers, I settled in New York. I was keen to find a group of people who based their hope for a new society on their faith in the fundamental principles of love and truth, instead of on law and expediency. I am tired of doing expedient things, furthering desirable half-measures. I believe very firmly that if we would only 'tell the truth, we would shame the devil.' Eventually, every individual would respond to truth. At present they are blinded by prejudices and opportunism.

I was eager also to be self-supporting. I had tried will-power, physical culture, determination, but had never developed sufficient endurance to do the strenuous and continuous work necessary to earn my living. I was hopeful that if I had definite work, and was obliged by necessity to do it, I could rise above my lack of strength and accomplish it. If I dispossessed myself of my property, I would have to swim or sink, and I hoped I should reach my long-desired goal of being economically independent.

The problem of being dependent on my own exertions worried me continuously. Could a woman at forty-seven, with no previous specialized training, and a life that had not tended to develop endurance, find work which would supply her needs?

I felt that I had no right to the private ownership of property, but I could not see how to rid myself of it. I could not give it away to individuals. So far, every chance I had had to help other people get started had meant that as soon as they were on their feet, their wants increased, and I had simply added one more to capitalistic society with capitalistic wants and demands.

Neither could I find any institution on which to bestow it, because I had no faith in charity or philanthropy. We shall have to look forward to a radical change in society. If I were going to work at something that would change society's ideals, it must be something much more radical than any of the palliative movements.

I went to hear Emma Goldman. I had hoped she would so capture me that I would hand over all my capital to her, and that, once free from it and forced to work for my daily bread, I would have the strength to do so. I admired her very much; I felt she was a brave, far-seeing woman, that she was leading an assault against special privilege, and that the work she was doing might be very necessary. But, and how those 'buts' have always been like forceful, hateful dragons in my way, I would gladly have turned over every penny to her, but her work was not the work for me. I do not believe in denunciation, even in dealing with an enemy; I am quite willing to think hatred may be necessary in certain stages of development, but it is not necessary to me. I saw Emma Goldman's goal, and claimed it as mine. I admired and respected her. Although I believe in freedom, I revolted from her determination to win freedom of thought and action for the oppressed, through assailing the enemy with bitterness. Was it only apparent vindictiveness which repelled me? I believe thoroughly in freedom for the individual, but my friends always say that the religious view-point of my youth so clings to me that I cannot postulate freedom without relating it to my faith in spiritual forces. To them, I shall never be anything but a Christian who fails of intellectual freedom. I laugh at them and retort, 'I am not afraid of words, no matter how much those words have been discredited by bad usage in the past.'

It seemed such a slight, personal reason for standing aside from what appealed to me as the best piece of work that was being carried on in New York. I thought if I could only take the jump and throw myself into the work of the anarchistic group, strength would come. I was haunted all the time by the fear that it was not my ideals that were deterring me, but my pride, that I did not want to suffer the obloquy that would ensue from linking myself up with the Ferrer Centre and the anarchist group. I was not afraid of any punishment of the law; but I am always afraid to say that, because, although I have been ready on several occasions to go to prison for my principles, I have never arrived there.

All winter I was wretched. Some days I could not go out at all, and I was all alone in the little apartment on 79th Street. One night at the Ferrer school I met Rachel. I had taught her some English in Toronto; then she left the city, and I had lost track of her. I gave her my address and asked her to come for dinner Sunday.

She was a frail, delicate little girl, with ambition and plenty of determination. She told me her experiences from the time she had left Toronto. It was very disheartening, her efforts to get work, and the constant unfair conditions in the industries, the attempt to unionize the factory, and her dismissal by the boss. It has been one prolonged, repeated struggle to find work, to fight for fair conditions, then lose her job and starve. She was pretty well run down when I saw her.

She came to my room a good deal during the winter, and it was the same old story. In the spring, when she was without work and penniless, I took her into my apartment with me. I cannot go out and stir the workers up to self-consciousness, yet it seems to me this is the first step to be taken. Some one who feels the ills of the present system must do it. It would be useless for me to go talk to the girls about loving their enemy, because the very first step for them is to have so much self-respect that they will refuse to accept the unfair conditions, even if refusal means strikes.

I thought, 'I cannot myself be a rebel and lead revolt, but perhaps Rachel may, so I will stand behind her.'

In the autumn, 1913, her brother Joseph came from Russia. What a dreadful winter was 1913-1914! The unemployed went to the churches. I was so filled with admiration for the anarchists who led them. The poor, underfed, shelterless men had had their manhood snapped by their dreadful situation; and yet there were leaders who did put sufficient manhood into them, so that they rebelled and went to the churches demanding food and shelter. Joseph, Rachel's brother, suffered from the lack of work. He preferred to starve, rather than do dishonest work, or work badly done because hurried and slighted for pay. He was the honest artisan but he would have starved in New York, so Rachel sent him to Canada.

New York
April, 1914

'Good-morning, may I come and live with you?'

I had opened the door in response to a knock. A little girl stood there, and in reply to my 'Good-morning,' asked me the question.

It was so sudden I gasped, then found breath to say, 'Come in, and tell me why you want to live with me.'

She was a little German girl, clean and neat, to whom I had spoken in the court as I passed in and out from my apartment.

'Father has a job; mother can live with him, but I can't. He said he would pay you, if you would let me live with you.'

'But dear, I have never seen your father,' I demurred.

'He will come to see you.'

'Very well, tell him to come and see me and tell me all about it.'

A very kind-looking man, with a strong face, full of character, came to see me that evening and introduced himself as the little girl's father.

'Little Helen asked me if I would have her live with me. I do not understand why she wants to come,' I explained.

'I have a job as steward in a club, and my wife has one as cook. I cannot take Helen, as no children are allowed. She wanted to come and live with you, and we would pay for her.'

'I have never seen you before,' I said.

'No, I have been living very quietly. I have been ashamed for anyone to know that I was letting my wife support me, so I have rarely left my apartment in the day time.'

A few questions brought out the information that he spoke six languages, and had been an interpreter for a consulate abroad, but had not succeeded in getting work in this country.

They had made no friends, and I was the only one to whom they could apply to take the little girl.

'I cannot do it, but I can arrange for a home for her,' I assured him.

Thirty families use my stairway. They move in and out at the rate of one a fortnight. It seems dreadful to meet people on the staircase and never to exchange a 'Good-morning.' They look at me in surprise when I greet them, but I persevere in smiling, as I meet the various strangers. That smile is the key to many a story. It has unlocked vast storehouses of loneliness and misery. Many of them are new people in a strange country, fearing one another, and shut in with their own small interests. The lady who has the apartment next to mine has lived here for four years, and has become acquainted with only two of her neighbors. I have beguiled her into my apartment, and have taken her to meetings with me. On stormy nights, when the milkman comes, I bring him in and give him a cup of tea, or when some poor tramp comes along, I do likewise. I have never thought of being afraid, but she has kept watch over me. She has always set her door ajar as soon as mine opened to admit a stranger.

May 10th, 1914

A month ago, about four o'clock, there came a knock at my door and my next-door neighbor, to whom I had not spoken before, asked, 'Are you going to be in this evening?'

'No, I have to go out about seven.'

'I ought to go to my job, or I will lose it. The woman who was taking care of my baby left me to-day,' she said in a worried tone.

'Oh, if it is imperative for you to go, my engagement can wait,' I replied.

'If I do not go, I will lose my pay for this week, and I need it. I will put the baby to sleep. If you will just look in once in a while to see if he stays asleep,' she almost begged me.

So I was embarked on caring for my neighbor's baby. I knew nothing about her, but discovered that she was married, that her husband was doing very well, and that had she had any knowledge of housekeeping and sewing she could have served the baby and the home better by staying in it than by going out. The independence of woman is only a partial measure. It is not a panacea for all the ills of society. There are women who could do better work as intelligent home-makers, who have had no respect for home-making implanted in them. They waste their husbands' wages and the resources of the country through lack of thrift and bad management, and the babies suffer.

The next woman on the same floor is a German. Her husband is an artist who makes beautiful bas-reliefs for Tiffany. He rises at six every morning and goes to a cellar room where the father of a friend has a little shop for sharpening and repairing machines and knives. Early in the morning, and after his shop hours, he and his friend are working on copper reliefs, hoping to be able to sell their work and amass capital towards some day having a studio of their own. Alone in a strange country, with no connections outside of the Tiffany studios, it seems to me a hopeless castle in Spain. The wife is a thoroughly domesticated German, a competent housewife, and a good mother, eager to help the husband realize his ambition, and yet with so much of the old-world feeling of neighborliness remaining in her that she would like to do a good service for a neighbor without pay.

She undertook to take care of the neighbor's baby, but, after doing it freely for a week, she was discouraged, because she found her neighbor spending money on things that were too costly for her own purse. She was in the throes of disillusionment. She wanted to help her husband. There seemed no way to do so except by earning money. She wanted to be neighborly, but, when she did not charge for her neighborly services, she was imposed upon. I like her and her husband very much. Last week, when their boy was sick, I called the nurse who lives on the top flat, and she came and told the mother what to do.

When I get old and have no strength for anything else, I can just settle on a stairway like this and help to humanize the people. Here they are of all nationalities and divergent interests. They have no common meeting ground. Simply to be human to each other, to try to establish the old relations of friendly interest, might revive some of the feeling that finds no vent now. To have commercialized all our neighborliness, our friendly services, to have a cash basis for everything, cheapens life. Surely, the reaction must come.

In another apartment is a young couple. The girl is a waitress in a restaurant and comes home at eight o'clock; the man is on night duty, and is rarely at home when she is there. What a miserable existence to try to be together under such difficulties! They have both been to see me in their spare time.

Then there is a policeman's wife who spends all her money and leisure on her clothes. 'I cannot afford any children,' she says, 'I will not have them in a city where they have no chance to grow up respectably.'

I shall know all the various tenants on the stairway sooner or later.

The young woman who collects my weekly rent told me that there was a futurist artist on the top floor, that she had told him about me, and he would like to meet me. Of course, I said the desire was reciprocal. I would never miss such an opportunity as meeting a real, flesh-and-blood futurist artist.

But the meeting seemed to lag. Some weeks went by, and I had not caught a glimpse of this wonderful artist, who, according to the collector, had a room filled with rare and bizarre things, and did such strange pictures.

I was helping the woman suffragists with their street speaking and wanted a banner for a large meeting we were going to have down in Wall street. I had an idea, and thought if I could persuade my artist neighbor to draw it for me it would prove very startling, a good publicity stunt.

I sought his studio, announced my desire, and he acquiesced. He was like some rare, sensitive flower, who dreaded the cruel dust-laden breath of the street. I was as gentle with him as with a babe. I liked his modesty, his gentle shrinking from noise and confusion, his timidity and dread of being exploited or misunderstood.

The next day I received a note from him, saying, 'I am exceedingly sorry to say that I find I cannot illustrate "The Man on the Fence"; and I never did illustrate, so why should I begin now spoiling things?'

I forgave him his fealty to his principles, and he brought me his book of poems to read. It did not matter to him what medium he used, whether it was the pen or the brush, his object was to arouse feeling in people. He explained to me how all the bizarre effects of the futurists were just so many prods to awaken the dead feelings of the sleeping people. When they once more became conscious that they had feelings, art would be able to appeal to much more delicate and subtle emotions.

I sat and listened with open ears, and wondered what psychological effect the pictures I had seen at the exhibit would have. I have grown very meek; I never distrust the pioneer, not even under my breath would I call the futurists crazy, now that I know that their object is to awaken the feeling of the crowd.

I liked my artist and I liked his poems better than his pictures. I could understand them. I arranged to mother him next winter.

Everyone drifted into my apartment, even the man who wanted me to find him a wife, because all the girls he knew were so extravagant.

'One day,' he said, 'I went to call on a girl, and she sent me to buy some peaches and cake for supper, and did not give me any money. I never went back. I did not want to begin to pay her bills for her before I knew her.'

Poor man! There was no girl like the old-time girls.

As I realized the heart hunger of the many people who passed up and down that city staircase, I wished that there were some one to tell their stories and tell them in terms of the ever present need for friendly services and sympathy. The longer I lived there, the more I felt that the chronicler of a city staircase must have a consciousness of new needs that have not yet been voiced. There must be new ways of finding co-operation and helpfulness, for the strangers of varying nationalities and different creeds and standards. There must be some great cause that will transcend the differences. I dream of the day when we shall have human understanding, and when all our little individual tastes and habits will sink into insignificance below the large fact of our universal unity.

CHAPTER XXII

New York
May 12th, 1914

Another new experience to-day. Shall I always go on tasting life's possibility of joy or woe by proxy, being but a spectator? I went into Marie Kirchkoff's rooms and found her fiancé there. They had been having a lovers' quarrel, and he was in despair. Evidently, life has not been going smoothly with them for some time. I always feel that ultimately they will realize that they are demanding too much of love. Some times we will destroy the illusions that surround lovers. We will demand less and gain more from personal relations when each one grants the other freedom and independence, seeking less absorption in each other, but more enthusiasm for some object of common interest. Searching for bonds of union which are impersonal, the personal tie will grow stronger, although less demonstrative.

Marie's flame of passion had been so strong that it had burnt itself out, and Abraham's had not yet exhausted itself. I could never make them understand that they would have a greater chance of their love enduring, if they made fewer demands on each other. Romantic love has its few rare moments when the two tread the mountain tops, but it has its daily life in the valleys, and times when the two are only conscious of a lack in each other. Well, I came upon them when life was bitter, and Abraham had drawn his pistol and was threatening to shoot Marie. I held his arms, and when I had quieted him, I took him out for a walk. I made him promise to hand over the pistol to me, and he went into a saloon to unload it, while I walked up and down out of doors, waiting for him and saying to myself, 'Suppose he becomes desperate and shoots himself,' but I could not work up any uneasiness. I was quite calm and confident that in time he would appear, and life would go on as usual.

Is that constant excitement typical of a Russian Jew? His lack of restraint, his thoughts and actions swayed by his feelings – they call it temperament; I call it lack of self-control – is it due to racial causes or to circumstances? When I consider their clannishness, which overflows towards whoever is friendly with them, I ask, 'Shall we have that when we have democracy? Will our Anglo-Saxon restraint, our years of self-sufficiency, vanish with the coming of democracy?' Surely life is full of interesting questions. The Jews are egotistical. To the self-sufficient Saxon, they seem aggressive, but their great atoning qualities are their wonderful vitality, their keen sense of life, and their excessive feeling. They ought to be a good opposite to the more restrained Saxon.

America is the opportunity for people of different racial characteristics to learn to live together. Shall we give the emotional foreigners self-control, and they give us a new sense of life?

I did not start off with the intention of being friends with the Jews. In fact, I never considered it. Like Topsy, 'it jus' grow'd.' Once, when I was crossing the ocean, I made a friend and corresponded with him for some weeks before it dawned on me that he might be a Jew. When I wrote and asked him, he confirmed my suspicions. To me, people are simply possibilities for a new interest, and I have no particular defence for classes or creeds. I find people everywhere whose personality attracts me, and I forget to ask their pedigree. The coils of interest keep tightening till, like a fly in a spider's web, I am powerless to escape. But it has not been unpleasant. I would like to have as many different lives as possible, and this is just sharing the life of another nation by proxy.

I came to New York to help with the garment workers' strike, quite unconscious that the principals were Jews. I was only interested because it was an attempt to gain the protocol, the most progressive measure that had been devised in industry.

Later, Rachel was ill and came to stay with me, and Joseph could not get work, so I encouraged him to go to Toronto. This all just came in the path of the next thing to be done.

Every new Jew I meet brings some other of her compatriots to meet me, and each one has her story of human interest. Yesterday, there was a young girl who had come out here from Galicia alone at seventeen. She had learned a trade, and then had given her savings to help her uncle bring his wife and the children. She had lived with them, six of them in two rooms; but now that the uncle was succeeding they could afford to have the two rooms to themselves, and she was all adrift.

She had no regret that all her savings had gone to get the uncle's family started. When I sympathized with her, she said, so simply, 'Why, they needed it.'

Sarah is another child of nature. She has had a dreadful struggle. Strongly emotional, needing affection at all costs, it has been her lot to have to support three husbands, or to have tried the matrimonial adventure three times, and in every case she had paid the full price for it. Her first husband she divorced because she loved another man. She had supported him from the time of their marriage. The second one lived with her for a time, and allowed her to support him, although he had made a good living previously. He deserted her. Him she still loves, and there is so much comradeship between them that when she needs him he comes to her help. Although she knows the gist of the modern writers, Ibsen, Maeterlinck, Sudermann, and their fellow authors and quotes them extensively, she has gleaned all her knowledge from hearing them discussed, and can neither read nor write. When she wants a letter written to her parents in Russia, she applies to husband number two to write it for her. Number three is a dreamer, an idealist who refuses to work for the boss, but is too impractical to succeed in running a business for himself. This world is 'out of joint' for him, and he allows Sarah to set it right. She has had her three matrimonial adventures, all unhappy, all unsatisfying, and yet is very indignant if anyone dares to suggest that she has not had a legal marriage with one and all.

'I must have some one; I cannot live alone' is her constant moan. 'I must have some one who understands me.'

Her great grief is that she has never been able to have any children. She is afraid that she has destroyed all future chances and her own health as well, 'but I could not bring a child into this world to suffer as I have done' is her extenuating cry.

She looks like a handsome gypsy, is as careless about her dress and personal appearance as any child of the desert, and is as uncalculating as any child. She shares what she has with whoever comes her way. If it is only a crust, it is given with grace and heartiness, and a welcome that sweetens the poorest meal.

'I have known so much hard luck that one bad time more or less does not make any great difference to me. Why should I not soften anyone else's path if I can?' she asks.

She will not accept anything in return; to give and give and still give of what she has is her habit. She works in a factory all day, and then comes home and does her house work at night, because she must have a home and it must satisfy her. She has a nice, well-furnished flat – the furniture bought in second-hand stores – and rents out three of her rooms to pay for it. I love Sarah for her lack of sophistication, her naturalness, her generosity, her love of her own home, and her calm sacrificing of the standards of the mass to attain what is her real need.

'If I were like you, rich and comfortable, I suppose I would not care how people lived, but when we are all miserable together, and there is no chance for us to have the things that would make life worth while, it is no wonder that we fight and make the effort to get some of the goods that life ought to give us,' she said to me.

May 15th, 1914

After the woman suffrage meeting yesterday, a well-dressed woman came over and sat down beside me. She talked about suffrage for a time, and then she abruptly asked me, 'Do you believe in New Thought?'

'Oh, to a certain extent,' I replied, 'I believe that we attract our own good or ill to us, that we determine our circumstances by our own attitude of mind.'

'Do you think that you can change your circumstances?' she inquired anxiously.

'Yes, I have firm faith in being able to control my circumstances,' I assured her.

'Well, I am a Christian Scientist, and I am up against it. I have spent all my money, and I cannot go for any further treatments. Your face looks strong, and I thought perhaps you could help me without money.'

I was very much amused at being appealed to for Christian Science comfort. What next? I may turn out to have the germ of all beliefs in me, to be a Buddhist, a Pantheist, a Universalist. Perhaps all the germs are there. It is only the way the bottle is shaken that brings the particular theory to the surface.

'Well, if you will walk with me to the street car, we will talk it over,' I said.

The hard times of the winter have caused a good many people who have made comfortable livings heretofore to lose their jobs. She has been one of the unfortunate ones. I took her home with me and gave her supper, as she had not had any food for two days. Then I kept her all night. In the middle of the night I woke up and suddenly recalled that I had not asked her name or her address. She had told me that she was carrying a dose of poison, so that if the worst came to the worst she could end her misery.

With my usual tendency not to face trouble until I must, I turned over and went to sleep. The next morning, when I woke up, she was dressing.

She will have to make a fight. For a time she must accept work that is badly paid, according to her standard of living, and she must keep her courage up. I have tried to convince her that the miracle would come from within.

'I believe in the creative power of courage, and in good, persistent work,' I told her in the morning. 'We do not understand how, but there is possible between us and the universe a harmony which we can realize through faith and actions. I am limited only by my lack of vision and faith.'

'Why, that is Christian Science,' she said.

'Oh, I never label my particular brand of faith,' I laughingly replied, 'but health and prosperity seem too limited ends to devote much religious enthusiasm to their attainment. Life is too intense, too vital, for anything less than the pursuit of some spiritual ideal which may bring prosperity, but which also may bring loss of health and success.'

'But how can you be content to be considered a failure?' she asked me.

'Perhaps because I want life rather than illusions. To live seems the only pursuit worth while. Depths of life come from the intensity of desire and not from its fulfillment. One may lose all the outer forms and keep the spirit, which is deeper than any external achievement.'

May 19th, 1914

I seem doomed to combat the temptation to suicide. If all people who were considering it were only Jews, I would lightly dismiss it and say, 'Oh, it is temperamental; nothing will come of it; they have to find some expression for their pent-up emotion; it will pass.'

I am always inclined to speculate a great deal on the extreme emotionalism of the Jews. Is it because they have been denied natural expression for their emotion? Has life been so full of danger and misfortune for them? Is it the braving of so much alien feeling that has made them tenacious of their own people and constantly expressing their feeling to them? Whatever the cause, the emotional dramatic instinct in those I know is very strong. It is such a contrast to my practical, matter-of-fact temperament that it is like living in a new world to associate with them. Their clannishness interests me. I only know poor Jews, or those who are in process of becoming well off. So long as the Jews are poor, at least the ones I know, they have wonderful sympathy and co-operation with all who are struggling. They do not stop to reason, if some one is in need, they offer whatever they possess. I am fain to believe that the Jews belong to two classes, one, of the calculating, bargaining class, and the other, the idealistic, unworldly. There are the two extremes.

My caller this morning, Morris Goldstein, was the romantic idealist. The last time he came he had just refused to take a position because some one else needed it. When I remonstrated with him, he said,

'Why should I not go hungry? He has a wife and child. If I suffer, I suffer alone, but if he suffers, two people suffer with him.'

'But this is a practical world. One must look out for oneself,' I said.

'Why for oneself, why is myself better than his self?' he retorted.

This morning, he had his phial of poison in his pocket, the second person in two weeks who had told me he had the intention or the delusion of ending his sufferings. His misery was due to a disappointed love.

He had brought the young lady to see me before, and she had attracted me very much. She was a thoughtful, interesting girl, far superior to him – needless to say, I had not told him so – and they had had a very happy time going to the best operas at the Metropolitan, and hearing the famous singers. They had read books on philosophy and social theory that were far in advance of anything I knew. They seemed to be having a delightful courtship, and now this morning he came up to see me.

'I have come to say good-bye.'

'Why, where are you going?' I asked.

'Out into the Great Beyond,' he said mournfully.

'Why?'

'I am alone.' With tears in his eyes, he told me, 'Miss A. has decided she couldn't marry me.'

He was so tragic I felt like laughing at him, but his face was sad. I restrained my inclination and tried to comfort him. Finally I suggested that he should try going on a farm for a time to see if nature would not bring him peace and solace. If living in the open with the free sky and the big fields might not restore his hold on life. He eagerly acquiesced, and I undertook to write to some friends of mine to see if I could secure him a place on a farm.

The life of a Jew is a regular herring bone. They are going in a certain direction, and suddenly they branch off to one side, and you think they have left the path for good; but by and by they return and continue to pursue the original direction for a time, and then there is a branching off again. By the time you have accepted this as their permanent course, they have returned to the original direction. If I could only be sure of the permanent direction, I would wait patiently for all their little excursions into the by-paths on the right and left.

June 24th, 1914

My last Sunday in New York was the crown of my six months there, because I did something that seemed extremely worth while.

In Colorado, the striking miners and their families had been living in tent colonies, had been beaten and shot by gunmen, and had machine-guns turned upon them. Their tent colony at Ludlow had been burned and three women and fourteen children had been suffocated; but so powerful was John D. Rockefeller that scarcely an inkling of the outrages had found their way to the New York papers. On Sunday morning I saw in the paper that Upton Sinclair had organized a parade of silent mourners to walk up and down in front of John D.'s church, in order to gain publicity for the fiendish acts of his staff. I hastily donned my black gown and hat and hurried to the church. I found only a score of people there, who were marching silently up and down. They were mostly working people, but I felt like taking off my hat or curtsying to them for their disinterested efforts to arouse John D.'s conscience.

As I paraded up and down, the ushers would come and look at me. One would go back into the church and bring out another. 'She is a lady, a real lady. What a shame that she should be there!' Then another usher would come to view me, 'Why she *is* a lady!'

The next day I was pacing up and down in front of John D.'s office on Broadway with an ardent single taxer, when some women made the same remark, and my colleague looked at me as if I were a snake in the grass. 'It is the last thing that I would like to have said of me,' he said. Poor me! Here I was, falling between two stools, the women who despised me because I was a lady taking part in the silent protest, and a man who could not escape looking as if he were a gentleman despite his negligée shirt, who despised me because of their recognition of me as a lady.

CHAPTER XXIII

Toronto
December 10th, 1914

Before I left New York in the spring, I arranged for Rachel to go to the country for the summer, and I hoped I would be able to help her secure training for the coveted position as trades union organizer. But when I reached Toronto I broke down, and for some months had to be carried from the house to the carriage every time I went out, so, as I had to allow her to shift for herself, she went back to the factory. I secured a position for Joseph on a farm. Whenever he comes to the city, he always comes to see me. He is making progress with his English.

Toronto
March 10th, 1915

Life is full, full to the brim, with interest. I have tried to persuade the various doctors that there is nothing wrong with me but too much joy in living. Even to be shut into my little apartment does not shut me off from excitement and experience. Jerry and Nancy have married and have the adjoining apartment. We have a connecting balcony, and use the two apartments as if they were one. Jerry always declared that if you shut me up on a desert island I would have an experience and a friend before night-fall. I am not going to break my record simply because I am shut into an apartment. I keep my proper sister-in-law scandalized, because when I try to walk I faint on the street. I assured her that the butcher, the baker, the candlestick maker, all bring me home, according to whoever picks me up. It is most unseemly to joke over such matters! But I have yet to discover anything that has not its joke, if you have only eyes to see it.

My great diversion this winter has been trying to teach my neighbor, Mr Saintsbury, to laugh. I undertook to do so on a wager. When I would be telling some experience with much gusto, he would look at me so pitifully, and say, 'Why! It is funny to you!'

Then I would redouble my laughter, and he would grow more and more perplexed. I used to call him up every morning and ask him, 'Have you laughed this morning?'

He would say, so quietly and in such a matter-of-fact way, 'Not yet.'

I succeeded in getting the whole family laughing. Mrs Saintsbury, or whatever child came to the 'phone, would immediately start to laugh when she heard my voice. I gave up my attempt to make Mr Saintsbury see the fun in life, before I won my wager.

I have had plenty of people to dinner, although I could not sit up, save with plenty of cushions.

A missionary from Japan whom I had been influential in sending there in my early days of missionary zeal came to see me. I invited my two brothers and their wives for dinner with him. Quite an ecclesiastical party! He had left Japan the day before war was declared and had had various trying experiences crossing Siberia. But what had disgusted him most was a lady who smoked cigarettes on the ship.

'Of course, she was very common; you would not expect very much from a woman who would do that,' he said.

I did not enlighten him, but I thought of a dinner party at a respectable house in Toronto, where nearly all the ladies smoked after dinner. The hostess was afraid to let her maid know she ever indulged in such frivolities. Amid much laughter, she diligently cleared her plate of ashes.

I certainly have been all things to all men this winter. I helped select the library for a theological college, decided on the course of study that my prospective nephew should take in the new theological seminary he was planning to attend. I helped to steer a secretary of social reform away from the dangerous shoal of having a new law against adultery placed on the Canadian statute books. Hard as I tried, I could not reach him by all my arguments of the necessity of overcoming evil with good. The reformer has so much stronger fear of evil than faith in good. I at least shook his complacency a little, so that he came to realize the subject of marriage is in the crucible, receiving worldwide discussion, and will not be settled by any hasty and ill-considered law. I think his efforts for immediate action will not be so strenuous.

Somehow, some day, we must arouse all these would-be reformers to comprehend that their nice little reforms are simply external, and we must dig deeper to nourish the roots of life, rather than chop off decayed branches.

I had letters from my erstwhile up-to-date maid. She and her family had gone West, and she wrote me, 'We are well off; I am a lady now. I do not have to work any more.'

I chuckled to myself, 'I knew it, I knew it, and in the next letter you will be president of the Woman's Club in Fargo.'

My letter from Miss Bruce, my colored girl friend, was not so encouraging. The struggle to be self-supporting and to study singing too has undermined her health, and she has broken down nervously. Poor girl! She had ability, but was too heavily handicapped. I did so want her to become a great singer, both for her own sake and the sake of her people. I shall keep my faith in her recovery and ultimate triumph. The rest of my family seem to be prospering.

I met a friend of Norman's this winter, a brilliant, successful authoress. She told me about his early days, after he was forced out of the university.

He came to Chicago looking ill, as if he might be on the verge of tuberculosis, but with his spirit unbroken. She said, 'It was wonderful how, though physically weak, he gave a new tone to the endeavors at Hull House. It is delightful to see him now, looking strong and virile and well-groomed.'

'He has an iron will,' I remarked, with new consciousness of his thoroughness and steadfastness in adhering to the régime of baths and exercises that kept him fit for his daily work.

'Yes, it was pure will power that has brought him success. He would come into the music room at Hull House too exhausted to talk, and I would play on the piano for him, my pity finding expression in my fingers.'

'Had he lost his radicalism then?' I asked.

'No, he was going through torture, deciding whether he would cling to his radicalism at whatever cost, or do the practical, expedient thing, and try to hold to his idealism.'

'He decided on the latter, and he has used great restraint, never being a loud voice to make much noise, but always quietly putting over the next progressive measure,' I said, with fresh appreciation of his force and resolution.

Norman has many clever, brilliant, successful, capable, women friends, all working enthusiastically for the cause of the people. Some of them are simply progressives, just following his example and doing good constructive work

along health lines, better care of children, broader education, more intelligent feeding of the nation, all desirable
ends. He has others who are bearing the scars of the radical
fight, and are losing their positions, but still fighting. I am
the one quiet wayside flower who has a thorn to prick him
because I am not convinced that the work he is doing is as
high as the life he might live. I wonder, when there are so
many distinguished women to be comrades with him, that
he keeps his slight connection with me.

Fruitlands
May 15th, 1915

In March and April, I made several excursions to the country to look for a place. I would like to buy a little farm
where I could make it possible for other people, especially
women, who have spent their lives in teaching or some
form of social work, ex-labor leaders, or the rebels who
have often blindly fought for some better way, and whom
society has not rewarded for their fight, could make a living on a few acres. If I were strong, I would risk everything
and buy one of the fruit places I saw, but I am not sure
enough of myself to take the jump. I remember that
William James tells somewhere that if you have faith to
make the jump, the very fact will probably land you on the
other side of the gully; but if you lack faith, the lack will
prove quite as true, and you will probably land in the
morass. I do not know whether my fear is a wise warning
to me to be careful just now. I cannot believe that there
will not come a time when I shall have more initiative and
more will power than I have to-day.

I rented a little workingman's cottage next to my friend's
place. I paid her the rent two years in advance, and she put

it in the shape I want. I shall be settled for two years. Oh, the relief of it! I have moved so often since mother died that the prospect of being permanently settled for two years is a great rest in itself.

I have downstairs a large living room, a sun parlor and kitchen, and upstairs two bedrooms, but no bath-room. This is the price I pay for moving to the country, and for a city-bred person this seems like going backward in civilization, but I have no doubt that I shall manage to be just as clean. I am going to try living in the country alone. I have lived alone in the city with a telephone at my right hand and plenty of friends within call, but how I shall like it here all alone I cannot tell.

My next-door neighbor is a German woman, married to a Scotchman. She is very clever and very progressive. It is interesting that I should come to the country to find some one more congenial and more in sympathy with my ideas than many I have known in Toronto. She is very nervous, living in an alien country, and is glad to welcome me because of my anti-military spirit.

I am interested, as I fancy I detect in her the national characteristics. She is very hospitable – too much so. If you go to her door, she immediately insists that you come into her house, and is offended if you refuse. Once inside, if there is the least excuse for so doing, she must serve you with food. She is very determined to do what she thinks best for you, irrespective of your wishes. Nevertheless, I find her a delightful neighbor and consider myself fortunate to have some one so congenial within reach.

My International stair is enlarging. Canadians, Americans, English, Irish, Scotch, Negroes, Russians, Jews, and now some Germans, have paused at least for a moment on it.

CHAPTER XXIV

Fruitlands
September 1st, 1915

A man knocked at my door this morning.

'Good-morning. Are you going to have a fire at noon?'
he asked.

'No, not just at noon. Why?'

'The foreman of the cook-camp has sent us down tea for
the gang of men working on the road, and he hasn't sent us
any teapot or kettle.'

'Oh, if that is all, you may come in and make a fire and
boil your kettle, even if I am not here.'

'Oh, I could not do that! I could not come into a strange
house and take such a liberty.' It was the English foreman
of the gang of Italians who were working on the road past
my house.

'Why, no one has ever done me any harm in my life, and
you will not be the first,' I replied.

'But I could not go into your house if you were not
there,' he demurred.

'Well, I will make a fire, if you will send one of the
Italians to chop some wood. I will leave the kettle boiling
when I go the station. When you are ready, you can make
your tea.

He agreed to that. I had some beets and potatoes in the refrigerator, and I rapidly gathered lettuce and parsley and left a nice salad for them on the kitchen table.

When I came back, they had had their tea and salad. The foreman, whenever I appeared in sight, would say, 'Good-day, mother,' and all the Italians in the gang would drop their axes and bob their heads and say it after him. So long as they worked on that section of the road, down went their shovels every time they saw me, and they waited for my greeting.

September 18th, 1915

Ten days later, I was coming down the road when one of the gang caught up with me.

'Have you potatoes?'

'No,' I answered, 'but my neighbor has some.'

'You know Italy?'

'Yes, I know Italy. I love Florence and Venice,' I said enthusiastically.

'You know Naples?'

'No, I have never been to Naples.'

'You eat Italiano macaroni and cheese?'

'Oh, yes, I have eaten it in Italy,' I replied.

'I make you macaroni cheese, Italiano,' he assured me with a beaming face.

Saturday morning, before I was up, my neighbor came to tell me that the Italian had been there to see me and had been hanging around for more than an hour.

I dressed quickly and went out to the garden. He had brought the cheese and the macaroni to make me his national dish.

He quickly built a fire and cooked his dainty.

While he cooked he talked, 'You live here alone?'
'Yes.'
'You good woman. I like you. You drink whiskey?'
'No,' I assured him.
'You good woman. The women this country bad women. I drink whiskey, sometimes. They drink whiskey all the time,' putting his hand to his mouth.
'I am sorry you do not know any good women in this country,' I said.
'Why you not married? All bad women, you good.'
'I had to take care of my mother.'
'I respect my father, he died ten years. I respect him, now I free to marry. I marry you. I chop your wood. I make your garden. I do your work.'
'Oh, but I am too old to marry.'
'I thirty-five. I marry you. Take good care of you. This clean house, camp dirty. I not live in camp. It too dirty. I live with you.'
'Oh, no, you must find a younger wife.'
'You good woman. I take you to show. I pay your way to the city. I take you any show you like. I pay your fare. You go with me. You good woman. The women in the city bad women. They take my money. They want me buy furniture for them, then they go with other men. I want you.'
Poor man! He showed me all the pathos of a foreigner's existence in a strange country, the absence of home comforts, the ignorance of any except the fast women of the city. I sent him adrift with much pity for his loneliness and many wishes that I knew some way to mitigate the evils of the foreign men who come to our shores without their women folks.
That was Saturday. Monday, just as I was getting lunch, another Italian appeared, a youth of twenty-five.
'I come lunch with you.'

I had to tell him that I could not have him that day, as I was expecting guests.

'I come see you this evening.'

'Very well,' I assented.

In the evening he arrived, dressed in his good clothes, a flowing Roman silk scarf on his neck, and a soft felt hat, which he kept on his head all the time. He told me about his people in the old land, and, as far as I could understand from his broken English, he had a farm there, and as soon as he should make enough money, he would return to it.

'Too bad you live alone!'

'I like it,' I said.

'You good woman. I sorry you live alone,' he repeated.

'I am very happy alone,' I told him.

'I come live with you,' he said.

'Oh, but I cannot have anyone live with me. I have no suitable extra room. I must live alone.'

'I marry you. You keep shop, I work in factory. Soon we make lots of money, then we go to Italy.'

I had to assure him that I could not marry him, either, that a shop and Italy did not move me.

'You kiss me, then.'

Poor laddie! I would not kiss him, but I worried about him for many hours.

The next day, I was walking up the track to the railroad station, when one of the other members of the gang overtook me.

I had my neighbor's little boy with me. He picked him up to carry him.

'Oh, you need not carry him; the child is old enough to walk.'

'Me carry him. Me have li'l boy in Italy. Me not see li'l boy two years. Me carry this boy.'

And when we reached the station, I shook hands with him, and he smiled all over. 'Good-morning, mother.'

Poor exiles from home and family! How I pitied them! How I wished that I knew how to mother them!

The threads of humor and pathos are inextricably mingled as they are woven into the texture of my days. As I bade my lonely Italian good-bye, the vision of myself as the proprietor of a little Italian grocery store, with its crowded shelves and its constant throng of just such lonely exiles wanting garlic, macaroni and olive oil, flashed across me, followed by a picture of myself as hostess at dinner given to distinguished savants in an English summer home, or a winter home in Canada. The contrast between the temptations of the little store and beautiful Italy, and the ease and luxury and work which my scientist has spread before me, sent me home in a wild state of merriment. Unlike Maud Muller, the gladdest words of tongue or pen are the glad, glad words, 'It might have been,' – and is not! Yet, somehow, I feel that my Italians lifted me another step by their faith in my humanness. I laugh at the incongruities, I go to bed excited with the many and varied possibilities of life, and awake in the mornings with the same spirit of fun. I begin my day with laughter. I hope it is a real form of prayer. I am much more regular and spontaneous in its outbreak than in my morning devotions.

September 21st, 1915

Norman was here to-day. He had intended staying a week or ten days in the neighborhood, but was recalled to New York, so only had a few hours. My German neighbor came to the door, and I insisted that she should come in and meet him. When she heard that he was leaving, she said, 'Why, you should not let him go!'

'I cannot help myself,' I answered, surprised at her contention.

'Why, hide his coat and hat and bag, then he cannot go. You cannot really want him to stay,' she said very positively.

'Yes, I am very anxious that he should stay, but I would not dream of interfering with his plans.'

She could not understand what seemed to her cold hospitality, while I resented any suggestion that I should interfere with his liberty to go and come as he wished.

He had just returned from his trip to the old land. In England there are all sorts of groups who are trying to work out ideals of brotherhood (simple but beautiful) and freedom of conscience and action. There are groups who carry on home industries, schools where the children have an education that tends to develop individuality, not only in work and play, but in their judgments of life, and there are resorts where kindred souls go for rest and inspiration, all with the same idea of simple living, high thinking, and the shedding of as many of the superficial values of life as possible.

In such a rest home Norman had met a little girl who had taken his fancy. He has asked to call on her when he was in London.

He had gone out to her home, and had found there a young French girl and a baby. He had taken his little new friend to the threatre and had discovered that she was a stenographer, earning eight dollars a week; that the French girl had formerly worked in the same office, and had married an American, but without a legal ceremony. She had had faith in the man, and thought he shared the same ideals of freedom as herself. However, when he discovered that motherhood was coming to her, he deserted her, sending her some money for her expenses. She had indignantly sent it back, had gone on with her work as long as possible, and then, after the baby was born, had been found by her fellow-worker in a state of destitution, and had been taken to her little flat, where she had been cared for ever since.

Norman said, 'I told her it was a man's job, and finally persuaded her to let me take care of the little French woman and baby.'

'That was fine of you,' I said.

'Oh, it is only fair that some men should help. You see, it is not simply an individual case, but we shall have many women who will suffer because of their faith in an individual man. You will never have freedom for women until the burden of the child's support is shifted from one man or one woman's shoulders to the state.'

'The state will never undertake it until it is forced to do so,' I said.

'It is just such experiences as that French woman's that will hurry the time when the state will care for all children,' he replied.

'Good for you, putting in your oar,' I said, enthusiastically.

'The war is going to break down many of the traditions that have prevented women fulfilling their own natures,' Norman said quietly.

'The few lucky women who achieve happy marriages are not going to have a monopoly of virtue in the future,' I replied, recalling the many women I had known who had been more keen for motherhood than wifehood.

'Every woman who insists on having her own child and her own independence, even if she cannot find the right man for daily companionship, will win the applause of the public. Economic conditions will sanction what society has previously declared immoral,' Norman asserted.

'Is it not interesting that if permanent monogamic marriages become a matter of achievement they will have ethical value? Now, however, when they are a matter of custom, much as their morality is acclaimed they are often immoral,' I said slowly, as I realized what freedom would mean.

'Unions between two people of opposite sex will be like a great many other customs, when they cease to be enforced through law we shall more easily discover a spirit in them. We shall go on cherishing the same old ideals of human conduct, but with new motives and new inspiration,' Norman assured me, giving me, as he so often does, a rude jerk upward. I am very stupid, I seem to have to repeat the same lesson over and over again. How many times have I faced it out that it ought to be possible for an unmarried woman who desires children to have them, and yet how timid I am in stating my conviction.

Norman is sane and fearless. He is always ready to face the development of the future without panic, and with an abundant faith in humanity that it will create new institutions to meet its needs. He would place no limits on the self-realization of individuals. He is always helping lame dogs, who have been maimed in their adventures in search of freedom, over stiles, while he keeps to the safe path and holds on to his law practice. This, I am sure he must feel, is in contradiction to his faith in men's ability to find the right way, without law and authority.

CHAPTER XXV

Fruitlands
September 29th, 1915

All my life my strength has been limited. I have wanted to do so many things, but always when I was in the middle of my desired work, my strength failed me, so I decided that I would try to make it possible for some young people who were eager to do similar work to carry out their plans. I took two hundred and fifty dollars and called it my human investment money. I used to loan it to one person, and when it was returned I would lend it to another. In this way, I had been able to get quite a few young people started in various ways. But I was troubled, that while I made possible a better life for individuals, I had done nothing to change conditions. If we are to have a better world, it is not sufficient that the few people I happen to meet get their chance; the myriads who have no one to be interested in them, whose abilities rust for lack of opportunity, what about them? Nothing will bring opportunity to that great army but a social revolution.

Life always seems to move in a circle. The few people in this world who keep warm their love for their neighbor and who, for the sake of increasing their earnings, refuse to sacrifice the little acts of kindness that they can do for friends, keep alive the spirit of good will in the world. Perhaps those few sparks may some day grow into a fire that will set the world ablaze. That is the way I comfort myself for my inability to undertake large movements. I do my little bit where I have opportunity, and then fall back into the class of people who live on the interest from capital. My conscience hurts me, but I have never found the work for which I had continuous strength, and so I endeavor to equip substitutes in my place. But alas, they rise no higher than I! They are overtaken by the thirst for things, their needs accumulate and they become wage slaves, the slaves, not of a master, but of their own increasing desires.

The boys and girls I have helped to start had callings that were socially useful, but they did not recognize the social purpose of their work. It is the motive that counts in life, the universal purpose behind the work.

As soon as I moved out to the country I sent for Rachel. She was worn out with the winter of fighting unfair conditions in the factories, and she was discouraged. She spent the summer with me and in September I sent her back with sufficient money from my human investment, or loan fund, for a meagre living while she studied for four months. Will she be my substitute in the labor world, or will she find some other avenue of work? I am like a mother, I must do the best I can and leave her free.

I am cherishing visions that as soon as Joseph is ready to work a farm for me I shall buy a farm, and we shall create all sorts of opportunities to make a living for men and women who wish to escape the noise and confusion, both mental and physical, of the city.

If I could have a panacea for the ills of mankind, it would be creative work in beautiful surroundings, urban or otherwise, with simple people or people with simple tastes. Simplicity, beauty, creative work, these are the essentials for happiness. Interest in humanity and sufficient individual sympathy to blend the universal and the individual, the good of the one and the good of the many – this is the spirit that most transfuses essentials. At present, each one seeks her own good and misses her goal of happiness.

I have ceased to believe in romantic love, in love that seeks absorption in one person, either lover or friend. It is a delusion which dies hard. One needs companionship in work and play, one gains *esprit de corps* in many common interests; fellow feeling, identity of purpose are the characteristics of pursuits and not of a relationship. People, especially women, love to deceive themselves by acclaiming the virtue of maintaining permanent loyalty to one person, neglecting the necessity for numerous common interests and diverse ones. With few exceptions the relationships in which two people *fully* satisfy each other, without stultification of one or the other, are so rare as to be negligible. We adhere to a tradition and lose the spirit. Faith in an exclusive, personal love in the past shut people's eyes to the universally extended opportunities for the expression of good will. Love is the precious thing; persons simply the desired means for its manifestation. Enlarging one's circle does not mean lessening the attraction of the centre.

My life is a series of circles, in the centre is the individual to whom I unveil myself most fully, who knows me more nearly as I am and as I know him, understands all, forgives all. Around the centre are the numerous circles for the men and women who share in varying degrees my ideals, my feelings, and for whom I have corresponding intensity of feeling. I am interested in each and all. My interest in them varies in degree, not in kind. Love is creative, that is the test in so far as love gives birth to feelings, thoughts, deeds, in so far as it breeds interest in the fuller expression of life through more and more individuals, I value it. The test of its value, of its intensity, is its inspiration to creation.

Fruitlands
September 30th, 1915

The desire of helping women and worn-out social workers back to a happy, healthful living on the land is always present with me. One night I went for a walk and fainted on the roadside. Mr Bertram, an author who many years ago had felt the lure of the land and had forsaken the city to spend his summers at fruit farming and his winters in writing and travelling, picked me up and brought me home in his auto. I wrote him a note, thanking him. Joseph was here when he called. The author took a fancy to him and offered him the opportunity to work his farm on shares. On it were three workingmen's cottages, and I thought my opportunity had come at last. We could offer people good wages and a chance to learn farming by experience. I immediately wrote to everyone I had ever heard express a wish to return to the land. They all promptly declined to take advantage of the professed long-coveted opportunity.

When Joseph took possession of the place, he found a hen and wee chickens hatched out late. He brought them up to the house. One died on the way up. He petted the poor, wee, dead chicken and looking up at me reproachfully, said, 'You do not seem to care, mother; some women would.'

Joseph has been one of my joys. He is in many things a child of nature. I was having a luncheon party one day, and when Joseph came in, he said, 'Why do you go to all that trouble for those people? They have it every day.'

'There was a tramp here yesterday and I gave him a meal,' I said.

'But you did not give him your pretty dishes. They meant nothing to your guests to-day, but they might have given the tramp some pleasure which would do him good, perhaps change him,' he answered.

'Am I not to have any pleasure?' I asked.

'You have so much, mother. When you have a party, you ought to invite people who cannot ask you,' he answered.

Another day, when he had been doing some work for a neighbor, he came in to me very enthusiastically.

'Mrs Morris thought I did a good piece of work and I am so happy that I pleased her.'

'Why, I am pleased, dear, that you had a good day's work.'

'Oh, mother,' he said, 'if I could always work like that I should be so happy – three people pleased – I, doing the work, Mrs Morris for whom I worked, and you.'

He went into the city one day and did not come back until very late. When at last he returned he had this story for me:

'Oh, mother, I had an experience, and I wanted you! I went to the moving pictures, and there was a nice young girl next to me. She started to talk to me, and when they were over she asked me to go for a walk with her. I went, and she took me to her house. She told me that she had to earn money for a young man. I gave her all the money I had, but I did not stay with her. I want you to go in and bring her out here. See if we cannot save her.'

October 20th, 1915

I have the same feeling about the war that I had about the trades union strikes and the anarchist movement. Strikes may be the means of awakening the workers to self-consciousness and self-respect so that they will demand fair conditions that make a decent standard of living possible, the fiery declarations of the anarchists may arouse the sleeping individualism of the masses, too prone to follow authority slavishly and unreasoningly, war may startle the people into the consciousness of the evils of imperialism and give them a vision of the brotherhood of nations; but they are costly and only partially successful methods. We shall not need violence when we have more faith in ideas, in the universal spirit of kindliness and good will that slumbers at present narcotized by fear.

I believe that the mass of people must gain freedom in the economic and political worlds, that for the arbitrary control of the few we must substitute co-operation of the many – of all; for imperialism, internationalism; but none of these measures will continue to be lasting panaceas without the spirit that seeks to express itself through them. When, then, should we not recognize that it is the spirit that giveth life? I keep my faith that we might conquer Germany through a new conception of brotherhood. In seeking to overcome her militarism through the force of ideas, we might lose our national life and save our souls, and eventually the ideas for which we stood without fear and in strong faith would conquer the world.

I am positive that the evils we go out to fight with violence we shall graft upon our own national life. Starting with hatred of our enemy's cruelty, we shall end by being cruel ourselves; detesting the subservience of the German people to their state, we shall become indifferent to the subservience of our people to our state. We shall lose our free institutions, free speech, free press, free assemblage, and have to struggle to regain them. I am afraid that Germany will impress us so strongly with her faith in organization and force that whoever wins the victory, her ideas will overcome the ideal of the allies. I have no misgivings but that the ideals of the allies are in advance of those of Germany; but I do not believe that you can ever disseminate ideas by force. We can only establish democracy by positive means, and not by destructive ones.

When the soldiers on their march pass my house and pause to lunch here, I go up and down the lines, saying, 'Thou shalt not kill; love thy neighbor or overcome evil with good. If necessary, die for your principles, but do not kill.' I feel that it is useless; but I have to do even the foolish thing in protest against the short-sighted, wasteful methods of trying to conquer Germany. Some of the boys come to my cottage door asking me what to do. I tell them that the fight ought not to be against German imperialism, but against selfishness everywhere, and then they say, 'We are powerless; we must fight; but why do you not arouse public opinion so that it will believe in other and more efficient methods of ending war.' Poor boys! They are the victims of our wrong thinking.

December 10th, 1915

Last week I went into Toronto to hear Hester McLean, who came to tell us about the Peace Conference the women had held at the Hague early in April. After the meeting, The Women's Patriotic League passed a resolution denouncing the women who had been sponsors for it. I immediately wrote a letter to all the papers, claiming the right of free speech and free discussion, and ending my letter with these words, 'There are people who believe that the surest way to conquer your enemy is to love him.'

The newspapers published my letter, but denounced me. One of them spent several columns condemning me, stating that Jane Addams and Hester McLean were unconscious emissaries of the Kaiser, and that I had fallen under their influence. I went into the editor's office and, bowing most elaborately, said, 'I am an emissary from the Kaiser. Of course, you will deign to hear me.' He laughed, and the laugh brought me the opportunity to reply through his pages. I used all the usual non-resistance arguments, attested my faith in overcoming evil by good, and urged that the allies should at once state the terms on which they would make peace and should endeavor in every way to show the German people that the spirit of capitalism and imperialism in the working people themselves, as well as their leaders, is the real enemy. My faith was unabated that Christ was a better psychologist than the men who were carrying on the war, that when he said, 'Love your enemy,' he was putting a stronger weapon in the hands of the people than Maxim guns.

When the public heaped abuse on my head, and urged that I be confined in an asylum or jail, I won further opportunities to reply and to urge that the spiritual principles in man were stronger than the temporal forces and that we could conquer by realizing that the kingdom of God was within us. No matter how long we fight, the ultimate outcome of this war will be a new sense of the potency of the spiritual life. Must we have years of bloodshed and the terrible waste of all we have gained through our material civilization to prove that war is futile; that the things that are seen are temporal, that the things that are unseen are eternal? Can people only learn through bitter experience? Is faith in the universal laws of truth only to be discerned by proving the utter failure of efforts at domination? I was so sure that we could conquer Germany by first conquering the injustice and the selfishness of our own country. If men had to fight to discover that their enemy was within their own breasts, that it was the desire for their own good at the expense of their neighbors that had blossomed into imperialism in the nation, I shall have to be patient.

I have learned to accept things as they are. It seemed a very costly way for men to have to learn that co-operation is better than hate; but if they elect to learn it through the failure of strife, I must hold to my ideals and my faith in the new consciousness of life that is coming.

Two editors of city papers who were writing the usual patriotic stuff in the papers, when they read my letters, wrote to me, 'If there is anyone who believes that Christianity is practical these days, we want to meet her; she will certainly be a *rara avis*. May we bring our wives out to call on you?'

They came, and we had a jolly day – such laughter, such discoveries of radical thoughts that they kept carefully buried, not dreaming that there was any place near Toronto where they dared express them. All my efforts to persuade them that they might lose their lives and save their souls if they became pacifists and expressed their real feelings in their papers were unavailing. Their excuse was that the public was not ready for it; they must give the public what it wanted. Editors must live. Oh, if out of the war will only come the end of that delusion! Why must a man live? The soldiers found something better than life; why should not idealists?

'What would you do about non-resistance, if you were a Jew?' they asked me.

'I do not know; I will ask the next Jew I meet,' I promised them.

CHAPTER XXVI

Fruitlands
December 27th, 1915

Last Autumn, when times were so hard in Toronto, Rachel and Joseph's brother David had been without work for some weeks and wanted to go away to New York to look for a job. He had run into debt while he was idle, and needed one hundred dollars to be able to leave the city. He had been working for his cousin in Toronto, who owed him one hundred dollars, but could not pay him. His cousin had the money owing him from a house-owner. I took a note from the cousin and advanced the money to David to allow him to go to New York. A few weeks later I went to collect the money from the house-owner. He was a self-made man, had started life as a day operator in a factory, and had progressed until he had become foreman in one of the big shops of the largest department store in the city. There were many stories of his injustice to his workmen, and how he demanded graft from them.

I went one Sunday evening to his house to collect the debt. He gave me a very warm welcome and asked me to stay for a party they were expecting. Always ready for new impressions, I accepted the invitation. The house had been most gorgeously decorated, and he had done it at the expense of the workmen whom he had not paid. He promised to pay me.

Soon the guests began to assemble. It was evidently a party to announce the engagement of his eldest daughter. The prospective groom's father and mother were there, and a middle-aged man and his wife. The man was the president of a large Jewish society and had a great enthusiasm for the cause. His wife was one of the big mother souls. You instantly felt she would share her last dollar with any one who needed it, and that she had come up through hardship and hard times and was sweet and unspoiled by either prosperity or adversity.

I liked them very much. There were half a dozen more guests, but my attention was absorbed by those four. I thought now is the opportunity to ask their opinion of non-resistance. I explained how I had been challenged to know what I would do if I were a Jew.

'Why, we believe in non-resistance,' both men exclaimed at once.

'As the Jewish people,' the older man added, 'preserved the ideal of one God, so they have been kept all these years, ofttimes in places where they could not resent the evils the community inflicted on them; yet they have been preserved to keep the ideal of non-resistance for the time when the world is ready for it.'

I gasped. It was so unexpected. Here they were, bemoaning that their temporal prosperity had lessened their hold on religion and openly lamenting that they were paying too big a price for their wordly advancement in losing the vigor of their religious faith.

'Has not the lessening of your religious observance deepened your freedom?' I asked.

'Yes, it has increased our freedom, but it has lessened the poetry in our lives, and we need flowers as well as food.'

Every few moments the Jewish president would turn to his wife and say, 'If Katie were only here, she could answer.'

Then he would turn to me and say, 'Katie has eight hundred dollars' worth of books; she would know.'

A few minutes later, he said, 'We have had no chance for an education, but Katie knows; Katie has a library.'

The older man volunteered to tell me a story.

'When my wife and I were first married, we decided that we would always set a place at the table for any stranger who should need a meal. One Sunday we had been six weeks without a guest, when there was a ring at the door. It was the immigration agent. "There is a party of Russian Jews over at the station. Will you not come over and see them?" I went over and met the men and asked them to come to my house. Then I went to the butcher's. It was Sunday, and it was against the law to sell anything on that day, but I said I would pay his fine if he were punished for selling to me. I had only $50.00 in the world, and an old horse and cart with which I collected rags and old things. They had cost me $35.00, but I thought I would trust the Lord, if the court should fine me. I got some meat and some vegetables. Then I went to the baker and got some bread. We had only one pot to cook in and a boiler for the clothes. As the pot would not hold so much food, my wife scalded out the clothes boiler very carefully, and we put the meat and vegetables down to cook. There was not room in the house, so we took the bundles of old rags and laid some boards across them to form a table in the yard. We put our best table cloths on it. We had only two, a clean one and a dirty one. When we were all ready, the men said they must go back to the station for their wives.

'I took the old rags and junk that I had been collecting out of the wagon and I harnessed up the horse and drove it over to the station.

'We put the bundles and children in the wagon and the women followed behind. We were a regular procession as we came through the streets.

'We fed them all and when night came we took them back to the station and I collected enough money from the people waiting for their trains to buy some apples and oranges for them all.'

I could not help liking the old man. He cried as he told his story, and when he added that thirty five of that group had finally settled in Toronto, and that they had done well and sometimes even now came to thank them for that Sunday meal, I rejoiced with him.

The ex-junk dealer asked me to go home in his auto. I could not wait so late, but I was glad that 'the harvest from the seed sown' in these meals prepared for the strangers in extremity had come back to him in an auto.

Janaury 15th, 1916

Last night I stayed in the city with my friends, the Saintsburys. I kept Mr Saintsbury constantly amused by my experiences. The other day, after telling some of my recent ones, he said in such a depressed way, 'I do not understand it. You have more experiences in a week than I have in a year.'

I laughed. 'It is all the seeing eye. My mother used to tell me that my swans were only geese. But if I saw them swans, they gave me quite as much pleasure as the genuine article. It is three-quarters enthusiasm that brings me my human experiences. I am interested in everybody.'

Mr Saintsbury was born a Puritan, without any sense of humor. Having forsaken all the old paths, he makes regular prison roads of the new. He started in life with a conscience. He was caught by the Salvation Army and served it faithfully until it disillusioned him. He felt as if its enthusiasm were manufactured, and then he turned to the church and studied for the ministry. But the further he studied, the more his mind worked. Instead of theology being a wet blanket to smother out all thought, it raised such a hot flame of opposition to its tenets in his mind that he threw over theology. He had learned to think.

Next he tried nature and found that chickens could not be raised on nice little theories of the delight of living as close to nature as possible. For a time he subsided into earning a living, but his old missionary strain was not eradicated and he returned to philanthropy. This time he is going to improve the municipal institutions and make them a more perfect expression for civic life.

He has a lurking suspicion that all endeavor is futile, that it is only the opportunity to try one's wings. One must have a machine in which to mount from this earth, but all machines are equally bad. The only virtue lies in choosing your own vehicle.

I think that I agree with him. I fought shy of the Salvation Army. Why? Not because I had some drawings towards it thirty years ago, but because I was too much of a social coward, too much influenced by the opinions of my little corner of the world. I tried the various panaceas that were to prove Morrison's pills for the amelioration of the ills of the universe and decided that they were one and all equally useless. My panacea now was to create a spirit of brotherhood. I was not turning religious like so many of the war philosophers, unless it be so to desire to maintain the integrity of my own soul unstained by fear or hatred. One enriches one's own life through enlarging one's human interests. I am interested in people because I like human beings. I want equality of income and opportunity because I shall enjoy my own more when that day comes. In the meantime, I have a sense of humor and always get more satisfaction out of my efforts to shove the world than I dream accrues to any one else. I am sure that I gain more joy out of my exertions than they cost me. All the bread I cast upon the waters comes back to me plum cake, and with the plums neither scarce nor small.

Despite my failure to create a spirit of laughter in Mr Saintsbury and to share with him my joy in living, he was a most stimulating man with whom to talk, because he was not afraid to challenge any opinion I chose to advance. His wife was as progressive in action as he was in theory. They were my brightest spot in Toronto.

Alas, alas, for the growing infirmities of age! When the war was announced, despite his bookcases filled with the works of modern writers and all my attempts to make him see that this war was the out-growth of conflicting feelings and ideas, and that the real fight must be waged against ideas and not against governments, he became patriotic and severely respectable.

This morning, when I came out of the Saintsburys, Mrs Saintsbury was very much distressed because I was so heavily loaded with parcels for my suburban trip home.

'What will you do? How will you get to the street car with so many and such heavy parcels?' she asked.

'Oh, I will smile and some man will volunteer to carry them for me,' I answered.

'You have more faith than I have in the efficacy of a smile,' she said.

'Wait and see,' I answered gaily.

My faith was not so great as it seemed, for I had noticed two men approaching, and as they stepped up to me the older one stretched out his hand for my suit case.

Mrs Saintsbury returned to the house laughing, and I went on much relieved. When we reached the car, my escort got in and sat down beside me. I discovered that he came from the North, that he was a successful farmer, and that he owned three or four farms that he sometimes rented out but oftener worked through foremen. He told me that I might send any of my boys, whom I wished to get back to the land, to him, and he would see that they got work according to their ability on the farm. Oh, he was such a nice, big-hearted countryman! The kind of whom you dream – intelligent, but unspoiled by city life. He had had real things.

'Do you like farming?' I asked.

'On the farm there is always something doing. We work hard, but there is constant interest, constant life. I cannot explain it, but it is far more interesting to look after living things than it is to work with dull, inanimate material,' he said.

'Do you like the country better than the city?' I questioned.

'Yes, yes, a hundredfold more,' he answered enthusiastically. 'Life is living; there is no word that goes beyond life, and city existence is dead. It is full of picture shows, it is full of excitement, but it is dead, dead. No one does anything of his own free will. Everything is machine-made.'

How he would have delighted Ruskin! How is it the people who read Ruskin fail to feel the awful deadness of modern life? We are drowned by noise and confusion and take sound and motion for life.

'Is not the moving picture show doing a great deal for the country?' I asked.

'They are spoiling the country trying to make it over into the city. What do we need of moving picture shows? We have real things and why should we be distracted from the real by lights and noise?'

'Are you not interested in making the country more attractive?' I enquired.

'Yes, but not in city ways,' he said. 'Let our boys and girls learn to love the trees and birds, to know the haunts of the squirrels, and learn where the wild flowers grow. All the lore which belongs to their own world should be increased. They are forgetting their old pursuits because the self-complacency of the city people make them think they are of little value. They are substituting city excitements for a day in the woods.'

When I was leaving the car, I said, 'My smile brought me a great deal this morning,' and gaily waved my hand at my passing friend.

CHAPTER XXVII

Fruitlands
April 1st, 1916

All my efforts to find a housekeeper for Joseph having failed, I am going down to live on Mr Bertram's place. I shall be glad to live with his trees for a season.

There is an aisle of pines, tall and stately, planted forty years ago. They are now stalwart watchers of a path carpeted with their needles and lighted by the sunlight which gently flickers through their branches. I have seen many of the cathedrals of Europe, but nowhere is there such an aisle as this one, built by nature with its pillars of pines. Aside from its beauty, there is the constant joy of the changing lights and shades, never the same. It is always a joy.

Adjoining the aisle is the wonderful nave, likewise girt with trees and carpeted with green grass. I shall surely say my prayers here if ever I pray again. The nave has pine trees for walls, but only the deep blue sky for ceiling. I shall be a tree worshipper.

The house is set back from the road and there is a high barricade of pine trees all across the front of the farm. They were planted to protect the fruit, but they will be a wonderful screen, shutting out the world. It will be almost as good as living on an island, for I shall be shut into the privacy of my own grounds. I can think myself a hermit if I desire. I am still hoping to find for the cottages on the farm men and women who want to get back to the land, and who will love to garden and pick fruit and live out of doors and forget all the artificial life of the city.

April 10th, 1916

I received word several weeks ago that Morris Goldstein, who was in New York, was anxious to come and try farming again. I had many misgivings. I wondered if he would succeed any better this time than when I sent him up from New York in 1914.

He was not able to get a position then anywhere, except in the heart of the backwoods, where conditions were very rough. He incensed the farmer's wife because he objected to washing in the same basin with all the family, and wanted a separate towel for himself, one that was not made out of an old flour bag or piece of sacking. Such unheard-of refinements for a farm hand were most shocking to the hard-working, rough and ready farm people. He had various hard experiences on farms that summer, but he said his zeal was unabated. He is very much a theorist, and coming from the ranks of the working people in the city, he overvalued his freshly attained luxuries. I had many doubts about his success, but consented to his coming.

The Open Fireside, Fruitlands
April 18th, 1916

A telegram from Morris a week ago announced that he was held by the immigration authorities at Niagara Falls. He had been searched and on him was found a letter from me, in which I said, 'my anti-military activities are causing my mail to be censored.' Such an innocent sentence to cause all this trouble! An agent of the government arrived the next day. He had a copy of my letter and asked me what some of the typographical mistakes meant.

'Oh, they are only the mistakes of an amateur typist,' I said laughing.

He looked at me to make sure that I was telling the truth, then he said, 'We thought they were some code.'

At which I thought, 'What will Norman, who always growls at the mistakes in my typewriting, say?' and then I laughed again.

He smiled, but felt that he must proceed to business.

'What anti-military activities have you been carrying on?' he questioned me sternly.

'Oh, just writing to the press and signing my full name to my letters.' I went to my desk and pulled out a whole sheaf of clippings. 'See, here are my letters with my name.'

'Is the surgeon-major of the —— regiment any relation to you?' he asked me.

'Oh, yes, he is my brother!'

'And the lawyer who raised such a large part of his country's war loan?'

'He, too, is my brother; and you must not forget the ministerial military member of this ultra-patriotic family.'

'Why, they are all patriotic citizens!' he exclaimed in surprise.

'Oh, yes! They are well-intentioned,' I said laconically.

'Umph' (such an expressive groan), 'you are no German spy.'

'Oh, no! I am only a patriot in advance of her time,' I said, laughing so heartily that he was obliged to laugh with me.

In a few days came a letter from the government, 'You have a right to your own opinions, but we cannot allow anyone who shares them to enter Canada. We must conquer Germany.'

I answered at once, 'Of course, we must conquer Germany. We all agree to that, only we think our methods would be much more efficacious than yours. Morris is an idealist. He cares more for the fragrance of a rose than the name of a battle, and the tint of a sunset than the name of a victorious general; but he can raise good potatoes, and Canada needs potatoes. We will be good, very good.'

A telegram came next day, 'Morris may enter. Good luck to your crops.'

When I told my nephew, I said, 'You see, Jack, that laughter carried me through.'

He remarked, with some disgust, 'It was your relations, and not your laughter.'

I am still simple enough to believe that it was my laughter!

When Morris arrived, we found him too romantic; he constantly bemoaned the destroying of his manicured hands, and hated all the essential, dirty work of a farm; he wanted to look after flowers or vegetables, not animals. We, who loved every single thing that had to be done on a farm, who cared little for the honest dirt, the good brown earth, and the fine yellow sand, had little sympathy for his dilletante tastes.

May 10th, 1916

The plan for this summer is merely tentative. I am anxious to learn how to make a living off of a few acres, so I can say to people, 'It is possible for you to be independent on a small holding, and spend your leisure in spreading the new gospel of life.' I cannot encourage anyone to make the attempt until I am able to demonstrate that it can be done.

I want to learn how to raise guinea pigs, rabbits, chickens, so that I shall know about them when I have my large farm, the farm that is to be, where I am to gather around me men and woman who will work eight or ten months in the year to gain a living, and who will spend the other two or four months in education, whether it be art or religion, or the heralding of the common brotherhood of man, when all society shall be organized for the common good and not for the benefit of the few. My courage fails me. How can I find the people I want for co-workers?

How can I perceive my objects so clearly that I can attract the people who are willing to live simple and natural lives, people who are tired of the artificiality of the city, and who crave the great out-of-doors, the freedom from conventions, fashions and possessions, and who have a common goal? I do not care whether that end be sought through socialism, art, or religion – whether they are Christian Scientists, orthodox ministers, artists, social reformers – I will even mother the IWW and be quite pleased if they are reaching people I cannot, and giving them a new human feeling. All I ask is that my group, when I find it, shall be swayed by unselfish motives. That they shall be seeking to bring the time when men consider their neighbors in all their dealings, in work and play, in buying and selling.

We shall work together freely, not through any rules or regulations, but through a common spirit of helpfulness. I am sure we shall win a spirit of tolerance for one another's pet hobbies and we shall – most glorious of all – be alive, not followers of dead precepts. We shall be liberated by our faith in a supreme reality, the foundation of all our aspirations, the source and essence of the spiritual qualities, freedom, understanding, harmony, unity, we desire to see expressed in human action.

I must know how far co-operation is possible, where we can have community action and where we must rely on individual incentive. Life is such a balancing of opposites. The old Greeks with their adage of proportion were wise. Did they lose some of the exhilaration of life by always balancing?

I should like to avoid the errors of the English colonies, where there was always some one ready to live on the rest of the community. Then there is the necessity of giving human nature some individual incentive to success.

This summer I am handicapped, I have little strength, I crawl across the field dropping my seed, and then I lie down and rest, and I crawl back, doing likewise, and rest again. I repeat it as often as I can, but the mere effort seems to deprive me of any desire for perfect work. It takes all the will and courage I have to accomplish the mere routine task. I have a great deal of sympathy with the people who are exhausted by bad air, bad food, overwork. I do not wonder they cannot rebel. It seems the height of foolishness for me to be cherishing plans with the limited strength I have, but I am determined to be ready to go on with them as soon as I have strength. I am sure that time will come; some day 'I shall arrive.'

May 29th, 1916

Bessie Field is staying with me. Last night was a glorious night, and we took our mattresses and spread them out in the cathedral nave, where we could watch God's altar lights – the stars. The blossoms from the apple trees were in full bloom, and added their incense to the beauty of the night. We did not think of churches or cathedrals or any of the institutions that man has made to try to voice his worship. We did not theorize or talk, we simply lay and enjoyed the wonderful night and the mystery of being out of doors among our own trees and surrounded by space.

Houses are like clothes, no matter how big they are, or how one may feel in them, they cramp the human spirit. There is no other sense of freedom so complete and satisfying as God's big out of doors, with only the sky and the trees with their wide loopholes through which one glimpses more and more space.

I crave space; space and freedom seem synonymous. I cannot imagine thinking or moving freely when I am confined in body or spirit, and spirit needs the great open with no clutter of houses or crowd of poor, sheep-like city dwellers without pleasure or initiative.

No, give me the country, the trees, and the open sky. Let me sleep there and feel that I, too, am a part. Let me worship in my cathedral aisle; let me offer the incense of the flowers to the spirit of life in the trees, always growing, always aspiring, never complete.

I think our zeal is unabated, and we still cherish dreams of persuading people to return to the land, but we shall make an economic necessity for them and have them come as wage-earners first. The trouble is that civilization has so destroyed all ability to live without parasitical pleasures that the people who have become accustomed to the bustle of the city do not realize the possibilities of the country. One of my friends was bemoaning the lack of art in the country. I promptly assured him, 'There is more art for me in seeing Joseph feed his pigs than there is in all the rural pictures in the academy, and the same is true of beauty all the time. Last week Joseph called me to come out the first thing in the morning to see a bird on the top branch of the tree, carolling his morning song. Every night we watch the shadows creep up over our pines and the glory of the setting sun. Why, the constant change of lights and shades, the glory and the mystery of each day enthrall us; we need no art gallery for the beauty of the universe lies so close to us.'

Once a party of young people had come out from the city to spend the day, and Joseph had taken them for a walk. When they were gone, he came in and threw himself down on the floor beside my chair, and said, 'Oh, mother, they never saw one beautiful thing! We went for the most beautiful walk, the lake was lovely, the sky was blue, we climbed such a glorious hill, and they saw nothing.' Poor laddie! He felt as chagrined as if some one had personally affronted him.

There was always a conflict between his desire to share his country pleasures with his friends and their lack of appreciation. He was quickly sensitive if they offended against any of my customs.

On Sundays and week-ends, a lot of his compatriots used to come to see him. They were Jewish working people, and I was rather at a loss what to do about them. Their standards were so different from mine. When I would pass them anything, or press any particular dish on them, Joseph would tell me later, 'Mother, you must just let them help themselves; they will not feel at home if you ask them to have things.'

The young girls and boys used to lie around on the grass in a state of abandonment. Not all my theories could quite reconcile me to their careless positions and their open affectionateness; but I was so sure that our traditions of carefulness and keeping the distance between boys and girls had not been successful that I was not inclined to interfere.

However, I winced a good many times at the rude breaking of my social conventions.

July 10th, 1916

I am a snob, a first-class snob, the only difference between me and other snobs is that I am conscious I am a snob. I try to believe that I am a really true democrat with congenial people, no matter what their social standing or their previous advantages or their intellects. So long as I am alone with them and no one is observant of my companionship, I am all right; but the minute that some one of my class – a horrid word, but nevertheless, I do belong to a class – watches my contact with some one who has not the same manners as my old friends, I wince.

To-day a labor leader brought his family, consisting of his wife and a little girl and boy, out for the day. About noon a friend brought her friend, whom I have never met. The Open Fireside is free to everybody who chooses to come, so long as it does not cost me anything in time or money or strength. I share the freedom of the place and all the beauty of the gardens and the fields and the blossoming trees and flowering shrubs. All that makes the glory and the joy of the country is free to everyone who can enjoy it; so my friend brought her friend, a woman of distinction, and dinner with her, arriving at noon.

We sat down at table. Whenever the labor leader or his family wanted anything, they would get up and reach for it. It might be half-way across the table, but nevertheless they would stand and stretch their hands. They helped themselves first without any regard to the others. All my naïve, gentle hints that I would pass things to them, or that Mrs Harris would like the rhubarb or Miss Hearn would have some bread, passed unheeded, and every time they offended against my social canons, I winced. The ladies laughed at me most heartily, after dinner, that with my boasted freedom, I was not able to allow people to act as they pleased.

I have the greatest admiration for the wife. She is a broad, progressive woman like many of my friends who have been in the labor movement. She has thought things out from her own experience far more deeply than many of my acquaintances who have been dependent on books for their theories and knowledge of life. She is a real joy to me – when there is no one else at the table.

Of course, I say I am not democratic about people who are not congenial, the people who are coarse or common. I have not yet come to the place where I call no man common. Snobbishness, snobbishness, I say it over and over to myself. I thoroughly believe that many so-called common people surpass me and my friends in their heights of heroism.

One of my boys who earns the usual painter's wages, who has a wife and child in Russia, and is very anxious to bring them to this country, had saved up one hundred dollars. His cousin came to him the other day.

'My wife,' he said, 'is much younger than I and she has fallen in love with another man. She cannot resist her feelings so long as she is seeing him constantly, and so I have sold my business.' (After long years of struggle, he was at last succeeding.)

'What will you do now?' David asked.

'I have sold it at a sacrifice. I am leaving for Chicago. Will you lend me one hundred dollars, so that I can make a fresh start and save my wife?'

'But why do you not let her go free if she loves the other man?' David questioned.

'I must save her. It would be wrong for her to love him when she is married to me, but he is young, and she is too. She must not do wrong, so I shall take her away so she can forget him,' the husband answered.

David gave him the precious one hundred dollars. Was not that chivalry in those two men?

I cannot help feeling that there was more heroism, more chivalry in them than in many a cultured, well-groomed man, and yet they were both simple working men.

If men could always stand revealed, the little formal things of life might decrease and the big things would come to their proper proportion. We, who get on in this world, grow so accustomed to count the cost of all our acts and to try to gain the best for all our expenditures, that I am commencing to believe that we cheat ourselves by our calculation. Life needs both thought and feeling, the humanizing of heart and head.

CHAPTER XXVIII

Fruitlands
July 10th, 1916

Norman has not been well and has gone to California. I have been worried about him and was relieved to receive a picture postcard from him this morning. I laughed that my joy at hearing from him made me accept gladly a picture postcard, which I ordinarily detest.

'The devil was sick, the devil a saint would be;
The devil got well, the devil of a saint was he.'

That was all that was written on the card, but my heart has sung all day.

Norman says I idealize him. I retort, 'I only treat him as a plaything, which I can dress up in all sorts of garments at my pleasure.' I wonder if a plaything has not advantages over a husband? I am never disillusioned, I am never satiated; I can dream on indefinitely. When I watch my friends with their husbands and see the limitations of their relations, I wonder if my dream man is not more satisfying than their present partners. It is rank heresy to admit such questions, but still I query if life is not very good to me to give me an idol, albeit sometimes a dumb one, that always remains a god through lack of intimate contact?

The last time Norman was here he asked me why I had never wanted to marry him. I thought I had. The question started a fermentation in my brain. So often I have lost the tangible thing I coveted and kept the soul, and have discovered later that the desired good would have conflicted with my inner purpose. Norman is my strong man, he comes nearer my ideal than any other man, but he would have dominated me and I would have compromised. I have groped my way blindly up my stairway, my subconscious self finding some way of lifting me over the obstructions in my ascent.

I am trying out Gorky's creed of the sin of possession, this summer, to a very limited extent. I do not know but it may be with possessions as it is with learning, a little renunciation is a dangerous thing! To let go of one's possessions piece-meal, to see your cherished possession, which has been worked for and saved for, calmly taken by some one with no sentiment for it, is a frightful stab. I feel sometimes, as one thing after another goes, that I am being slowly bled to death.

When I was eleven, my mother decided that I was too old to have any more dolls, but I wanted a doll, so I enlisted the help of an older sister of one of my friends, and she showed us younger children how to make a good doll's body. My mother relented, and bought me a head. That doll was my solace in many an hour of pain and disappointment; when cut off from the more lively pursuits of stronger children, I found refuge in her; and she has accompanied me on many a journey when my mother was not well enough to go with me. All the nieces and nephews and neighboring children who came to visit me have found pleasure in her. This summer, Bella, the housekeeper's little girl, demolished the head and the arms, and I felt as if I were losing a precious possession.

However, often as I went through the pangs of sharing my possessions or seeing them appropriated with pain, there was one appropriation that brought me some gain. The various people who used to come to the Open Fireside were very much taken with my English sandals, and used them without asking leave, and so carelessly that very soon they were strapless. Then, one day, finding myself sandal-less, I went out in the soft grass in my bare feet. I felt like a peasant, rejoicing in the good brown earth.

One may dream about the grass and the lovely, fine sand of the farm, but nothing but bare feet, with their close, intimate touch on the earth and grass can give the wonderful feeling of being transported into a new world. The wonder of it was the feeling of joy, of elation. I was treading on air, I had enlarged my own nature so that I was both bird and human. Why should such a little thing as discarding a flat piece of leather, the pressing down with my own feet the lovely, clean, yellow sand, and the running in the grass where each blade seemed to caress my ankles, affect me so? Why should that give me such a sense of exhilaration? The delight of the physical I might understand, just as the joy of swinging, but the new world, spiritual as well as physical, was beyond my comprehension. It was being re-born, a new emancipation.

I could not understand it. But never again will I return to sandals in the precincts of the farm.

It is strange how every little advance takes a lot of courage. Last summer, I was scrubbing my kitchen floor and I kicked off my sandals. A little neighbor boy came to the door and found me in my bare feet. I was as intensely chagrined as if he had caught me half dressed. For several years, whenever I have been in England, where some of the people have worn sandals without stockings, I have been delighted to follow their example and do likewise. At home, in my apartment, I had gone in stockingless feet and sandals and last summer, for the first time in the country, I had done it out of doors in America. It was incredible to me that being found without a sole and a few straps on my feet by a little boy should cause me so much annoyance. I must be a hide-bound conservative, when every wee break with custom causes me so much pain.

I never went in sandals beyond the precincts of my own farm. I lacked courage to do anything so unconventional in the eyes of the inhabitants, as to go further than the gate, while in England, where people have become accustomed to seeing individuals do so, I have roamed in sandals all over the village. Such is life. It is the unaccustomed that is terrible in the eyes of human beings. Custom is the great enslaver.

And now, this summer, I have gone a step further. I have walked about without even the sandals. Of course, the neighbors would occasionally pass through the farm and it spread among them that I went barefoot. Their consternation was great, but not so great as that of the good church people when I used to go to church without gloves. I was born with a craving for freedom, I love to stretch and twist my body, every part of it, as I will; and feel that there is nothing confining me. Alas, alas, it is sadly discounted! My hands get dirty, my nails unclean, and I look at them sometimes with dismay. How I would rather endure the dirt than gloves few can understand; but hands are easily washed!

Once when I was at a Walt Whitman dinner in New York, a gentleman was introduced to me. He immediately asked, 'How did you ever come out of Lakeside?'

'Oh, my radicalism was very slight. I would not wear gloves, and when I asked people to dinner, I would not serve elaborate refreshments,' I answered smiling in re-

membrance of the consternation of my friends at my de-
fiance of those conventions.

'I did not think that anything radical could live there,' he
said, still unbelieving.

'Oh, my brand of rebellion was very mild. I suppose it
was the things for which people denounced me behind my
back, and wondered to my face how I could be so brave,
that saved my soul. My great wonder is, once I have shaken
off the dust of the home town, will my desire for freedom
find some expression worth while?'

That was two years ago. My sandals have followed my
gloves. 'What will be the next bandage to go?'

Eight years after I had won my freedom such a little thing
as going barefoot meant such a lot of questioning. I was enjoying it immensely, but it was one more thing to separate
me from the people. It was the old question, how far must I
conform to the usage of the group, in order to throw my
influence on things worth while?

Is it really worth while to be true to one's own instincts,
when you do something that upsets the equanimity of the
herd? Is it more important to strengthen some desirable
propaganda by refraining from offending prejudices of the
masses, than to be true to your own ideal? I feel that non-
resistance, not in the sense of acceptance of evil, but in the
attempt to return good for evil, to substitute for the outgrown ideal of conflict a world-wide, positive ideal of good
in which all would share, is the only right path for a nation
to follow. Your willingness to attest your faith in the truthfulness of your position by any sacrifice, even your death if
necessary, appeals to your opponent and must ultimately
convince him of the truth and sincerity of your position. I
believe in truth, 'the almighty years of God are hers.' Truth
does not need violence or any evil actions, justified on the
ground of expediency, to ensure her ultimate triumph. If

the nations had stated that they were willing to deal justly with all nations, if they had attested that they were willing to lose their lives so that justice might prevail, they might have lost their lives and saved their souls.

Non-resistance is only possible to men and women whose faith in this being a spiritual universe is strong. I have had a hard time to decide what my individual action should be, because I realize that there are few people who believe that the spiritual forces in life are greater than the armies of the Germans.

I have come to the place where I feel that no one can tell how the new social spirit may come. I believe the pacifists have glimpsed the coming world ideal. It may be possible, however, that only through conflict and the welding together of the peoples would that world ideal of the fusion of rights emerge for the mass. It is the motive that counts, and all the people who are sincerely sacrificing for a broader democracy will gain from their sacrifice. It may be the privilege of the conscientious objectors to see clearly the end that the armies have only glimpsed, that we shall make possible their final triumph. If there had been sufficient number of people in Britain with comprehension of the power of non-resistance, overcoming evil with good, we might have conquered Germany. Ideals must, in the end, win. I realized that the statesmen had not yet grasped an ideal that would make possible co-operation between all nations. I decided that, however far in the distance the ideal I stood for might be, I would be true to my own belief in the brotherhood of nations, the abolition of special privileges for individuals and states and the fusion of rights between individuals and between countries. But for the people around me, the most heroic thing that they could do was to throw themselves disinterestedly into the war.

Going in bare feet discredited the principles for which I wanted to stand, and yet it increased my own sense of freedom and my own consciousness of unity with nature. Should I give up my joy in that simple act for the sake of increasing my little influence in the community?

My friend, Eleanor O'Brien, argued with me. She was much more radical in her thought than I, a clearer thinker, but she managed to conceal her radicalism and just voice the opinion, or persuade to the action, that was a wee bit in advance, the people with whom she was in contact. She usually carried them a step further towards her goal. She was a good diplomat.

I cannot do that. I am perfectly willing not to obtrude my ideas and to allow everyone equal liberty, but it is difficult for me to hide my opinion, especially for a purpose.

There are people in all stages of belief. There are the radicals who are so far in advance of their times that everything they stand for seems chimerical. Again, there are the progressives who see the next thing to be done to-day and the conservatives who hold fast to yesterday. With whom should I align myself?

Finally, I decided to stand for the thing that was true for me. To everyone who questioned my anti-militarism, I said, 'You may be doing the thing that is true to you. God bless you. It may be the next step for you to take. It is not for me, and I must stand for a different ideal, even if I stand alone.

'You may be following the immediate duty, but the duty of to-morrow must be prepared for to-day. We shall have to do away with individual privilege, the seeking of every man his own good and all the selfishness it entails with its ultimate expression in world war.' In refusing to be disturbed by the jealousy of one nation for another, in having faith in the ultimate triumph of brotherhood, in trying to find some universal principle that will transform life, in everything I do, I am trying to keep before me the creation of a spirit within myself and hope that that spirit may spread.

After the armies have proved the futility of force, and Roosevelt, the superman with the big stick, has passed into oblivion, and after the liberals who are trying to build a bridge between the past ideal and the coming with their diplomacy and armies, using both means to conquer each other, have done their work, then we idealists will be heard, who from the very beginning of the war, yea, before it started, were urging that there was a new sense of life in the world that would prove more potent than armies. If the present conflict grew out of the selfishness of individuals developing into imperial ambitions, the new era will come from the recognition that 'each for all, and all for each' is a higher aim. We have passed through our stage of acceptance of the right of the stronger to a time of conflict of rights, and we are coming to an age when we shall all believe in the fusion of rights, equality between individuals and internationalism among nations.

CHAPTER XXIX

Fruitlands
July 21st, 1916

Our cottages are filled with people who have come out to holiday, and for this year we must forego our dream of enticing anyone back to the land, or to share in any co-operative plan. We have had many candidates who came out for the week-ends and played at farming over Saturday, but by Monday they were quite convinced that they must stick to the city because they could make more money there. Canadians have not yet tasted deeply enough of so-called civilization to make them long for country life. They are not yet sated with the excitement and confusion of the city. External things are still their measuring stick for all life values, and they do not realize that freedom, beauty and creative work are more satisfying than possessions.

To-night, as I walked by the lake, the moon was shining and the long reach of the waves carried me away from my surroundings. I was conscious that Marion was beside me. I seemed to commune with her.

'As the years slip by, I commence to understand you better, Marion. You were so much more widely read, more brilliant, cleverer, than I in every way. Your wisdom surpassed mine. I wonder if you realize now that our bond of union was that one man had given us the same ideal of him. Our common desire for truth, democracy, simplicity, freedom, beauty, united all three of us.

'Did we not think that Norman might be another Edward Carpenter, a Tolstoy, a Christ – the free man?

' "Out of the jungle of custom and supposed necessity, into a new and wonderful life, to new and wonderful knowledge,

Surpassing words, surpassing all past experience – the man, the meaning of it all.

Uprears himself again."

'You were deeper than I. When Norman and you used to talk, I did not understand, I felt. My faith in you softly buried your seed thoughts until my soil was ready for their growth.

'You gained early a dim vision of the wonderful possibilities of the creative spirit in man but before it had come to full consciousness, you put it aside for the sake of immediate gain; you married and threw yourself heart and mind and soul into his work, that he should do it in the best way and together you should keep your idealism, your faith in the age to come.

'You were the first to realize the futility of the work you did, and you quietly fell asleep.

'Norman has persevered. Because of his quietness and lack of ostentation he has been able to further many a radical movement. He has been an opportunist, doing the next thing, but never losing his vision. I did not understand, I only felt that your experience must not be in vain. I could not accept work from Norman, when he might give life. As of yore, we never talk, speech seems too commonplace, life too intense to find utterance in words, but he knows, and I know that he knows, that you and I both desire the same from him – to be the free man.'

July 26th, 1917

How often can one be born again?
I was re-born to-day.

I entered the world this time as Pan, and I danced with all the gnomes and fairies, with all the spirits in the grass and the little imps in the winds and soft little wooing sprites in the rain-drops. I cared not what guise they wore, whether it were wind or rain or grass or tree or flower. I was one of them. My body was but the cloak that concealed my spirit, but my spirit was one with theirs.

It rained, and a whisper came to me to go out and dance in the rain on the lawn hedged in by the tall pines. Once I was there, shut in by the trees, all alone with the rain and the clouds, I shook my clothes from me and forgot for one mad hour that I was human. I was simply one of nature's children. I danced with the wind. I bowed to the flowers. I courtesied to the grass. They were all my partners. My body was like theirs, just part of nature. I was in a new world, a world of spirits of life, of pulsating, exulting emotion. I stretched my arms and all the earth was mine. I stood erect and pulled the sky down. The sighing trees, the driving rain, and the thunder played the orchestra for me, and the lightning was my illumination.

I think I flew, that my feet left the ground as I pressed it with my tip-toes. I wanted to be a bird and career through space above the trees, to look down on this old sordid world. Oh, it was wonderful! I did not know that such joy was reserved for man or woman. To be one with nature, to be one with everything that was being refreshed by the rain. The big drops pelted me like warm caresses, the little drops soothed me. They were the quiet touch of the great big mother of us all. I left time and space and cities and peoples and forms and ceremonies and all restraints; they all fell from me with my clothes.

I can live an uneventful year in the memory of that hour. I cannot measure its glories or sum its joys. For one hour, I lived! Life, glad exultant, infinite, was mine for one short hour.

July 30th, 1917

The Fishers' little two-acre place is at the back of this fruit farm. There are four children and they are the most wholesome, best-trained and most original children I know. Mrs Fisher has simply the wholesome English woman's domestic instinct. It is not any theory or any particular intelligence due to books or learning that guides her in directing those children. The other day Bob came over to the house. I was busy in the kitchen.

'Why does the fire smoke?'

I was busy and did not want to bother with him, so I said, most indifferently, 'I do not know.'

'You ought to have a father like mine; he would tell you.'

'Does your father know everything, Bob?'

'Why, of course, and he always tells me. It is too bad that you have not got a father like mine.'

He was very sincere and earnest about it.

He was very much interested in our horses, and he used to come over every morning trying to persuade Joseph to sell one to him.

'How much can you give, Bob?' Joseph asked.

'I have eight cents in my bank, and I will give it to you for Peter.'

'But Peter will need to be fed.'

'Well, I will bring you every cent that father gives me.'

'Well, Bob, I will tell you what I will do; I will take you out with the horse whenever I go for a drive,' Joseph promised him.

Yesterday I went over to ask Mrs Fisher if Bob could come with me for a drive.

'Well, what do you think, Bob? This is Wednesday afternoon. You know father will be home, and it is his only afternoon home. Did you not promise to help him dig the drain?' asked his mother.

'Yes,' came very soberly from Bob.

'Do you think you would like to disappoint father?' queried his mother, and then he turned manfully to me, 'I am sorry; I cannot go.'

'I am sure that you will be glad, Bob, that you kept your promise to father,' was the commendation of the mother.

That was the wisest bit of child training that I had seen; Bob had been strengthened in keeping his promise, when it cost him to do so; he had been loyal to his father, and he had made the decision himself. It seemed to me that should be the keynote of freedom in education, wise direction with emphasis on right choice, but freedom for the child to make it himself.

CHAPTER XXX

Fruitlands
August 29th, 1917

Trying to work this place on shares has not worked out very well. Joseph is young, well intentioned, but headstrong. I had no voice in the management, as the bargain was between Mr Bertram and Joseph, but I have acted as a constant go-between. I am learning by experience the functions of law. People well-intentioned do not always understand agreements alike. It is necessary for each party to have a clear, definite statement, their understanding should be as nearly alike as possible. Therefore, they should be stated in clear, succinct language. That is where the present law practice seems to have strayed as far away from the desired procedure as possible. Mr Bertram has found an older man, and wants the house.

A letter came from Jerry a few days ago. He wrote, 'I recollect dimly a good old Lakeside Methody spasm from you shortly after we parted with tears. And I seem to recollect starting an answer thereto, something about the mental honesty of somebody who impugned the moral honesty of anybody who could eat, drink, and be merry though in debt, but the rest slips from me, and heigh-ho – why not? The world would run as ill on what tracks I would lay down for it as it would run on yours. There is no indication that the poor thing will have to run on either. Summer is here, and there is Scotch in the decanter, and beer in the ice chest, and wine in the cellar, and cigarettes and cigars and pipes and books, though the bills – several of them are still unpaid, and though I walk in the valley of the shadow of the Liberator, and though I read Norman the Happy, good and Walter the Lip-mann, my chief concern remains: How to get me a Ford that my lady may take the air? How to get me the time from bridge and books and music to write a little, if only letters? And how to decoy that social dynamite, yourself, within reach our loneliness?

'Here be a nifty little place; here be companionable folk of wealth, to shock to thy heart's content; here be nifty little cottages, to be had for the piping of a silly refrain; here be second-hand Fords of unimaginable ingenuity and stubbornness; here are good roads to race over, the woods to explore, interurban trips for the taking; moreover, here is a very considerable leisure of thy friends, and it may be an inconsiderable job for thyself, where thou mayst salve thy Methody conscience with the syrup of belief that thou earnest the excellent grub that would be dispensed to thee here. Here (altogether, and to make an end of it) is just such a paradisal spot as I should not ask you to, lest you find nothing to grumble about, did I not know that the pearly gates themselves would not cure your divine discontent.

'My lingo is a little mixed, but we are both bluffing, and we are both called. (Many shall bluff, but few be called, but we shall be called.) For I know as well as your amiable self that, accordingly, you will discount my description of B – some ten per cent, but nevertheless, will conclude that it will be tolerable, containing us, and you will come; and we shall get a cottage and a Ford; and have a scrumptious time until the least calloused of us can stand it no longer – and then a new deal. (I bet you deal next, too.)

'Every paragraph ends with your coming eventually. Why not now? The girl wants a machine, and I want an answer, so I pause to end this, but my muse goes on by wireless, conveying love and all sorts of disrespect and pleasant memories and keen anticipations.'

The letter was the hand beckoning me to Boston to renew the pleasant experiences of living with Nancy, and Jerry thrown in. I am going tomorrow to hunt for a farm, whence they may commute daily to Boston.

Hearthstone
September 20th, 1917

Could anyone guess the reason that Joseph gave for wanting to come to Hearthstone with me? 'Oh, mother, if you die there, there will be no one to put flowers on your grave.' I chuckled over that. But, after all, Joseph feels a son's responsibility for me. He may talk about my grave, but it would worry him to have me live alone. I left him to pack the furniture and bring the horses to Hearthstone. My German neighbor wrote me that the last seen of him at Fruitlands were his wild attempts at the station to keep Caruso, his dog whom he had taught to bark in an ascending scale, under one arm and his pet rooster under the other.

Hearthstone
October 10th, 1917

Jim and I went for a drive in the auto to-day. I do not wonder that people mortgage their houses and face ending their days in the poor house, all for the sake of owning an auto. My ideal of bliss is to fly. Always when I am happiest in my dreams, I am gently flying through space, floating on airy nothing. Autoing is as near as I have ever come to realizing my dream. To skim along over the ground with so little apparent effort, so little consciousness of motion! Yes, I shall go hungry, if need be, but I shall auto whenever I can buy a gallon of gasoline. Last week I had a letter from friends, saying that they would be in Boston in the morning. I straightway sold a pair of hens so that I could auto in and bring them out. I may become a habituée of pawnshops, pawning my valuables in seasons of hard luck for the money for gasoline.

If I arrive in the poor house for my last day, I shall be glad that I arrived there in a flivver, and that I had Jim for my chauffeur. We looked a wild couple. He is handsome, and sits as straight as a god, and looks as if he had conquered the world. He wears an old white yachting shirt, not over clean, and wears it as if it were a knightly robe. He has had an adventurous career. He was turned out of his home and sent adrift by his father. He landed at Yale, where he earned his way by playing poker, until the authorities likewise turned him out. Then all the wealthy friends whom he had made there introduced him to their families, and the female members at once fell in love with him. But he would have none of them, because he did not think he could retain his freedom and be supported by a wife. So he turned his back on the wealthy homes of New York, and took refuge in Greenwich Village.

He shared a seven-room flat with some brother artists as impecunious as himself. There was no way of heating the apartment except by stoves, of which they had none, and grates, for which they seldom had the fuel. A friend, one day, found him and his chum perched on a step-ladder. They maintained it was warmer near the ceiling. However, he managed to fall in love with the wife of a fellow artist, as poor as himself, but his ideal of the sacredness of the family made him flee New York. From New York, he went to New Jersey to try the Tolstoyan return to the soil that he might be really self-sufficient and independent. He worked for six months. Then for six weeks he visited some friends of mine who sent him on to me with a note that 'Jim was reacting against all artificial life of society, and was seeking simplicity in food, clothes, and living conditions. He was courting hardness and endurance.'

My friends had told him my feeling about sharing my possessions, and they had sent him, hoping that I could make it possible for him to earn his living. His idea was that he was to work for his board three days a week, and be free to paint the other four. He was quite indifferent to what he received for the three days' work, so long as it paid his board. His only other need was for tobacco and, if necessary, he could renounce that.

I hailed him with joy. Here at last was a young man who felt the same need as I for out-door free life, who was suffocated by the crowd, the dirt, the noise, the ugliness of the city, and all the second-hand thought and amusement there. He wanted space and opportunity to live his own life. I was full of hope that we might work out some plan whereby we would make it possible for others of similar mind to live in the country, earn enough for simple needs and spend their leisure in work that was worth while to them. Jim is twenty-two, and I am fifty-two, thirty years difference in our ages, but I am hopeful that the life that I crave and have never known how to gain for myself he, younger, stronger, more enthusiastic, and full of the idealism of youth, will work out.

He has been here three weeks, and I am beginning to understand the temperamental difficulties of an artist. The conflict is between his firm belief in following feeling and the effort at the same time to hold himself down to such regular work as is essential to earning his quota of the household expenses.

He and Joseph do not agree. They are jealous of each other. If I smile on one, the other frowns; and when I smile on the other, the first one scowls. It amuses me to see them so jealous. I, who never had admirers as a girl, to have two young boys fighting each other for my smile. The irony of life!

It is great fun testing one's theories. I, with all my theories of simplicity in dress and my desire to ascribe half the ills of the feminine world to the tyranny of clothes, find it somewhat trying to drive through the streets with hatless Jim in his soiled white shirt. I wonder what the people say. Freedom is a very scary thing. To be well-dressed in conventional clothes, or, at least, so that I am not remarkable, to be not noticeable for any idiosyncrasy, was the keynote of my early training. Here am I, wincing every time I have to put my theory of freedom of dress to the test.

October 29th, 1917

How far is non-resistance possible? How far is it wise? It is very easy for me to practise it, but I am never sure that it does not hurt Joseph. When he is impertinent to me, I feel that he does not hurt my dignity. I cannot get angry with him; that is not my temperament. Jim was very indignant with Joseph to-day, indeed he will not speak to him, because he resents so strongly his rudeness to me. I tried to explain to Jim that Joseph had not known any women except those of the peasant type, who were accustomed to being dominated by the men, who would feel that their men did not like them if they did not boss them. I can get rid of Joseph at any time, I can send him adrift. I do not get angry. I do not resent his conduct, violently. I literally fulfill the scriptural injunction of turning my other cheek, but my very meekness enrages him, and his temper grows as he fails to stir me up. Full of sorrow, I watch him. I cannot resent his anger any more than I could resent the senile talk of a drunkard. His temper is to me a sort of disease. I am not sure that I am not as weak in my lack of temper as he is in his excess.

I tried to explain to Jim that all peasant women have to endure much more from their men folks than I from Joseph. Here am I, independent of him economically, mentally, spiritually. If I cannot conquer him by gentleness, the whole theory of non-resistance breaks down. If it breaks down with Joseph, where I have every advantage, then it would break down with Germany. It would break down between nations. I must try every plan my ingenuity can suggest to arouse his better self.

November 20th, 1917

I have sent him away to-day. I have given up the fight. Gentleness, kindness have failed, and I have sent him out into the world. If one only had vision! I am sure that I could do right, no matter how hard it was, if I could see what was right to do. I am glad that I am relieved of the never-ending problem of how to deal with Joseph. It is restful, having no conscience to consult, but just living without thought. I am not at all sure that trying to be a Christian is not just being a weakling, that continuous gentleness is not mere lack of virility. If I were stronger, I should probably think more vigorously and act accordingly.

November 25th, 1917

After being away a week, Joseph came back to-night thoroughly penitent. 'Mother, I am not all bad. You are sixty-five per cent good; but you have some bad in you, too. Will you not believe that I have some good? I am sixty-five per cent bad, but there is thirty-five per cent good in me. Will you not let me stay with you until I am sixty-five per cent good?'

Who could resist that? He is such a dear boy when he is good. If there were only some way of overcoming his egotism and self-will, I feel that there would be a great future for the boy. My one hope is that he will learn from his failures. Eventually that he will realize that his temper is due to nervousness, and that he must take precautions to gain control of his nerves by building up his nervous system. There is always the question in my mind, whether he will gain poise and self-control when he has gained his right work and place in life. My little knowledge of psychology makes me think that some of his temper and self-will may be due to unfulfilled and, in his case, unknown desires.

Rachel, after her years of struggle, is at last succeeding. Her few months at school, of which she made such good use, fitted her for a better position. She has always aspired to go on the moving picture stage, and now a manager has promised her an opportunity. I hate moving pictures. They are an abomination to me, but she must be free to take the chance she desires. She is one more of my foster children to succeed. What use will she make of her success?

December 17th, 1917

Once more, my ideals of freedom are being rudely shattered. My two friends, Nancy and Jerry, who is a poet, have been with me six weeks. The war has destroyed their business. They are inordinately and passionately fond of bridge. They would play all day and all night. In fact, they start at two o'clock in the afternoon and, stopping only for dinner, play until two in the morning. Some time, between then and daybreak, the poet gets up and writes a couple of lines of verses and thinks he has done a good day's work. Jim has caught the bridge fever, and has given up all his work, and is running rapidly behind with his board. While I might be willing to help him if he were sacrificing for some ideal or principle, if he were trying to find his way to some simple mode of life that would increase the possibility of having things worth while in this world of false values, I do not feel it is essential for me to feed him and give him shelter that he may spend his days and nights playing bridge. He is leaving on Monday, owing me six weeks' board.

This question of sharing one's earthly goods grows more and more perplexing. Here am I, willing to share all I possess with people of like mind. I am not willing to share with people in order to give them opportunities to spend on things I cannot afford. It is the old problem. Every society of which I have ever heard, which has been organized to help people, has been victimized by some who were unworthy. I had a friend, who was a member of a Tolstoyan colony in England, and who believed most thoroughly that she had no right to goods that some one else needed more than she. The trouble was that there were plenty of people to join the community, who had overwhelming needs, but lacked energy to supply their own. If we all started equal, and there were no unequal distribution of wealth, it might be easier for us to let the people who want things struggle for them.

I wish to enjoy my own possessions without any qualms.

I would be quite willing to abide my choice, to do without something that other people have in order to have things I desire, if other people could have a choice likewise and have what they desire on the same terms. Equality of income would be a wonderful relief to my conscience.

December 29th, 1917

My Christmas house party was a great joy to me, for if I have not solved the problem of equality of goods, I have at least an international house. On December 25th, 1917, while the war was raging in Europe and the enemies were reviling one another, around my table sat a Polish count, whose brother was mayor of one of the Polish cities under German jurisdiction; a Belgian refugee; an Englishman; an ardent supporter of the Allies; two Americans, who sympathized with Germany; a Russian Jewess from Kiev; and myself, a Canadian and a strenuous pacifist. The Belgian refugee wanted the Germans crushed, but the rest of us wanted a peace without victory. I think there were few celebrations of the season of peace and good will where it was so adequately recognized. Soon I shall have all nationalities gathered on my stairway, and realize, through friendly relationships, 'that God has made of one blood all the nations of the earth.'

Lakeside
March 15th, 1918

Jerry accepted a position in the West, and Nancy followed him, hoping to find a position near him. Joseph went to the Agricultural College at Amherst for the short session. I did not want to stay alone in the house during the cold weather, so came home. One day I met an elderly woman, shabbily clad, whose face was familiar, although I could not recall any circumstances connected with her. I bowed to her pleasantly as I passed her. After I had gone a block, I heard some one calling my name, and turned to find her hurrying towards me, calling as she ran. I turned and retraced my steps and waved my hand to her. When she came up to me, she clasped her two hands together and shook them so enthusiastically, saying breathlessly, 'It is you; it is you; I had to come back to make sure, and to see you smile.'

I asked her a few indefinite questions, for I could not place her, then shook hands with her and turned away, saddened by the meagre life that had treasured a casual smile ten years.

Lakeside
March 22nd, 1918

A letter came from Norman to-day. He has been called to Washington to advise the State Department on International Law. I am as happy as I can be, and almost ready to say that I have been wrong, and he has been right. He has gone on quietly gaining his knowledge of International Law, avoiding being mixed up with radical groups, often because of his prestige and his known good judgment able to help the radical cause more than if he had been openly identified with it. Now he will be in a position where he can stand for justice in the coming peace terms, and do a work of world-wide significance.

I wrote him at once, begging forgiveness for my pertinacity in demanding that he should forsake the old paths and come out as a rebel against all the traditions and customs of to-day. I have been sure that only a new spirit, a new social ideal, could ever bring us world peace, and that there must be pioneers who would be content to live the truths they believed, even if the living brought them opprobrium and misunderstanding, so that they were denied the chance to work for the new civilization we desire.

Norman chose to combine work and theories, he would say, and events seem to have justified him. I still cling to my faith that the new social order must come from people living the truths they profess to believe, from the spirit within man, clinging to an ideal and ignoring all motives of expediency.

CHAPTER XXXI

Hearthstone
August 21st, 1918

My neighbor is a large-hearted Irish woman, although I doubt if she ever saw Ireland, with a heart large enough to embrace everyone who comes within her reach. The charitable societies in the city who feel that they are doing a meritorious work in finding homes in the country at a very low price for little street gamins struck a bonanza when they found Mrs Kelly. She has nine children of her own, six of them married. She works on the farm all summer, and in winter she goes into a factory. She manages her house and family, keeps her eye on her children's households, does her own sewing; if a neighbor is ill, she is the first one there with a loaf of bread or a pie for the good man's supper. She is general medical adviser for the community. She seems to be able to do about three times as much as any one else, and does it easily and cheerfully. She is a big sister and brother all rolled into one, and something added. She never stops to think of herself nor her good deeds, she has no self-consciousness.

Seventeen children arrived at the farm one early summer. There was Jimmie, whose two aunts wrote to tell Mrs

Kelly, 'Please be good to Jimmie; his mother's dead, and we're sixty. It's hard for us to get enough work to buy food for the three of us, but we can't part with Jimmie. Don't let him make hisself sick by eating too much. He's only had bread and water all winter, and might be tempted to ate more than is good for him.'

Mrs Kelly let him eat and vomit, and do it again the next meal, and the next, and the next, until Jimmie grew accustomed to having a full stomach and put on flesh.

There was also Tommie, whose father and mother drank, and who arrived holding his pants back and front, because it was safer than leaving them to the gaze of the public. Mrs Kelly soon rushed him into bed and stitched the pants up on the machine, and the child forgot that he had trousers on.

Many a story I heard of the 'country-week children.' The first thing when breakfast was over, it was, 'Mrs Kelly, please come and play!'

'Mrs Kelly, we will wipe the dishes, if you will come out!'

'Mrs Kelly, we will dig the potatoes, if you will go to the woods with us.'

With one voice they proclaimed their willingness to do all the work for Mrs Kelly, if she would only come out with them. Once, when the day came for them to go back, they clung to her, begging her to keep them just one day more; but the time had come and they had to return. Another seventeen were coming to take their places. The next night Mrs Kelly was watching for her girl and boy, whom she had sent to the mill with the old horse and wagon. Every once in a while, as she got supper, she would go to the door to look out to see if they were coming. Finally she spied the wagon coming over the hill, and in it were four children. There were Effie and Charles, but who were the other two?

She ran back, put two more places on the table, cut a few more slices of bread, and came back to the door to watch who it could be.

'Why, my sakes alive!' she exclaimed at last, 'if it isn't Tommie and Jimmie!'

Such waving of hats and shouting when the boys caught sight of Mrs Kelly! Bedlam let loose!

'Why, boys, where did you come from?' she screamed. 'Sure as the devil, it is Tommie and Jimmie, I sent back yesterday.'

'We came! We said we would! We're here! We left Boston this morning, and we walked all the way to Walpole!' they shouted back to her. 'We were bound to come!'

Such excitement!

'But does your mother know?' Mrs Kelly asked Tommie, as soon as the hugging and hand-shaking had subsided.

'Oh, she won't care.'

'But if you did not tell your mother, you must go back.'

Their faces fell in dismay and tears were very near the surface, when their attention was attracted by a carriage. The boys had stopped at a house in Walpole to ask for something to eat, and a lady had answered their knock at the door. She had heard all about the country week at Mrs Kelly's, and how the boys had walked the twenty miles to get back. She was so restless after they left that she had her horse harnessed and had followed, to see farmer Mustard pick them up and carry them to the old mill, but she could not turn back. Before she reached there, Effie and Charles had them in the wagon. She was not content, even when she saw their long tramp was ended. She drove on, arriving at Mrs Kelly's to hear her tell them they must go back, and see their disappointed faces.

'Oh, Mrs Kelly, if they wanted to come so badly that they walked twenty miles to get here, we cannot send them back! If you will go into Boston and see their parents and gain their consent, I will pay your fare and that of the boys into the city, and I will pay their board.'

The somersaults the boys turned, although not the conventional method of thanks, were quite satisfying to the interested lady.

Next morning, Mrs Kelly went to the city with her two runaway boys. At Tommie's house, she found the mother and father both lying on the floor drunk. It was the typical drunkard's home, no furniture, no food, and hungry children crying. Of course, the first thing she did was to feed the children. She did not think that they would miss Tommie, so she did not wait for the parents to sober up to gain their consent. When she told the lady about the home, she said, 'Oh, Mrs Kelly, if you will keep Tommie, I will pay his board!'

Mrs Kelly's big heart at once adopted him. She clothed him herself, and worked hard to give him his chance with her own boys. The lady contributed only a very modest sum, not nearly enough to pay his cost in the lavish establishment of Mrs Kelly.

He stayed for three years, until he was able to earn his own living and, like the proverbial story, he became a successful man.

He is only one of the many fresh-air children that Mrs Kelly has fed and mothered and started on the road to being good men, and her heart is still as large and unseared by life's hardships as of yore. The first Sunday that I was at Hearthstone was the first time she and her husband remembered sitting down to their Sunday dinner without a stranger to share it.

Many a dainty has Mrs Kelly brought me during the year. She managed my farm for me, looked after my cow, and generally mothered me and pulled me through the summer. What would I have done without Mrs Kelly?

She is sixty, and has not a cent laid up for a rainy day,

but her spirit is undaunted. 'Why should I worry about to-morrow, it is enough if I do what needs to be done to-day. How could I be happy myself, if some else were in trouble, and I had not done my bit to help him?' she asked innocently.

August 25th, 1918

Mrs Kelly brought her mother in to meet me to-day. She is eighty years of age, but full of energy and enthusiasm as any young girl. She is the other side of the modern story. She married young, against the wishes of her family, and discovered, as so often the young and wilful do, that her people had been right in their discernment of the hardships that she must endure. Her husband was a very hard worker, thrifty, devoted to her, and a good father to his children, but he was poor. He worked in the lumber camps for a dollar a day, and they carefully saved his scant earnings to make payments on the farm. She found that poverty had all the drawbacks her parents foretold, but she also found a joy in overcoming it that compensated. When she realized the hardships that she would have to endure she determined to make the best of them. 'I had made my own bed, and I knew I must lie in it, and I was confident that I could add some feathers to it.' She said this with so much spirit that I could imagine the grit with which she had conquered her early difficulties.

'Were you unhappy when you realized the hard work ahead of you?' I asked.

'I was determined that no one should hear me complain. I had to look after the farm when my husband was away. We kept cows and sheep, and I had the bread to make, the butter to churn, the wool to spin and weave. After working all day in the fields, I would come in at night and spin and weave my wool. I used to weave a hundred yards every winter. There was very little I could not do. I dug potatoes, pitched hay, loaded wood, made maple sugar.'

'Did you never want to be relieved of your bargain?' I asked.

'No, I had promised to take him for better, for worse, so I knew that I must keep my word. Soon there were two children, and then I had to stand by and help for their sake. I had to do sewing for the neighbors for fifteen miles round to earn the money for necessaries. My husband went twice a year to the store for our stock of tea, flour, molasses and the few other groceries we bought; everything else we made on the farm.'

'Do you think it was worth while to endure so much hardship and work so hard?' I asked, with intense interest.

'Certainly,' she said emphatically. 'I had eleven children and I raised them all to manhood and womanhood, and never paid ten dollars for a doctor's bill. I nursed them through all their diseases and raised them to be good citizens. I am not ashamed of one of them.' She said it with such a feeling of pride in something accomplished that I felt like applauding her, for she had accomplished her task under difficulties which I believed had but added to her zest.

'How did you do it all?' I asked, because she seemed such a frail little woman to have done such strenuous work.

'I was ambitious,' was her simple answer. 'When my children had diphtheria, their father was in the lumber camp; no one would come near us, and I was left alone. A neighbor brought some beef and placed it on a stone in the yard, so I could get it when he was gone. He was afraid to come nearer the house. When his children fell ill, I nursed them all. I used to attend all the confinement cases. I was doctor and nurse too. I ushered more than seventy-five babies into the world, and I attended the dying and prepared them for the grave.'

'Why, how could you do it when you had so much to do for your own family?'

'Why, I did it because it needed to be done. I have to love my neighbor and help him when he was in trouble, if this was to be any kind of a world for me and my children to live in.'

Now, at eighty years of age, she is enjoying the evening of her life. Her courage is still unabated, and her zest in living is keen. She is the life and spirit of a Bible Class of forty-five women, visits the sick and aged in her church, and is the unpaid pastor's assistant. Before there were institutions and hospitals and district nurses, she was expressing the spirit of helpfulness to her community. She was Good Will. So much that we have shoved off our shoulders on to paid workers she had done from sheer fellow-feeling, and I would rather trust myself in her or Mrs Kelly's hands than any paid specialist with a staff of highly trained nurses. It is not scientific, but I confess I think I would discount the danger of germs if I could have either Mrs Kelly or her mother look after me if I were ill. I shall commence to believe that Christian Science and New Thought have a real basis in human experience, that good will, unconscious of itself, is more potent than drugs.

There was no lack of interest in life for the old lady. There never had been any lack. Every member of her community was her friend, whom she had succored in times of need, and everyone within a radius of fifteen miles had felt her kindliness. 'Why, everyone was the same; we all shared and gathered alike,' she explained to me; but somehow, I felt that she had been a Christ in her community. Every age has its own Christs, the few who recognize that living and loving are more important than having, and it is better to give than to receive.

Every time I realize that there are no differences in the aspirations of varied groups, that each creed has its own advocates in every circle, I am jostled into another step upward.

CHAPTER XXXII

May 28th, 1919

A friend brought me an armful of old clothes she had found in her attic. To-day, I have run up a seam, darned a hole, stitched a patch or sewed on a missing button, trying to make the garments worth sending to the destitute children of Europe. The time since you, dear mother, left us, thirteen years ago to-day, has vanished. I was not here in my own house, but back in the old home. My sewing machine stood just outside the square alcove window where your large, leather, platform rocker used to stand, and you were sitting there with your workbasket on the low bench beside you, and a roll of small garments which your persevering fingers had fashioned. In the opposite chair in the alcove sat the constant procession of your daily callers. Your boys came and went, with their morning stories of success or failure, their hopes and ambitions. Their wives and their children made their daily calls. The minister, the Sunday school teachers, and the workers in the various church activities all occupied the guest chair in turn – each with his or her problem. Outside were the people who had come a block out of their way to pass your window, and who looked eagerly for your smile and cheery wave of the hand. How often have I come back from some errand down street to find you lying exhausted and in pain on the divan, but bravely asking me, 'What news?'

I would reply, quite sincerely, 'I did not hear anything,' and then you would tell me many items of human interest which had been poured into your ears by your various callers. I would recall that I had heard many of them before, and forgotten them, but to you they were full of interest and personal significance. You could truly say, 'Nothing human is indifferent to me!'

As some of the garments which I had carefully mended to-day opened up visions of need of the little children in Europe, I wished for your purse, that always lay in your basket, ready for all demands upon it, kept filled by your sons, who said, 'Our wives have all their desires fulfilled. We want our mother to be able to gratify hers. If giving is her greatest pleasure, then her purse shall never be empty.' Their gift brought double joy. You were so happy in their thought for you, and you rejoiced in all the avenues of helpfulness it opened up to you. The struggling school boy needing books, the country minister desiring a magazine subscription, the Bible women in Japan, and your sick neighbor shared the gift with the various charitable and church societies.

As I sat and stitched, my friends of the past thirteen years came and took their places near my mother, and poured out their hearts to her. She was big enough to listen to them all, but they did not strike quite the same note to her. They were more apologetic for their failures, less sure that they had been blameless. I tried to imagine how her sympathy, her consciousness of a universal Father, her belief in the imperatives of right and duty, would have met their problems. Would they have been saved from some of their wanderings?

Her son, in whose home her chair rightly sits, because he

has inherited the largest portion of her spirit of unselfish, quiet service, came to tell her that at fifty-six he was going to risk sacrificing his future and join the army, because he believed his specialized knowledge could be of service. Her God was the universal Father, including the Germans as well as the Allies in His care. She told her boy not to forget that this great calamity has come upon us because of our sins – 'that we have forgotten God, and turned every man to his own way,' and out of the maelstrom of opposing, selfish desires has come the world war. She sent him on his way with her blessing, reminding him that while we were expiating the sins of the world no peace but a just peace would ever be lasting. Her grandsons and granddaughters, who went also to 'do their bit in France,' she warned that we must create the world, that God desires. His laws are inherent in the world, and as we obey them we shall succeed in having a world in which justice and good will are supreme. She was big enough to send them forth with her blessing to take their part in the struggle with all its horrors, and yet big enough also to give her blessing to the daughter who stayed at home to fight for free speech, truth about our enemies and a peace that would mean justice to all peoples, irrespective of their past sins.

I told my relatives who supported the war, 'You are denying the faith in the teachings and spirit of Christ that you have professed to believe, but perhaps this may be your "fall," and after you have eaten of the "tree of knowledge" you may know good and evil.'

They asked me in shocked surprise, 'Are you not a patriot?'

And I laughingly replied, 'No, I am something much more rare; I am a Christian.'

They did not like me!

The tenants of a city staircase, my Italians, the friends I

made in the various strikes, whose names I have forgotten, who were but 'ships that passed in the night,' to whom I signalled a message of good will, to-day in mother's room you sat in her guest chair and I told you that I had simply passed her message on to you.

Garden City is gaining in size, but also in conventionality. The fact is appearing there that when men put their faith in any order, any form of society as an end in itself, rather than as a temporary expression of continually expanding life, they defeat their own longing. The desire for the growth of the Garden City, for the enlargement of the tangible thing, has led the officials to offer inducements to many people who came for the advantages of the place and were not in sympathy with the spirit of the first comers. Some of the early residents felt that the war upset all the theories on which they had founded their faith and supported the government in its militaristic activities. There were others who were true to their faith that you cannot conquer evil through violence, that the kingdom of peace and good will must come through a change in men's spirits and motives, be a spiritual re-birth and not a political organization. They suffered all the penalties inflicted on the conscientious objectors. There are still many individuals in the Garden City who cling to their belief that we need neighborliness and service in our daily lives, not limited or adequately expressed through any medium less versatile than life itself.

Mabel and Arthur have held their faith in love being the great creative force in the world. Arthur has spent most of the time of the war in prison as a conscientious objector, and Mabel has done any work she could find; but she has always had a crust to share with some other person who was persecuted for faith's sake. Mother would not have understood their absence of a legal marriage, but she would have been quite sure that 'the blood of the martyrs is the seed of the church,' and that, after all the horrors of war are over, the seed of the people who have been true to their vision will bear its harvest in peace times.

Mother would rejoice that Mary Stone has achieved success in her business. Her step-children have brought her honors from their university, and she has taken her place in the activities of the Western City, happy in the respect of her community.

Jim is now flying in France; and seems to bear a charmed life. He fell three thousand feet from his aeroplane and escaped unhurt. Will he return to work out his ideals of simpler and more beautiful living?

Jerry and Nancy are so busy that they have forgotten how to play cards. Jerry is steadily forging ahead as a leader of liberal thought and Nancy is turning the conservative benevolent welfare work of a factory into progressive democratic control by the employees.

Norman is back from Paris thoroughly disgusted with the futility of his work in the Department of State. The Peace Conference stands to him for all the things which we professed to hate in Germany and have incorporated in our own and our Allies' national lives. He is planning to attempt some new phase or reform of existing institutions, hoping that he will be able to assist in the reaction that is sure to follow the present stupid attitude of the world. He does not see that we have had unnumbered reactions and changes of external forms and they have been fruitless because they were always aiming at correcting abuses rather than creating a new spirit. I cannot believe that we shall always be ignorant victims, swinging on a pendulum from one extreme to another. I have faith that we shall discover the cause of life and growth.

Would mother have succeeded in instilling in Joy Bruce

missionary zeal and faith in duty, so that she would have gone back to work with her people, abandoning her own individual ambition and saved herself the nervous breakdown? Was the nervous breakdown too big a price to pay for the struggle that intensified her vision of the need for beauty in her own and her race's life?

Would she have inspired the young woman on the steamer with courage to make a real home for the father of her child, and the faith 'that the best pleasures come in the wake of duty done'? I am afraid all my influence tended to make her true to herself rather than loyal to a relation that had no virility in it.

Rachel is back in the labor world after her short sally into the struggle for personal success. She has come back to identify herself with the working people, and to rise with them. Would she have avoided her brief forgetting of her ideal if she could have talked to mother? Are there mistakes for sincere people? If one chooses to be true, is she not held to her purpose despite apparent wanderings?

Joseph is on a farm in Massachusetts, working hard and studying in every spare minute. Every time I see him I rejoice in the way he is developing. He has gained control over himself and is forging ahead to work out his ideal of brotherhood. He will always be the vindication of my faith in non-resistance. Would mother have directed him so wisely that his self-will would have been subdued by the ideal of a God of Righteousness, whose laws far transcend individual finite thought. Would he have been saved the suffering that has come from the conflict of his individual desires with the sublime ideals of his race, but have lost the glow of growth, stagnating in a belated faith? Once when I was remonstrating with him, he said to me, 'You always say that you attract your own good or ill, so you are responsible for my badness to you.' It was not polite, but it silenced me. Was my own restless spirit responsible for all the groping people, searching for some dimly discerned good, who sought me with their stories? Would they have told different stories to my mother, and would she have sent them away silenced, quieted by her faith in universal righteousness?

Mother would have made her appeal to an ideal authority whom she called God. I made my appeal to the ideal in every man which I do not name 'the light that lighteth every man that cometh into the world.' Her faith was in a Supreme Being, who existed perfect, complete; mine, in a life force present in every man, which must grow and develop.

Step by step my faith in laws, institutions, customs, enforced on me by some external authority, whether of church, state, or Mrs Grundy, had to be destroyed, to be replaced by faith in the life within me. Through my contact with others I had to learn that in them as in myself was the craving for freedom to express the love, the life, within them. Alike we have traversed arid roads of selfish individualism, self-will, egotism, that we might rid ourselves of the garments that choked the life within us. From experience we had to learn that there are eternal verities deeper than our caprices and that the real satisfactions in life come from making universal ends our own. Having discarded the externals, the idols men have made of God, the sanctions of custom, the valuations of the mob, we have gained a new and larger comprehension of the unity of the universe, the life whose eternal laws are truth and love. We march towards the new day when faith in love as a vital force in all human relations shall make men free. To him who loves, 'the golden age is ever at the door.'

POSTSCRIPT

Hearthstone
June 10th, 1919

I wrote Norman last week to ask if I might dedicate my books to him, and he replied, 'As for the dedication you propose, I would not wish to limit in any way the expression of your feeling, though I cannot imagine how I have contributed in the least to your accomplishments, unless it has been as a hard taskmaster – though not an unsympathetic one, in spite of appearance to the contrary – who insists on your finding yourself in the only way one can find oneself – alone and unaided.'

Why did that innocent paragraph arouse me? I sat down and wrote with haste and passion, 'Do you remember the first night, eighteen years ago, that I met you, when I had two of my nieces in Buffalo, and your wife invited us to dinner? When we left your house the moon was shining, earth was illuminated. I crossed the park that night simply flying on space. It was the greatest event of my life. I had met a god, and although I have had to recognize the clay feet, I have always kept my faith that some day those clay feet were going to be burst by the life within you growing. You have never wanted me to be dependent on you and, in the sense of any dependence that would in any way bind or fetter us, I have not been.

'The greatest gift that any one can give to another, you gave to me through no volition on your part. I have tried many times to make you understand the depth, the intensity of my feeling for you, whose great good for me was not your response or lack of response, but that you had discovered to me something deeper within myself, deeper than anything I could have had without this experience.

'Of course, I have suffered, but suffering is a small price to pay for the vision of the reality of life and love, the reality that there is something in me deeper than tradition or expediency or possession. Do you not realize that in the most fundamental way I am quite content to live my own life and satisfied to have you live yours? If there were any way in which I could make it possible that you should have the strong feeling for another that would give you faith in your own soul, that would turn you from expediency and all the various catch phrases with which we deceive ourselves, I would rejoice – no matter what the cost to me – to have that someone give you what I fain would, but could not. I believed in the life within you, I do believe in the life in you; I think it is a small matter who tears the bandages from your eyes, but I am sure that it will be done through feeling, not through reason. When your eyes are unsealed, you will know that only truth gives freedom, and the joy of freedom never grows stale. Every day is a fresh creation, needing almost a superman to endure its glory.

'Life seems a blind alley. You give to me unwillingly, reluctantly, and I, with all the intensity of desire of which I am capable, am powerless to give to you.

'I wish I could help you to understand that love is the basis of creation, love that is the surrender of ourselves to some life force deeper than our individual wisdom, that carries us out into the wide ocean of humanity. You cannot create alone, I cannot. We have each to find the love that is life, and through living and loving, the faith that in every man is the same desire for freedom, for beauty, for truth, for love. We shall change the world when we change our attitude to the world. Our outworn institutions will drop away when we neglect them and put our trust in the ever-growing life in people. Another spiritual renaissance will bring back the joy and splendor of living.

'You cannot comprehend that nothing you do or leave undone affects my feeling for you. That is not you, it is I, the I that you have discovered to myself, the I that makes life worth living to me, and for which I can make you no return. Very well I am still I, always loving you.'

I have built my stairway, and from the top I can see the level road of security and certainty stretching ahead. I have gained the faith that will illuminate the road. I shall march serenely. 'The future I can face, for I have proved the past.' I shall go singing all my days, 'I know what I have believed.'

I have won my freedom.